LANGUAGE, SYMBOLIZATION, AND PSYCHOSIS

LANGUAGE, SYMBOLIZATION, AND PSYCHOSIS

Edited by
Giovanna Ambrosio, Simona Argentieri and Jorge Canestri

Essays in Honour of Jacqueline Amati Mehler

Routledge
Taylor & Francis Group
LONDON AND NEW YORK

First published 2007 by
Karnac Books Ltd.

Published 2018 by Routledge
2 Park Square, Milton Park, Abingdon, Oxon OX14 4RN
711 Third Avenue, New York, NY 10017, USA

Routledge is an imprint of the Taylor & Francis Group, an informa business

British Library Cataloguing in Publication Data

A C.I.P for this book is available from the British Library

ISBN-13: 9781855755857 (pbk)

Edited, designed, and produced by
Florence Production Ltd, Stoodleigh, Devon
www.florenceproduction.co.uk

CONTENTS

FOREWORD

Giovanna Ambrosio and Simona Argentieri

ἄνευ γὰρ φίλων οὐδεὶς ἕλοιτ' ἂν ξῆν ἔχων τὰ λοιπὰ ἀγαθὰ πάντα

Aristotle, *Etica Nicomachea,* VIII, 1

"without friends no one would choose to live, though he had all other goods".

Aristotle, *Nicomachean Ethics,* VIII, 1
Translated by W.D Ross

Paradoxically, it is not easy to write about a person whom you have known, esteemed, and loved for such a long time. Not only because so many thoughts come to mind, so many episodes of shared emotional and professional life, but also because you wonder whether the recipient of these pages will recognize herself in them, whether she will consider that her thinking is reflected in the chapters written by the many eminent colleagues who have wanted to contribute to this book, and in the more private images that emerge from our introduction.

Several years ago, on the occasion of the publication of a book by various authors, Jacqueline was the only one who did not want to publish her date of birth at the beginning of her chapter, a touch of feminine coquettishness that assumed the tone of an amusing paradox in a personality as rigorous and authoritative as hers. The publication of this book, however, is specifically to celebrate her seventieth year, but the situation is reversed because, today, the coquettishness consists in openly declaring her eminently respectable age and measuring it against all the things that she has accomplished and continues to accomplish with such unyielding self-assurance.

To borrow the words of Hugo von Hofmannsthal's title (*Buch der Freunde*, 1922), this can truly be called a 'book of friends', addressed to friends – but not only to them – in order to celebrate together a person who holds a really special place in the panorama of contemporary psychoanalysis. These pages contain contributions from many well-known colleagues dear to Jacqueline, although not all of them (they really would be too many!); others have encouraged the initiative and have lent us their continuous affectionate support, even 'from a distance'.

Jacqueline was born in Barcelona where her parents had gone to live at the end of the 1920s in order to leave behind the suffocating, anti-Jewish culture of their native Mitteleurope. But after a few years, the civil war in Spain forced the Mehler family to emigrate once again. Her father, a brilliant and adventurous businessman, first chose Paris and then – foreseeing the tragedy announced with the Anschluss – Buenos Aires. And so all of Jacqueline's family are polylingual and polycultural – true citizens of the world; and the coming and going between nations and continents will always characterize their lively and courageous style of life and relationships.

Although Jacqueline grew up in Argentina, she went to an English school. After obtaining her degree in medicine, she followed her husband to the University of Pavia in Italy where she began to study paediatrics, and then, in Milan, psychiatry. After two years, they moved to Boston, and it was here that she began to develop an interest in research on the functioning of the mind and the importance of relationships in therapeutic vicissitudes. She worked in the Department of Psychiatry of Harvard University where she researched into hypnosis and memory, and subsequently she specialized in adult and child psychiatry and psychotherapy at the Harvard Medical School.

This brings us to the 1960s – the golden age of enthusiastic collaboration between psychiatrists and psychoanalysts, when analysts such as the Bibrings, E. Zetzel, the Deutschs, the Ranks, A. Modell, and many others were called upon to teach psychodynamically oriented psychiatry. It was more or less inevitable that a promising and enthusiastic young psychiatrist would decide to undergo psychoanalytic training. But the events of her private life once again took her elsewhere, and it was in Italy that she would undertake her training as a psychoanalyst, with Eugenio Gaddini as her personal analyst.

With an affective and cultural background such as this, Jacqueline's continuous and fertile communication with psychoanalytic societies all over the world has been a natural consequence. For alongside her scientific activities, she has always been passionately interested in societal policies, but not in politics, in her conviction that the survival and transmission of psychoanalysis are closely linked to the organization and good functioning of the relative institutions.

Over the years, Jacqueline has held important positions in the International Psychoanalytical Association (IPA) and in the Italian Psychoanalytical Association (A.I.Psi.), during which time she developed a close network of cultural exchanges, esteem, and friendships to which this book bears witness. From 1987 to 1996 she was a member of several IPA committees, among them COMPSED (Committee for Psychoanalytic Education); from 1988 to 1993 she was a member of the European Board of the International Journal of Psycho-Analysis; from 1989 to 1993 she was IPA Secretary under the Presidency of Professor Joe Sandler; from 1992 to 1997 European Associate Editor of the IPA Newsletter; from 1994 to 1997 European Representative of the House of Delegates in the Executive Council; from 1997 to 1999 she was elected Vice President of the IPA; and in 1997 she was a recipient of the Mary S. Sigourney Honorary Award for Outstanding Contributions to Psychoanalysis.

In 1992, together with colleagues who were also close friends, she was one of the founders of A.I.Psi., of which she was President from 1994 to 1999, and Director of the Training Institute from 2004. In 1997, she and a group of colleagues founded the A.I.Psi. journal *Psicoanalisi* of which she is Director.

Due in part to human nature, but also to her renowned uncompromising character, her interventions have not infrequently been the cause of resistances and sometimes of keen arguments; but even her opponents have always recognized in her a fair-minded, straightforward adversary, who, regardless of personal conveniences, is capable of providing lively – although sometimes unpopular – solicitations to our psychoanalytic thinking.

Besides, paradoxes and complexities have always been a constant feature of Jacqueline's life and personality: on the one hand, her strict secularity, but her fondness for Hebrew tradition; her readiness *ante litteram* to enter into the world of computers (she was the first of us to acquire one in 1989), but her permanent struggles with their binary logic; her passion for jewellery and lovely clothes, but also for fast cars and for music both heard and performed (she studied as a child with Heinrich Racker) and for her long, leisurely holidays on the coast of Sardinia; on the other hand, her tirelessness and intransigence – especially with herself – on any occasion involving work, and, above all, her reliability, her absolute sense of friendship and of loyalty.

It is hard to understand how, over the years and in spite of her generous commitment to all scientific and institutional activities, she has been able to constantly maintain her full-time clinical work, a prodigious daily feat that is repeated in her family life. She and all her close relatives – her two daughters, her five beloved grandchildren, her sister Sidy – herself a well-known psychoanalyst – her brother Jacques who is an internationally famed psycholinguist – are all scattered around the world and yet they are constantly in touch with each other as they come and go across the oceans in a kind of *moto perpetuo* for holidays, birthdays, and family festivities.

Such a wealth and multiplicity of encounters and affects is also testified by the authors of this book; not only do they come from many geographic areas – from North and South America and from Europe – but they represent very different schools and traditions of psychoanalysis and are today, in their turn, excellent exponents of various theoretic orientations. This is one of the main points of interest of the book, because it compares different psychoanalytic thinking and models – all of a rigorously Freudian stamp – on issues of great theoretic and clinical importance. The contributions of these generous friends concern some of the themes that Jacqueline Amati-Mehler has investigated with such dedication during the past twenty years – 'Language, Symbolization and Psychoses'; three concepts of vast theoretic and clinical importance that are significantly interwoven with each other both in personal development as well as in the atypical and individual forms of pathology. The authors have thus endeavoured to reply to one of the foremost queries that has occupied Jacqueline's thinking: whether and how the acquisitions of modern psychoanalysis have brought about changes in our criteria of analysability; whether our increased knowledge has lead to a greater therapeutic capacity, as she believes; and whether, as a consequence, we must endorse the so-called 'flexibility' of the setting and the classical methods, as she does *not* believe.

We could mention other issues to which she has dedicated her writings: polylingualism in the intrapsychic and relational dimension, migration and nostalgia, hope and hopelessness in clinical work, love and impotence in men, studies on the concepts of 'ego' and 'object', representability, the technical and conceptual differences between psychoanalysis and psychotherapy. So many thoughts that could perhaps provide the material for another book in the future! This present book, however, is our way of honouring Jacqueline now, apart from the 'celebrative' rhetoric, in the hope that its contents of critical and dialectic confrontation on fundamental issues of psychoanalysis may enrich not only the intimate circle of her friends, but also the wider audience of all those who today love and practice psychoanalysis.

Acknowledgements

We should like to thank all the contributors, without whose affectionate and willing participation it would not have been possible to promote our editorial adventure. Special thanks are due to Jill Whitelaw-Cucco – secretary, translator and friend – whom, during the time of her most intense IPA activity, Jacqueline used to call her 'alter-ego'; she has shared many years of work with Jacqueline, and continues to do so, and has enthusiastically and affectionately participated in our project with her customary professional competence. We also thank our publishers, Karnac, and particularly Oliver Rathbone who trusted in us and helped us transform a wish into reality.

(Translated from Italian by Jill Whitelaw-Cucco)

References

Aristotle, *Nicomachean Ethics*, Book VIII, 1. Translated with an introduction by David Ross, revised by J. L. Ackrill and J. O. Urmson, Oxford University Press, Oxford 1998.

H. von Hofmannsthal (1922), *Il libro degli amici*, Adelphi, Milano, 1980.

ABOUT THE EDITORS AND CONTRIBUTORS

GIOVANNA AMBROSIO is a Full Member of the Italian Psychoanalytical Association and the International Psychoanalytical Association. She is also the Secretary of the Italian Psychoanalytical Association and Chief Editor of the Journal *Psicoanalisi*.

She is the current overall Chair of the IPA Committee on Women and Psychoanalysis (COWAP) and former european co-chair of the Committee on Women and Psychoanalysis (2001–2005).

Her main scientific interests include the field of the intrapsychic interaction relationship between 'truth and false', the meanings of 'lies' and issues related to the well known problem of the 'confusion of tongues'.

SIMONA ARGENTIERI is a Full Member of the International Psychoanalytical Association, Training and Supervising Analyst of the Italian Psychoanalytical Association. Her main interests include the mind-body relationship, psychosomatic medicine, and gender identity. She has published extensively in these fields.

Besides her full time clinical practice she has been involved in the field of bio-ethics, in teaching at Universities and in active psychoanalytic divulgation in the mass-media.

She has dedicated much thought to the relationship between psychoanalysis, and culture and art, particularly the cinema. She is the author of many essays and books on the above subjects.

HAROLD P. BLUM, MD, is a Clinical Professor of Psychiatry and Training Analyst, New York University School of Medicine, Department of Psychiatry.

He is also Executive Director at the Sigmund Freud Archives, Library of Congress and Past Editor-in-Chief of the Journal of the American Psychoanalytic Association, Past Vice President of the International Psychoanalytical Association.

He is Author of more than one hundred forty psychoanalytic papers and several books and recipient of numerous awards and lectureships including the inaugural Sigourney Award, Mahler, Hartmann, and Lorand Prizes.

JORGE CANESTRI, MD, psychiatrist, psychoanalyst. Training and Supervising Analyst for the Italian Psychoanalytical Association (A.I.Psi) and for the Argentine Psychoanalytic Association. He is Director of the Institute of Psychoanalysis of the Italian Psychoanalytical Association (1992-1998); Full Member of the International Psychoanalytic Association; Mary S. Sigourney award recipient 2004; Chair of the Ethics Committee (IPA 2001-2005); Chair of the Working Party on Theoretical Issues of the E.P.F. (2001-2006); Chair of the 42nd Congress of the International Psychoanalytic Association (IPA) in Nice (2001). He is also member of the Conceptual and Empirical Research Committee (IPA); Professor of Psychology of Health at the Roma 3 University; Editor of the Educational Section of the International Journal of Psycho-Analysis; member of the Editorial Board of the International Journal of Psycho-Analysis.

Jorge Canestri has published numerous psychoanalytical papers in books and reviews and is co-author of *The Babel of the Unconscious. Mother Tongue and Foreign Languages in the Psychoanalytic Dimension*; Editor (with Marianne Leuzinger-Bohleber and Anna Ursula Dreher) of *Pluralism and Unity? Methods of research in psychoanalysis*; Editor of *"Psychoanalysis: from practice to theory"*. He is Director of the webpage: *Psychoanalysis and logical mathematical thought.*

FIDIAS CESIO, MD, is assistant professor in Psychiatry at the University of Buenos Aires and researcher in psychophysiology. In 1948, in training analysis with Marie Langer, he entered the Training Institute of the Argentine Psychoanalytic Association (APA) and began to take seminars. Since 1951, he has been a professor of that Institute and since 1956, a training analyst. Since the beginning of his training, he has been intensely active in psychoanalytic clinical practice. His teachers in psychoanalytic training were especially Angel Garma, Arnaldo Rascovsky and Enrique Pichon Rivière.

He was the Director of the Institute of Psychoanalysis, Scientific Secretary of the Executive Committee and President of the APA and Delegate for Latin America to the House of Delegates of the International Psychoanalytical Association.

He has published numerous contributions to psychoanalysis, especially in the *Revista de Psicoanálisis, La Peste de Tebas* and other journals. He has also contributed in book form.

The main subjects of his contributions are the Actual Neuroses, in particular Lethargy in the analytic situation, the Oedipus tragedy and the Negative Therapeutic Reaction.

GEMMA CORRADI FIUMARA is a Training Analyst with the Italian Psychoanalytic Society, and professor of philosophy at the University of Rome. Her books include: *The Symbolic Function: Psychoanalysis and the Philosophy of Language, The Other Side of Language: A Philosophy of Listening, The Metaphoric Process: Connections between Language and Life, The Mind's Affective Life: A Psychoanalytic and Philosophical Inquiry.*

YOLANDA GAMPEL (Psychology Department, Tel Aviv University. Psychotherapeutic Program, School of Medicine, Tel Aviv University) is a Training Analyst of the Psychoanalytical Society of Israel, and the International Psychoanalytical Association. Vice-President EPF, 2001-05; International Hayman Prize, 2001; European Chair for ING, 2004; Sigourney Award, 2006.

ALAIN GIBEAULT, PhD, philosopher, psychologist and psychoanalyst, is a Training Analyst of the Paris Psychoanalytical Society and Director of the E. & J. Kestemberg Centre for Psychoanalysis and Psychotherapy (Mental Health Association of Paris 13th). He has played an important role on the international scene as Past President of the European Psycho-Analytical Federation and as Past Secretary General of the International Psychoanalytical Association. In this function he has contributed to the development of psychoanalysis in Eastern Europe after the fall of the Berlin wall and especially in

Russia, where he has been nominated in November 2006 Honorary Professor of the Lomonossov Moscow State University. He is the co-editor of *An Anthology of Contemporary Psychoanalysis* published in Russian. Well known for his publications on symbolisation, he has published many writings on psychosis, on the theory and technique of individual psychoanalytic psychodrama and on prehistoric art.

ADOLFO PAZZAGLI graduated in Medicine and Surgery, and specialized in Nervous and Mental Disease. He obtained Tenure in Nervous and Mental Disease and in Psychiatry in 1980. Professor of Psychiatry at the School of Medicine and Surgery of the University of Florence, he was also Director of the Graduate Schools of Psychiatry and Clinical Psychology of the University of Florence.

He was President of the Faculty Assembly of Psychological Disciplines at the Medical Faculty.

He is a Full Member of the International Psychoanalytical Association, a Training and Supervising Analyst of the Italian Psychoanalytical Association (A.I.Psi). Full Professor of Clinical Psychology of the University of Florence (Italy), he is also Vice-Director of the journal *Psychoanalisi;* Co-Director of the journal *Adolescenza,* and then of *Infanzia e Adolescenza.*

His main interests concern psychology and psychopathology of parenthood, the dynamic psychopathology of phobic and psychotic patients, the psychotheraputic treatment in schizophrenia and the borderline Disturbances of Personality.

He is Author of about 250 publications, several of which were published in important international journals and of some books on the above mentioned areas

ETHEL SPECTOR PERSON, MD, is Professor of Clinical Psychiatry at the College of Physicians and Surgeons, Columbia University, and a Training and Supervising Analyst at the Columbia University Center for Psychoanalytical Training and Research. Dr Person along with Dr Arnold Cooper and Dr Glen Gabbard edited the *APPI Textbook of Psychoanalysis*, published in 2005. She is the Author of *Feeling Strong: The Achievement of Authentic Power*; *The Sexual Century*; and *By Force of Fantasy: How We Make Our Lives*. She is privileged that in 2006 American Psychiatric Publishing, Inc. reprinted her book *Dreams of Love and Fateful Encounters: The Power of Romantic Passion.*

She has edited 11 other books and contributed over 100 papers to the psychiatric and psychoanalytic literature.

FRED PINE had his PhD from Harvard University in 1956 and developed a career in research, academia, and clinical psychoanalysis. He is currently Emeritus Professor in the Department of Psychiatry at The Albert Einstein College of Medicine and on the faculties of the Columbia Institute for Psychoanalytic Training and the New York University Postdoctoral Program in Psychoanalysis. His writings have been broadly in the intersect of developmental theory and clinical psychoanalysis, and are largely collected in three books: *Developmental Theory and Clinical Process* (Yale, 1985), *Drive, Ego, Object and Self: A Synthesis for Clinical Work* (Basic Books, 1990), and *Diversity and Direction in Psychoanalytic Technique* (Other Press, 2003).

ANA-MARIA RIZZUTO, MD, an Argentinian born psychoanalyst, is a Training and Supervising Analyst at The Psychoanalytic Institute of New England, East, Boston, MA, USA. Dr Rizzuto is the author of *The Birth of the Living God. A Psychoanalytic Study* (1979), The University of Chicago Press, *Why did Freud Reject God? A Psychodynamic Interpretation* (1998), Yale University Press. She is the co-author with W.W. Meissner and Dan Buie of *The Dynamics of Human Aggression* (2004), Brunner-Routledge.

ANNE-MARIE SANDLER was born in Geneva, studied with Jean Piaget and was for a time his assistant. She then came to England where he trained in child analysis with Anna Freud, going on to complete the adult training in the British Psychoanalytical Society, where she is a Training and Supervising Analyst. She has been President of the British Society and of the European Psychoanalytical Federation, and Vice-President of the International Psychoanalytical Association. She was formerly Director of the Anna Freud Centre. Many of her published papers were written in collaboration with Joseph Sandler and published in various psychoanalytical journals. They also published a book *Internal Objects Revisited* published in 1998.

THEODORE SHAPIRO, MD, is a Training and Supervising Analyst at the New York Psychoanalytic Institute, Faculty member of The

Columbia Association for Psychoanalytic Medicine and Professor Emeritus at the Weill Cornell Medical College. He has contributed to the Psychoanalytic literature and lectured widely focusing on the interplay of linguistics, development and psychoanalytic theory and practice. He also has written on his and his collaborator's empirical studies of language and affect in Early Infantile Autism, normal development, and most recently, his collaborative studies of hypnosis and neuroscience. Further contributions to the literature on the pursuit of meaning in clinical practice are forthcoming.

ADRIANA SORRENTINI, MD, is a psychoanalyst with a private practice in Buenos Aires, Argentina; She is Full Member of the International Psychoanalytical Association; Training Analyst of the Argentine Psychoanalytic Association (APA);

Training supervisor of the APA; Professor of the 'Angel Garma' Training Institute of the APA;

Full Member of the Latin American Psychoanalytic Federation; Member of the Referee Committee of the journal *Psicoanálisi.*

RICCARDO STEINER is a psychoanalyst belonging to the British Psychoanalytic Society. His work, together with Pearl King, on *The Freud-Klein Controversies 1941–1945*, Routledge, London, 1993, was acknowledged as 'The book of the year' by the American Association of Psychoanalysis 1993 and by the Paris Psychoanalytic Society in 1995. In 2001 he was awarded the Sigourney Prize for his contributions to psychoanalysis. He has a personal chair as Professor of Psychoanalysis applied to Literature and History of Ideas at the University of Westminster, London.

LOUISE DE URTUBEY was trained in Uruguay. When, still rather young she was already Full Member and was directing the Training Commission, she left that country, which was under a dictatorial situation and where the professional secret was not longer respected. She came to Paris, where she was elected Full Member with training tasks of the Paris Psychoanalytical Society.

She also is twice a PhD, in psychology (Uruguayan University) and in psychopathology (Paris VII, Sorbonne).

She has published a great number of papers, particularly in French for the *Revue de Psychanalyse* from Paris Psychoanalytical Society, for

Psychanalyse à l'Université (from Paris VII and Prof. Laplanche), once in the *International Journal of Psychoanalysis*, for which she belonged for ten years to the Reading Commitee.

She belongs to the Committee of readers of the Journal of the Italian Psychoanalytical Association *Psicoanalisi*.

She has also wrote several books, *Du côté de chez l'analyste* (2003) and *Si le psychanalyste passe à l'acte* (2006).

Language, symbolization, and psychosis: an introduction

Jorge Canestri

The title of this book, in which a group of eminent psychoanalysts express their friendship to Jacqueline Amati Mehler and at the same time pay tribute to her contributions to psychoanalysis, clearly indicates its subject matter. From different points of view and using different theoretic formulations, its chapters explore a fascinating and problematic area of psychoanalytic knowledge – the relationships between symbolization and serious pathologies – including the role that speech and the different languages play in psychoanalysis, the 'talking cure' *par excellence*, and how they are used in the cure. All these themes have been the object of Jacqueline Amati Mehler's attention and of her papers during the many years of work that she has dedicated to our discipline.

Symbolism, as we know, is one of the great themes confronted by Freud, from *The Interpretation of Dreams* until his final works. His contribution is determinant, even in the eyes of those who do not agree with some of his hypotheses. Many disciplines have taken an interest in 'symbolic facts' including semantics, logic, rhetoric, hermeneutics, aesthetics, philosophy, ethnology, psychoanalysis, poetics; and probably none of them can claim to have fully deciphered this specific activity of the human being. A reasonable position could be to study the various ways of understanding and defining the 'symbolic facts' and the modalities through which the individual succeeds (or does not succeed or only partly succeeds) in *symbolizing*.

A certain discrimination of the elements in play when we speak about symbolism could be useful in order to limit the field. The three terms of symbol, symbolism, and symbolization frequently appear on the scene. The first, and indeed the others, is defined differently according to the discipline involved. Semiotics, for example, suggests a definition of symbol – and here again, it varies according to the semiotic theory chosen – that is not the same as that deriving from psychoanalytic research. In both *The Interpretation of Dreams* and *Introductory Lectures on Psychoanalysis*, Freud hypothesizes that the symbol depends on an unconscious shared universal knowledge limited to a few elements. His disciple Ernest Jones (1916), as we know, wrote a paper that, even though it is controversial, is considered by many to be one of the milestones in the psychoanalytic theory of symbolism. In it Jones emphasizes certain rigidities of the Freudian model and claims that only that which has been repressed becomes symbolized and, furthermore, that only the repressed needs to be symbolized. Like Freud, he believes that only a few elementary ideas (body, family, birth, death) are destined to be symbolized and that the other associations are conscious or are susceptible to becoming so. These latter would not be symbolic but metaphoric. To this form of symbolism in a strict sense (i.e. reduced to a limited number of essential elements), several authors in the psychoanalytic field have contrasted symbolism in a wide sense (cf G. Rosolato, 19.) in which any element of a dream, or any association linked to it, can be considered symbolic. Following Jones' essay, numerous psychoanalysts have put the accent on the concept of symbolism rather than on the definition of the symbol itself; that is, on the 'symbolic operations of the mind' rather than on a concept that, for the semiologist Tzvetan Todorov, is not the essential notion of symbolism. The names of Melanie Klein, Hanna Segal, Jacques Lacan, Herbert Rosenfeld, Wilfred R. Bion, Donald W. Winnicott, Marion Milner, Pierre Marty, etc., are evidence of a persistent interest in a theme that the passing of time and the increasing pluralism of psychoanalytic theories has not dimmed.

The evolution of psychoanalytic theories has probably brought with it a displacement of the accent in the basic conception of symbolism. What would seem more pertinent to our discipline today is not so much a definition of the symbol itself, or a rigid and limited characterization of symbolism, either from the semiotic standpoint (the sign already constituted by language functions as a signal in an association with a symbolic sense) or from the standpoint of unconscious symbolism postulated by Jones; but, rather, after the pioneer work of Melanie Klein and Hanna Segal following the forgotten works of S. Ferenczi, the greater relevance acquired by symbolization as a process – a process that the mind can bring (or not bring) to fulfilment and that can assume various characteristics and undergo not a few distortions.

It is inevitable, therefore, that in the perspective of symbolization as a process, the different psychoanalytic theories on the development of the mind or of the psychic apparatus should assume a central role, and that the hypotheses on the symbolization process should depend on the theories of development that are chosen. One example, but there are many others, is the relationship between symbolization and the depressive position according to Melanie Klein.

In making what we might provisionally call the 'symbolic function of the mind' the centre of its interest, psychoanalysis has partially drawn near to the cognitive conception of symbolism. According to the cognitive conception of symbolism, symbolic interpretation is not a decodification (semiotic theory), but is based on implicit knowledge and on unconscious rules that constitute an autonomous 'symbolic device' that forms part of the inborn equipment that makes experience possible for the human being. I say 'partially' because although psychoanalysis may easily reject the classical semiotic theory of symbol (I emphasize 'classical' inasmuch as certain works of C.S. Peirce, R. Jakobson, I. Fonagy, and others suggest a semiotic theory that is more convincing) and, at least from my own point of view, the conception of Jones, the problem that interests psychoanalysis is not essentially the autonomous symbolic device of the cognitive sciences, that may take its place among the 'x' of the Freudian complementary series, but the fact that the subject can make use of it procedurally. It is in relation to this question of how the subject uses the symbolic device in his developmental process that the relationships between symbolization and the serious pathologies of psychoses, borderline and psychosomatoses, intertwine. This question, that is of fundamental relevance in contemporary psychoanalysis, is dealt with in some of the papers in this book.

The title of this collection of papers also includes language. Nor could it be otherwise seeing that language intervenes predominantly

– though not alone – in the whole process of symbolization. But the language that these papers speak about is also the language of the communication between analyst and analysand – the language that intervenes in the listening and in the interpretation, the language that, as we said before, manifests itself in different tongues. This linguistic diversity, its role in the constitution of the psychic apparatus and of the representations that are part of it, and in the relationship between representation, affect and analytic experience, has always been one of the privileged areas of Amati Mehler's reflections. Some of the authors included in this book develop different ideas on the theme.

Fourteen authors, from Latin America, Europe, and North America, have contributed to this homage with their papers. In *A psychoanalytic enquiry into Pandora's box: symbol and metaphor*, Harold P. Blum discusses the Greek myth of Pandora's box in a way that comes close to Freud's original view about certain symbols representing an unconscious shared universal meaning. 'Inextricably related to psychoanalysis, the myth is also interpreted as symbol and metaphor in the social sciences, art, and literature.' From a psychoanalytic perspective, Blum considers that Pandora's box refers to structurally distinct symbols and metaphors (Sarnoff, 2003), to conscious and preconscious secrets, as well as to repressed unconscious metaphorical danger, or traumatic experience. If released from repression or suppression, and/or projected externally, the contents of Pandora's box 'would be perilous to the individual, the family, and/or society.' Blum focuses on the fact that such 'mythical dangers', are the opposite of the psychoanalytic process aimed at lifting repression and revealing secrets in the service of therapeutic action. However, because Pandora's box contains evil as well as gifts, Blum wonders whether clinical situations in which unconscious forces of censorship and repression, 'in keeping the unacceptable contents under wraps and a lid on the jar' may be in the service of mental health. 'For persons with fragile reality testing, massive denial of external and internal danger may eventuate in a psychosis. Pandora's box could lose its symbolic or metaphorical meaning and encapsulating function.'

Fidias Cesio, in *Deciphering the secrets of oblivion*, follows in the conceptual wake of Freud's actual neuroses and proposes two differentiated categories of memories: those that are unveiled in the field of transference in transference neuroses ('psychic memories'), and those that, in contrast, manifest themselves but cannot be remembered ('actual memories'). The 'actual memories' are supplemented by what Cesio calls 'the buried', i.e. the Oedipal tragedy, the primarily repressed material and a component of action. The 'texts' that derive from these elements cannot be decoded – that is, interpreted; this category of memories must be the object of *constructions* in analysis. The construction, which the author conceives as 'a kind of distant translation of the original', is the means of access to this specific kind of memory. Each memory has interrelated components: actual, action, psychic, and texts (a set of gestures, signs, and spoken words that express an idea). The author attributes a special place to the soma, which is considered to be the source of origin of the drives and the foundation of the ego. According to Cesio, the 'actual memories' are essential because they are intimately linked to the serious pathologies but also because, after a correct analysis of the psychic component of the memory, the analyst comes up against the barrier of the actual memories foundation. If he does not understand this passage correctly and uses the constructions as well as the interpretations, then he may find himself faced with a negative therapeutic reaction and a therapeutic failure. Through his original vision that reinstates the concept of 'actual' (Aktuelle) in psychoanalysis, Cesio numbers himself among those who study those elements that escape the declarative, explicit, and retrievable memory.

In *Self formation, symbolic capacity, and spontaneity*, Gemma Corradi Fiumara notes that the process of mentalization is a real challenge in psychoanalytic research. In this process, defined as 'the core of the inner vicissitudes which sustain our growth and survival', one of the principal factors is the development of the symbolic function. When compared with what has been said above about slipping from the symbol and symbolism to the concept of 'symbolic function of the mind', Corradi tends towards this latter direction. She bases her theory on the well-known works of Peter Fonagy on mentalization and on Winnicott's concepts relative to 'mirroring', 'playing', and the 'good-enough' parent; but the main aim of her paper is to develop the consequences of the possible failures – attributed essentially to the inadequate response of the environment – in the process of mentalization, and to analyse in greater depth the analytic work that is needed in order to contrast them. Useful technical and clinical notes for working with the serious pathologies can be drawn from her considerations.

Corradi emphasizes that, following Winnicott, there is no denying that we need 'sufficiently good' parents, 'but we specially need the capacity to deal with the 'partially bad' parents . . . because affective support and emotional corrosion are often so interwoven in our growth as to become indistinguishable.' This capacity should also manifest itself in the analysis since not even the analyst exclusively represents the 'good-enough' parent. The symbolic capacities (or the symbolic function) can deteriorate and be used destructively, creating a spiral of falsification: 'Symbolization is often used as an all-powerful (and hence false) means of imitating the world and, therefore, of simply "extracting" reality out of the subject, instead of laboriously coming to recognize it in persons and nature.' These are pseudo-symbolic processes. Language itself, which, as the author says, is our symbolic domain *par excellence*, can be passively imitated, and our linguistic potential suppressed or crystallized in some kind of ideology that is transformed into 'spoken subjects'. To these pseudo-symbolic processes, Corradi opposes a genuine symbolization that can be developed only subjectively.

From the clinical and technical analytic point of view, the author examines the contribution that 'spontaneity' can make as 'something more than interpretation' that many authors search for in order to produce progress in the cure of certain pathologies or simply to make the cure itself possible. She says that: 'Experiences of spontaneity do not correct past empathic failure by means of the analytic relation, as they do not compensate for past deficit. Rather, something new springs to life in the relation which transforms the quality, level, intensity of the bi-personal field.'

As the title of her paper, *A language for remembering the future*, suggests, Yolanda Gampel deals with the object of W.R. Bion's speculations, especially as the author of *A Memoir of the Future* – something that we could call 'the very first thoughts', 'the premature personality' or 'primitive parts of the self' or even 'primordial elements'. The author tells us that in Bion's thinking: 'Remnants of the premature personality continue to exist alongside the post-mature occupier of the same soma-psyche. There develop psychosomatic reactions, somato-psychotic demands, unfamiliar elements which, on their appearance, we sometimes construct as illness, psychosis, neurosis, borderline state, and so on.' In clinical work on these 'remnants of the premature personality', the well-known Bionian concepts of alpha function, reverie, constantly operative paranoid-schizoid/depressive oscillation, the container-contained relationship, the negative capability and the selected fact, are privileged instruments of work. The author emphasises how, in the development of his thinking, Bion explores increasingly primitive, prenatal elements preceding the 'birth of the mind', remote and undecipherable, that lead him to wonder in *Emotional Turbulence*, 'When do things begin?'

Gampel writes: 'What we can say is that the mentalization of those primitive parts of the self is very different from the processes which psychoanalysis is supposed to probe. These primitive parts of the personality think with the body. The laws governing them are closer to neurophysiology than psychology.' As proof of this, the author then introduces us to other lines of thought that could serve to think the unthinkable: Taoism, Amos Oz, George Perec, F. Pessoa. When thinking about Jacqueline Amati Mehler's 'psycho-archeology', 'those so-called "underground precursors" of speech which become manifest through a series of paralinguistic elements, that ever growing complex network of polysensorial associations which make possible the transition from the concrete to the abstract, from the bodily to the mental', Gampel enters into the heart of that which animates the deliberations of a considerable part of contemporary psychoanalysis and is also the object of many of the papers included in this book.

In *Symbolization and psychosis: the mediating function of images in individual psychoanalytic psychodrama,* Alain Gibeault develops a similar argument, although from a different point of view linked to a specific practice – the psychoanalytic psychodrama – that for a long time has been at the centre of his reflections and also of his clinical work with serious pathologies. Gibeault refers to Freudian theoretic thinking, and hypothesizes that the mental images are intermediaries, and lie somewhere between the unconscious thing-presentations and the word-presentations. The author says that if we accept the Freudian hypotheses on the unconscious, then we must accept the existence of some kind of thought process that precedes the advent of the word. Freud's thinking in *Constructions in Analysis* seems to lean in this direction when he suggests the existence of true hallucinations in non-psychotic patients, and this is what enables Gibeault to hypothesize the importance of the role of the image and of pre-verbal thoughts in order to guarantee access to the conscious, to remote memory traces, primitive sensations, and pre-verbal thought. The quoted works of C. and S. Botella relative to the importance of topographical and formal regression follow this same line of thinking. The psychoanalytic psychodrama, by provoking a 'movement' of images, a lateralization of the transference and motor and verbal action, facilitates work with psychotic patients. The strategy and the interpretative tactics seek to 'encourage' symbolization and to reduce the splitting of the ego, thus favouring the transition towards mental states that are less split and closer to the conflict. This chapter offers abundant clinical material that well explains the work done by analysts and operators as they follow psychotic patients in their vicissitudes with symbolization and thought processes.

In *'White psychoses': silence and delusions,* Adolfo Pazzagli underlines how the term 'psychosis' in psychoanalysis does not truly correspond to a psychiatric diagnosis, but, rather, covers a vast and variegated area of phenomena characterized essentially by serious limitations in the personal sense of self-fulfilment, in the capacity to feel pleasure in interpersonal relationships, and a strong limitation of self-liberty. These phenomena combine to define, with a certain stability, a personality structure or a psychotic mode of mental operation.

Pazzagli recalls how Jacqueline Amati Mehler insists on the 'co-existence of different levels of narcissistic and psychotic psychic functioning, but also of non-differentiated areas of mental functioning in severe patients'; he then describes those pathological structures 'with few or non apparent symptoms of psychosis', that in the French literature are called 'psychoses blanches' (white psychoses). In this type of pathology, which illustrates the paradox of 'psychotic operational levels' with no or with only occasional symptoms, Pazzagli thinks that Amati Mehler's note on the non-differentiated areas of mental functioning is essential. In order to produce a flourishing psychotic symptomatology, there must be a structure, no matter how immature or incomplete. The psychotic symptoms, the author says, produce anxiety, but they are also manifestations of useful – though primitive – defences.

By mentioning Winnicott's idea of an unintermediate area – the problem of relating what is perceived objectively to what is perceived subjectively – the author is able to make a hypothesis on the specific nature of the disorder of 'white psychoses'. Even in white psychoses this intermediate area is lacking, and the patient cannot make the necessary distinction between the realms of objective and of subjective perception. 'The two realms appear to be either separate or jumbled one with the other. Rigid separation, if maintained, leads to the presence of symptom-free psychotic modes of operation (white psychoses).'

Fred Pine, in *When actions speak louder than words*, describes a particular clinical phenomenon in which, due to an incapacity to symbolize, actions occupy a prime position in the clinical experience. Pine hypothesizes that these are patients with 'a history of the strain trauma of childhood internalized, carried, and repeated', following Kris' ideas on the subject. These patients cannot transform passive into active, they could locate no experience of their *making* it happen.

On the basis of this consideration, the author points out how specific aspects of the common working method of the analyst may be re-traumatizing for a particular patient. He suggests that it is important, for a period of time – i.e. until the patient acquires a certain level of agency or of ego function – to eliminate transference interpretations that are perceived by the patient not in terms of content, but as actions arousing feelings of passive victimization. In the second clinical example presented by the author, it is the fact of speaking 'with certainty' – i.e. the tone of conviction – that represents, in the mind of the analysand, the passively suffered action. Incidentally, since we are dealing with language and the use of language, these observations emphasize the importance in clinical psychoanalysis of considering the pragmatic value of language extremely carefully.

It is evident that these psychopathological conditions, precisely for the reasons above mentioned, emerge and manifest themselves in the interaction between analyst and analysand; therefore, 'empathic failure becomes a central issue with these patients'.

Pine mentions that in his paper *Unconscious wishes and human relationships*, J. Sandler (1981) hypothesizes the existence of 'primary needs for recognition, confirmation, and respect for boundaries', which become crucial in psychic life when they are not observed.

It is not sufficient, therefore, to understand and interpret the specific vulnerability of these subjects, inasmuch as metaphorical repetitions of an incursive invasion of the patient's self are inevitable in the transference. In Pine's view, this phenomenon of insufficient symbolic representation, which does not allow the analysand to transform from passive into active unless it is possible to put into effect an experiential correction in analysis, suggests to the analyst that he should carry out technical modifications, such as not interpreting the transference and responding to the patient's demands.

Ana-Maria Rizzuto, in *Reflections on listening to and speaking with the patient during analysis*, considers the specificity of listening and speaking in analysis. She refers to the words of the great Russian linguist R. Jakobson: 'we speak to be heard and need to be heard in order to be understood.' As Rizzuto reminds us, this evidence does not diminish the immense complexity of the task in psychoanalysis. What do we listen to and how do we listen in analysis? What theoretical and technical instruments have we developed in order to convey the complexity of analytic listening?

Rizzuto points out that we have to listen and speak to the analysand as 'an autonomous adult self, in a dialogical symmetry of equal participation and asymmetrical functions'. Addressing our listening and our discourse to the constantly invested adult is not the opposite to listening and talking *simultaneously* to the 'suffering child still alive in the patient experience with us'. The supporting nucleus of analysis as a correctional experience, therefore, consists of the fact that the analyst offers the analysand what he/she has never known before: a relationship in which the analyst listens and speaks to the autonomous self but facilitates the regressive re-experiencing simultaneously. This becomes possible to the extent that the analyst offers the analysand an 'emotional object constancy and investment' and never fails in his/her commitment, which must not be in any way altered by the patient's defensive manoeuvres. The author says that this concept of *analyst emotional object constancy* goes beyond the therapeutic alliance inasmuch as the latter is based on the conscious capacities and commitments between patient and analyst, while the former refers to an affective disposition of the analyst.

In her conclusions, Rizzuto reminds us that the psychologist J. Bruner theorized that parents stimulate their children to use the language they consider appropriate for every moment of development (Language Acquisition Support System, LASS). The analyst, too, *mutatis mutandis*, accompanies the analysand as an adult partner searching for better instruments to live his/her own human experience. An interesting clinical case, of great pertinence to the issues dealt with in the rest of the text, supplements the author's theoretical reflections.

Theodore Shapiro, in *The mystery of the unsaid name: commonalities between God and Rumpelstiltskin*, considers the question of the 'power of naming', first from a linguistic and then from a literary and cultural viewpoint. He feels authorized to use material lying outside clinical work by the fact that Freudian and post-Freudian analysis have extended interpretation from the couch to culture, thereby considerably adding to its models. In his theorization, besides well-known concepts deriving from 'classical' linguistics, Shapiro introduces other concepts belonging to the 'pragmatic turn' that, in the contemporary study of language, implies recognizing the contribution of pragmatics (to do things with words, as Austin so well expressed it) to semantics and, in some cases, the pre-eminence of pragmatics over semantics and syntax in the construction of the meaning.

In my opinion, these concepts are essential to the study of the symbolic function and of symbolization. 'Every utterance in words is an interpretation' the author reminds us; every interpretation defines the dimensions of meaning that we take into consideration. Freud elaborated a complex transformational system that allows access to the conscious, naming them, of constellations of unknown elements linked to the affects. Many of these elements come from pre-verbal infantile experiences of which no declarative memory is possible. In this system, Shapiro assigns an important role to the 'naming' and, consequently, to the 'unnamed'. Naming and saying have a specific power of delimiting the meaning of the object and constrain it into a cognitive frame. The speaker and the listener are provided then with a sense of the power of utterance. On the other side, 'the "unnamed" protect us from the banality and confined humanity of the named': i.e., the 'unnamed' acquire a significance and a symbolic value. The 'unnamed' God, Shapiro suggests, 'is a reference to an abiding and unfettered creative force'.

The careful and original analysis of the fairy tale by the Brothers Grimm, *Rumpelstiltskin* – one of those medieval oral creations in the 'Spinnstuben' where women met to spin together – allows the author to significantly link the fairy tale to the prohibition to pronounce the name of God and to the psychoanalytic operation that helps us to understand 'the roots of awe that are also features of our symbols'.

Adriana Sorrentini, in *Texts and pre-texts in psychoanalytic clinical practice: languages and idioms*, differentiates between the representations spoken by free association and 'the actual presentations'. When these actual presentations break into the discourse through silence, anxiety, somatic manifestations, pain, lethargy, etc, their dialectic differs significantly from that of the known languages. This is transference of a different nature, with an intense actual-experiential-drive quality, that invests the analyst as 'an original object' and qualitatively and quantitatively diverges from the usual representation of the libidinally invested analyst, as in the psychoneuroses.

Sorrentini reminds us of the Freudian statement in *Outline of Psychoanalysis*, about certain coincidences between the id that represents the inherited constitutional past, and the superego 'with the influences of the past assumed by others'. The ego, instead, appears to be governed by what has been experienced. Analysts do not have access to the non-repressed and non-representational – therefore *actual* – unconscious material through the interpretation. They must resort to construction. This technical recourse, the object of one of Freud's most interesting later texts, should allow us to deal with a 'prehistoric' material that presents itself in the clinical experience as 'actual' (Aktuelle) and with a-temporal modalities. The task of the analyst, the author says, is similar to that of 'translating an archaic text into a shared and contemporary tongue, to name the unnamed, to transform tragedy into drama, to passing from prehistory to history and thus having memory, representation recall and word'.

Finally, in this text, as in others in this volume, we are aware of a common preoccupation concerning the possibility of 'translating' the archaic material (in this case theorized as 'the buried underground' of F. Cesio) and which are the best instruments to use.

In *Symbolism in love and sex,* Ethel Spector Person proposes yet another different point of view. The author reminds us that, as mentioned at the beginning of this Introduction, there are many questions that still await a shared solution concerning the complex issue of symbolism in psychoanalysis: the origins of the symbolic process, the developmental stage in which symbols are organized, etc. Her attention, however, turns towards the role that symbols play in love and sex, and also to the role of culture in the processes of symbolization.

The author states that what is often omitted in discussions on the concept of symbolism is the communicative component of the symbol, and, by quoting P.M. Bromberg, she stresses the importance of the interpersonal aspects of symbolism in language and in free association. From this angle, the process of symbolization and its vicissitudes is seen as 'a continuing task built into the analytic structure'. The amorous symbol of our ideal pre-exists the meeting and makes us attribute to the other the image of the type of lover we wish for. This is the *Lover-Shadow* of H.G. Wells, a product of our mind, constructed on the model of the primary relationships belonging to the subject's past.

However, symbolism and sex differences between men and women are culturally and historical conditioned: romantic and sexual symbols change with the cultural *Zeitgeist*. Person offers the reader an interesting panorama of the differences between the symbolism of the past and that of the present relative to the romantic and sexual symbolic characterizations. She points out how variations in the symbolization of male sexuality – when compared with the past – are less significant than those that refer to female sexuality; in the same way, there are fewer novelties in the theorization of male sexuality than in female sexuality.

Person says that because of the significant cultural innovations of the past 50 years, including birth control and the economic and social independence of women, 'the culture acts to re-codify symbols such that they differ to a greater or lesser degree in different cultures and different epochs'. In agreement with other authors, and also with myself, the author emphasizes how, in H. Loewald's model (1988, *Sublimation: Inquiries into Theoretical Psychoanalysis*), symbolization is part of ego development, without the traditional emphasis on defence, as happens in E. Jones' theorization.

The reader of Riccardo Steiner's chapter, *Index, Icon, Symbol? Can Peirce's Descriptive Classification be of any Use to Psychoanalysis?*, will find himself immersed in a fascinating and scholarly account of the conceptual history, in Kleinian psychoanalysis, of the symbolic equation and symbolism. The journey begins with a series of clinical vignettes, which he subsequently analyses according to the historical-conceptual examination that he conducts in this chapter.

This historical-conceptual examination begins, obviously, with Freud, and emphasizes how Freud in *Studies on Hysteria* (1895) states that pre-verbal and non-verbal 'language' lies at the heart of the symbol. This point is important, together with a reference to the thoughts of the father of psychoanalysis on schizophrenics, in order to indicate how many of Freud's reflections, together with Ferenczi's and later M. Klein's (1930, *The importance of symbol formation in the development of the ego*), lead to the conceptualization of the symbolic equations, descriptively speaking.

Following Klein, Rosenfeld, Bion, and Money-Kyrle, Steiner suggests a developmental sequence beginning with the early symbols (that Steiner calls 'normal symbolic equations, different from the pathological symbolic equations of schizophrenic children) and that, going beyond the depressive position, leads to fully-formed symbols. This developmental sequence continues throughout a person's entire life and is subject to a regression to symbolic equations when projective identification 'is used as a defence against depressive anxieties, symbols already formed and used as symbols and sublimations may revert to symbolic equations'. The author says that this sequence highlights one of the problems of the Kleinian model: 'the lack of an explicit developmental model of the psychic apparatus, beyond the first year of life of the baby.' This leads him to wonder whether there exists an intermediate state between symbolic equation and proper symbolization, a state that would certainly require a more mature and integrated self than the one involved in the symbolic equations.

In the final part of his chapter, Steiner – in my opinion, happily – turns to some ideas taken from the semiotics of Charles S. Peirce and Roman Jakobson. From the former, he recalls the difference propitiated between index, icon, and verbal symbol, concepts that Peirce conceived 'as related and implying each other'. This semiotic model may prove to be extremely interesting from a psychoanalytical point of view, for it is a fairly open model and its elements are interconnected. The model of the Russian linguist Jakobson follows in the same direction, connecting verbal language to non-verbal language, to the body and to gesture and visual language. All these elements should be absorbed and integrated into verbal communication, and Jakobson theorizes this function as an 'intersemiotic function'. Steiner rightly considers it as another way of naming and conceiving Bion's alpha function. While index and icon are related to a static notion of time, says Jakobson, the symbol contains a 'to be in the future', a sense of time that can be developed. This, Steiner points out, is similar to what Klein, Segal, Milner, Rycroft, and others have tried to say regarding the symbolic function in psychoanalysis.

Louise de Urtubey, in *The foreign language*, presents a work that, like almost all writing on multilingualism, is enriched by a great deal of autobiographical information as well as clinical notes. The author wonders about 'certain anxieties and defences when faced with a foreign language and what is foreign in general'. In the first Freudian theories, the unconscious appeared as a 'foreign body', like Satan in diabolic possessions; even 'The Uncanny' shared those same characteristics that lead the foreigner to be thought of as feared and dangerous. The possible double meaning of 'Unheimlich' (uncanny), revealed by the combination of what is familiar (Heimlich) to the subject and its denial (Un-heimlich), tells of the effort to place outside what frightens us from the inside (projection as defence, negation of similarity, narcissism, rationalization of prejudice against the projected bad object, the disavowal of the capacity of others through envy or sense of danger). What could be the reason for resistance to learning a foreign language? Urtubey postulates a particular and partial defect of symbolization: all these fears about the foreigner 'show an underlying wish for unity, for narcissistic fusion and non-differentiation'. Symbolization is impossible without the existence and recognition of a third party: there is the object and the word that corresponds to it, but there is no space for a third element, the foreign word.

What hypotheses could be suggested to explain this partial defect of symbolization? A fragile narcissism? A functioning of the ego that hates external reality? The author reminds us that before children fully acquire their linguistic capacities, even parents and adults speak something that for the child may appear as the equivalent of what would be a foreign language for the adult. The foreigner, in this case, 'will dwell more in the superego than in the ego, from where he will prohibit the possession of that which belongs/ belonged to the parents, in a sort of auditory primal scene'.

Anne-Marie Sandler writes about *The past unconscious and the present unconscious*. In only a few lines she provides one of the most complete summaries of her model of the functioning of the mind (shared and created with Joseph Sandler) that I have ever had the opportunity of reading. She begins by noting that many of the chapters in this book contain new insights or reflections that could lead us to a clearer understanding of how our minds work. In the same way, these contributions should help us to find new and better ways for listening to and interpreting analytical material, especially the clinical material of severe patients where serious difficulties of symbolization prevail. It is with this intention that the author re-proposes the concepts of the past unconscious and present unconscious, elaborated with J. Sandler, that she considers a helpful frame of reference.

These concepts are very well known in the psychoanalytical world, and I would not know how to present them more clearly and concisely than Anne-Marie Sandler has done. I particularly wish to underline how the author connects the concept of past unconscious – its direct inaccessibility and the real impossibility of being remembered – to concepts deriving from the neurosciences, such as the concept of implicit or procedural memory systems – 'just memories of procedures in which experiences are encoded as roles of functioning.' These structuring organizations, or 'basic dynamic templates', stemming from the past unconscious 'give form to all the intrapsychic content that arises in the depth of the present unconscious', exerting a constant pressure on the analyst who must identify and interpret them in the transference and countertransference work.

Having reached the end of the book, the reader will be able to identify in the variety of proposals and arguments, a common thread that, in different ways, runs through all the chapters. All the authors – strengthened by their clinical experience with severe pathologies that come to analysis more frequently than in the past, but also thanks to the greater theoretical and technical ability of the analysts – question themselves and work around the precursors of the symbol, the very early processes of symbolization and the deformations that this process may undergo. As we have seen, while the theoretical models used diverge, the lines of research converge. In these chapters, as Anne-Marie Sandler says, I think that the reader will be able to find many interesting points for a continued reflection on an issue that is so central to contemporary psychoanalysis.

CHAPTER ONE

A psychoanalytic enquiry into Pandora's box: symbol and metaphor

Harold P. Blum

The Greek myth of Pandora's box has been within our personal and collective imagination through the ages. In contrast to many other mythological characters, Pandora has remained familiar and has never lost her psychological and social vitality. Over time, the myth has been altered or modified but the essential features and outline have remained relatively intact. This paper will discuss the myth of Pandora and her box as symbol and metaphor in psychoanalysis, as well as in Western art and literature. The Pandora myth, inextricably related to psychoanalysis, represents the repressed, the return of the repressed, curiosity, and censorship. In the psychoanalytic process, the myth additionally represents resistance to analytic inquiry and insight. Clinical examples will be used to illuminate the over-determined, complex meanings of the Pandora myth. These include focus not only on the traditional interpretation of Pandora's box as the female genitalia and reproductive organs, but also additional meanings as concealed and revealed secrets. The myth of Pandora is further elaborated as representing basic human ambivalence, and universal unconscious fantasies related to individual and familial secrets and secrecy.

From a psychoanalytic perspective, Pandora's box refers to structurally distinct symbols and metaphors (Sarnoff, 2003), conscious and preconscious secrets, as well as to repressed unconscious metaphorical danger, or traumatic experience. If released from repression or suppression, and/or projected externally, the contents would be perilous to the individual, the family, and/or society. These mythical dangers, however, are the opposite of the psychoanalytic process. In clinical psychoanalysis, lifting repression, suspending censorship, and revealing secrets all contribute to therapeutic action and progress.

There are numerous permutations of the Pandora myth. In the typical narrative of the Pandora myth, she was the first woman, a beautiful woman. Formed of earth and water, either by Prometheus or Hephaestus, she was animated by Athena or with the aid of fire stolen from heaven by Prometheus. Pandora was completed by all the other gods, each of whom gave a gift, thus the name 'Pandora' – 'all gifted'. The gifts of Aphrodite and Hermes were malevolent rather than benevolent so that Pandora, always with the box bestowed by the gods, became a symbol of ambivalence, 'a beautiful evil' (Panofsky & Panofsky, 1962). Though Prometheus warns his brother, Epimetheus, against Pandora, the latter, nevertheless, takes her, with her sealed box, as his wife. She subsequently becomes the mother of suffering and sorrowful humanity. Unable to resist her insistent curiosity, she opens the lid of the sealed box, releasing every evil into the world with permanent destructive consequences. Only hope remains in the box or jar. While hope is not lost, neither is it available, since it is resealed in the box. Pandora's box is like the Trojan horse, betrayal and fatality disguised as a gift. Pandora's box is clearly related to our vernacular expressions, 'opening a can of worms', and 'curiosity killed the cat', etc.

The biblical myth of Eve is a modified version of Pandora within another culture in the Western tradition. Eve is warned against eating the apple from the Tree of Knowledge. She too is curious, and cannot resist the temptation of the forbidden fruit. As a result, Adam and Eve are expelled from the utopian bliss of the Garden of Eden, which becomes lost paradise. This lost paradise is never to be regained and the offspring of Adam and Eve, humanity, will henceforth experience such negative affects as pain, shame, and guilt. Exiled by the formerly loving but now punitive God, humanity will have to work and sweat for its existence. Humanity will have to contend with love and hate, good and evil, destruction and death. Immortality is now gone forever, and humanity must struggle with uncertainties and hardships in a finite life span.

Pandora and Eve are related to the sirens of Greek myth whose seductions are irresistible. Anticipating the gifts of sex and love, the men are betrayed and led to their own death. The sirens might be compared to the modern-day version of the seductive woman who seemingly offers boundless gratifications, which are inherently dangerous. The relationship has the potential for seduction and destruction.

Pandora is the *femme fatale* of the world's literature, drama, and art. She has been variously and vividly represented by such great writers as Calderon, Voltaire, and Goethe, as well as by artists. In literature, her representation has been influenced by issues of gender, culture, and language (Amati Mehler, Argentieri, & Canestri, 1993). In some of the literature, Pandora, as in the traditional version of the myth, wreaks havoc and disseminates disease, disasters, and death. In others, the converse is the case. Pandora turns vice into virtue, is a humanizing and harmonizing influence, and brings happy endings to former conflicts. Representing a variety of allegorical and metaphorical meanings, the beauty and charms disguise the deceit and destructiveness of femininity. In Calderon's drama, *The Statue of Prometheus*, Pandora is not the first mortal woman, but rather retains the image and attributes of a goddess. Presented with a very attractive box as a present, Pandora is curious but unsuspecting as she disregards the prohibition and opens the vessel. The two brothers, Prometheus and Epimetheus, and their allies fight over her and all sing in despair 'Woe to him who saw good change to bad, and bad to worse.' (Panofsky & Panofsky, 1962, p. 119) In the end, Prometheus marries Pandora with the union as a metaphor for the harmonious fusion of art and science.Voltaire wrote an opera, *Pandore* (1740), in which Pandora is depicted as a traditional foolhardy woman whose unrestrained impulsive curiosity unleashes evil upon humanity. Pandora has a loving but frail character and the opera has a happy ending.

In Voltaire's view, she did not deserve punishment. She opened the lid for love, and with the assistance of hope, conquered all.

In 1773, Goethe wrote a play about Pandora, a life-long interest. In the play, Prometheus stoops before the image of Pandora, addressing his self-made statue with a paean of praise: 'Pandora, sacred vessel of all gifts that are delightful under the broad sky on the infinite earth . . . all that which I have ever tasted as a pure radiance of heaven and a calm pleasure of the soul . . . all this – my Pandora.' (Panofsky & Panofsky, 1962, p. 123). She is presented as an innocent, beautiful, bright girl who has learned from her father the secrets of life and death. Later in 1806, Goethe was attracted to a lady whom he gave the pseudonym Pandora. When she left, he wrote a second play, *Pandora*, in which Pandora loses her lover and is left with grief and longing for his return. Goethe suggests a connection between the myth and madness, and the relationship between art and the irrational.

Pandora has been painted and sculpted by artists of the ages in many different styles. Henry Moore did several sculptures of Pandora. For Dante Rossetti, Pandora is depicted as a sensuous beauty with deeply shadowed eyes, holding a golden box from which a cloud of evil spirits escapes. Swinburne described the painting as 'among Rossetti's mightiest in God-like terror, an imperial trouble of beauty, shadowed by the smoke and fiery vapor of winged and fleshless passions crowding from the casket in spires of flame-lit and curling cloud around her fatal face and mourning veil of hair.' (Panofsky & Panofsky, 1962, p. 109) Paul Klee's drawing (1920), conveys the traditional psychoanalytic symbolic meaning of Pandora, representing Pandora's box as a kantharos vase with evil escaping as vapor through a thinly disguised representation of open female genitalia. Max Beckmann's painting (1947) depicts an explosive, fiery scene, as a metaphor for devastation. In this connection, Pandora is not infrequently encountered in the writings and cartoons of the news media, i.e. with reference to the horrors of war, the Holocaust, and the epidemic of HIV. Pandora's box has become a general metaphor for the eruption of violence and destruction. Pandora, in the ancient myth, also represents the phallic, castrating, devouring witch of literature and fairy tale. Faced with the technological capacity to destroy civilization, humanity, like Epimetheus, may become wise too late.

Although not mentioned explicitly, the myth of Pandora figures prominently in Freud's choice of 'Dora' as the pseudonym for his famous patient, as well as in the case report. Freud encountered Pandora in the form of Theodora, in the theater, while studying with Charcot in Paris in 1885. Theodora was a Pandora-type figure in the form of a Roman empress. Freud played upon the titles of the playwright Sardou's dramas, inventing such titles as Thermadora, Equadora, and Toreadora; he imagined a play named Dora . On April 16, 1900, Freud wrote to Fleiss, 'since E hates to suffer through all my technical and theoretical errors, I actually think that a future case could be solved in half the time. May the Lord now send the next one.' Freud called this case 'Dora', a gift from God (Malcolm, 1982; Decker, 1991). There were boxes in two famous dreams in the Dora case. The best known is the jewel box, which Freud interprets in terms of Dora's virgin genitalia. In Dora's famous dream, she was attempting to flee her burning house but her mother wanted to stop and save her jewel case. Her parents had failed to protect her. She was exposed as a young teenager to Herr K, her father's friend who pursued her with gifts, blandishments, and courtship. She was to be the bartered bride, given to Herr K in exchange for her father having an affair with her Herr K's wife. Herr K had given Dora a costly jewel case, which in idiomatic German was slang for the female genitals. Freud interpreted that Dora was to give him her jewel case in exchange for his jewel case. Dora's precious jewel case referred to her virginal genitals, and to her virtuous ideals. For Freud it was clear that Dora was consciously or unconsciously conflicted about defloration by Herr K (and unconsciously by her father and Freud). At that time, Freud had written that the case had smoothly opened to his existing collection of 'pick locks', then unaware of his intrusive, invasive countertransference in the analysis of an eighteen year old in the culture of her time and place.

In both of Dora's dreams, while the box unconsciously represents her genitals, metaphorically, its highly meaningful hidden contents represent preconscious personal and familial secrets as well. Dora's family secrets were a heavy burden. Her father's extramarital affair with Frau Kay was supposedly a secret, as were Herr K's designs on Dora. Her father having been treated for syphilis was another secret. Further, Dora secretly believed her mother had been infected and degraded by her father. Her conscious adolescent fantasies were associated with fears of being shamed and degraded like her mother, dishonoured by losing her virginity before marriage, and exploited as a bartered sex object. Behind Dora's contempt for doctors and her negative transference to Freud was her contempt for her father's inheritable disease, his infidelity, and deceit, as well as contempt for her mother's passive complicity. There was secret collusion among the Ks and her parents. Her mother managed to not be curious, to not know or disavow what was going on in her own family. Dora's mother silently colluded in the familial secrecy and duplicity. Dora, however, in some measure wanted to understand and be understood. While inhibited, she also wanted to lift the veil of secrecy within the family. Like Pandora, she struggled with keeping the lid on the bejewelled box, despite her thoughtful curiosity and her perception of the deception and hypocrisy of her parents, the Ks, and Viennese society.

Dora's reluctance to be treated by Freud had been preceded by her refusal to see new doctors. For Freud this meant that she was afraid that each doctor would uncover her secrets. He referred to her secret masturbation, the secret of her childhood enuresis, and the secret of her vaginal discharge. These secrets were linked to her shame and humiliation over her mother's vaginal discharge and her father's venereal disease. Dora, like so many women of that era, had experienced maltreatment or lack of treatment at the hands of male doctors in authority. Freud's interpretation of Dora's contempt for physicians was that the inept physician had been unable to discover her secrets. When Dora opened and shut her reticule (a small cloth purse), opening it, Freud interpreted this behaviour on the couch as a masturbatory equivalent. Freud then declared 'no mortal could keep a secret. If (the patient's) lips are silent, he chatters with his fingertips; betrayal oozes out of him at every pore.' (Freud, 1905, p. 78) While there is a balance between the wish to conceal and the wish to reveal, the demand to withhold and the command to confess, it is not possible for the analyst to define every patient's secrets. All patients are Pandoras in degree, more or less inhibited, and initially reluctant to lift the lid and reveal their deepest secrets. Some patients reveal such secrets only in the terminal phase of their analysis and others keep some of themselves in the closet for a lifetime. For example, Anna Freud stated that she was taking some secrets with her to the grave. Many homosexuals in public life formerly remained 'in the closet' avoiding social stigma and possible economic and political repercussions, the secret often kept from spouse, family, and friends. Throughout history, such issues as illegitimate birth, abortion, adoption, corruption, and imprisonment have been associated with secrecy.

As with Pandora, however, some secrets are best left as secrets. Culture often determines what is secret and what is overt. For women in some cultures, menstruation was an overt or covert taboo, a secret that is sometimes more apparent and sometimes more opaque. Menstrual blood, emanating from Pandora's box, was frightening and hardly recognized as the only form of normal bleeding. Menstruation activated fantasies of mutilation and castration in both sexes with cultural and religious ritual, to avoid 'blood contamination'. The menstruating female could be kept 'boxed up', forbidden to have physical contact with the rest of her family. Long regarded as the 'curse', and the woman as being 'unwell', the blood and vaginal discharge were among the ills which Pandora released. As a personal and social secret, menstruation was kept in a sealed box in ordinary discourse, and in the art and literature of past generations.

Freud had imagined a plaque commemorating his discovery of 'the secret of dreams', and kept his specimen dream of Irma's injection a secret from Fliess, his figurative analyst, for five years (Freud, 1900; Blum, 1995). Freud was aware of his growing contempt for Breuer by the time he wrote *The Interpretation of Dreams*, but then was only dimly aware of his rising secret devaluation of Fliess. A closed box figures in Freud's correspondence with Fliess, and then among the specimens of unconsciously motivated forgetting described by Freud (1901) in *The Psychopathology of Everyday Life*. He wrote to Fliess on August 7, 1901, 'I have promised Miss L. that I would buy her a small iron strongbox in which she could keep her valuables, but I continually forgot about it. Eventually, she reminded me, . . . it must have been somewhere in an easy to find location in the inner city. But I was absolutely unable to find this place on my walk. So I resolved to look it up in the phone book . . . but then I forgot about it again on five successive days. Finally I forced myself to remember and look up the address. Where is the place of this (store) window with the iron box? Brandstatter, across from Breuer, where I must have seen it several thousand times.' Freud's conflicts concerned Breuer and money, for Freud was resentful about having been in Breuer's monetary debt, for which Breuer had refused repayment. Freud may also have been consciously or unconsciously disparaging of his own father for being unable to support his large family. The actual sources of financial support of Jacob Freud's family remain among history's secrets.

As previously indicated, Pandora's box with dangerous content, not to be opened, represents the repressed, disguised unconscious. Freud's provision of psychoanalytic access to the unconscious, and to the unruly child in the adult, was tantamount to opening Pandora's box, but with beneficial rather than harmful effects. Conscious secrets were linked to silent daydreams and then to the unconscious pathogenic components of infantile neurotic phenomena. Pandora's box represents the unconscious forces of censorship and repression that keep the unacceptable contents under wraps and a lid on the jar.

In the Pandora myth, Prometheus had warned his brother, Epimetheus, not to accept the gift of Pandora from Zeus, just as the biblical Eve was warned never to eat the apple from the Tree of Knowledge. The fear of opening Pandora's box is directly related to the ever-recurrent opposition to psychoanalytic findings. This is not to say that psychoanalysis should be immune from scientific challenge or criticism. Nevertheless, much of the criticism and invective levelled at psychoanalysis and the flogging of Freud in the media is based on an irrational visceral opposition. The lid must be kept on Pandora's box and the unconscious must be kept out of conscious awareness. The iron strongbox must be kept safe, intact and its dangerous unconscious conflicts and fantasies kept permanently locked and sealed against any form of escape.

Pandora's box also represents the conscious or preconscious personal and/or familial secrets, contained or suppressed within the box. Shared secrets, in silent collusion, become important components of the relationship between the secret sharers. Secrecy and silence of the object world exacerbates traumatic experience, often associated with the isolation of affect, with parts of the self and object kept compartmentalized in a Pandora's box. The traumatized person, often sensing that a dark secret is being withheld, is afraid to open the box; curiosity is inhibited. The traumatized person may be left in doubt about what happened in reality. Affective awareness may be further blunted by concern for the welfare of love objects. In the case of child abuse, an adult authority's false claims that nothing really happened, or that all that happened was innocent will further the child's denial of reality. The child may be left in perpetual doubt. If the child feels caught in an abusive quandary with no exit, then hope too is sequestered in Pandora's box. For persons with fragile reality testing, massive denial of external and internal danger may eventuate in a psychosis. Pandora's box could lose its symbolic or metaphorical meaning and encapsulating function.

The following clinical vignette illustrate Pandora's universal dilemma, to conceal or reveal, and with what cost and consequences. The locking of Pandora's box may also lead to a learning inhibition, avoiding enquiry and comprehension. Before entering puberty, X had been a lively, vivacious, and popular girl who enjoyed school and was a good student. She got along well with her teachers and peers, spontaneously attended to her homework, and wanted to have a college education. By the time she was fifteen, her attitude towards school had noticeably changed. She seemed no longer involved in her studies and class participation. Her grades gradually declined and then plummeted to the point of her being on the verge of failure in most of her school subjects. When pressed to prepare for examinations, she would study for a great deal of time, but with impaired concentration; she was unable to absorb the subject matter. Panicked by their daughter's development of a learning block and the threat of failure in school, her parents brought X for diagnosis and treatment. What emerged in the modified analysis of this adolescent were shared denials and rationalizations involving the entire family.

With adolescence, X became much more interested in her appearance, clothes, cosmetics, etc. This interest was more than matched by her mother who presented her daughter with a lavish wardrobe complete with ostentatious, impressive accessories such as pocketbooks, shoes, bracelets, etc. X was learning about a world of high style.

We gradually came to understand that X was bewildered about how her mother managed to present her with such a large and expensive wardrobe. Her parents both worked, earning an adequate, but not high income. They were upwardly mobile, living in a middle-class home in a middle-class neighbourhood; no one in the family had won the lottery or had a significant inheritance. X was gratified, but also bewildered and distressed by her costly wardrobe. Pleased with the way his wife decorated their home and their daughter, her father seemed serenely unconcerned with the source and signs of luxury. He would not look a gift horse in the mouth, and wore blinders as a way of life. He was in silent collusion with his wife about avoiding perplexities regarding family finances.

Family and personal secrets are often associated with important repressed conflicts. (Jacobs, 1980) The fantasy of sexually acting out now emerged in X's treatment. In one area of her personality she had traditional values and ideals. She wanted to be respected and respectable, postponing sexual relations until she was an adult and in a love relationship with 'prince charming'. Unconsciously, she had prostitution fantasies with fears of dire punishment in the form of incurable venereal disease, infertility, and social disgrace. These conflicts proved to be associated with the forbidden daring inference that her mother was having an extramarital affair or affairs. Her mother had unconsciously represented promiscuity and prostitution that inwardly frightened her. Her defence had been a massive learning block characterized by, 'I see no evil, I hear no evil, and know no evil'. With the lifting of the veil of denial and repression, X began to learn at home and at school. She began to understand her distrust of me, as well as her inability to make connections about family life and finance. Her incestuous temptations emerged in the transference alongside her immense disappointment in her parents, especially her mother. Were material rewards truly as important as they seemed to be to her mother? Becoming inquisitive and perceptive, she noticed that one of her mother's charge accounts had a strange name or title. Perhaps this was previously noticed, but disavowed. To question the account could be devastating to herself and her parents. Pandora's box was ajar, partially open, partially shut. X no longer accepted her mother's gifts, made only modest purchases, and immersed herself in schoolwork, about which she had previously been so inhibited. Her mother was upset that X would no longer accept gifts. Pleased with X's progress, and probably sensing her daughter's suspicion, X's mother decided that she was now cured. X was very sorry to leave but also relieved. She had learned enough, and in unconscious compliance with her parents, did not want to learn more. She had by then assumed that her mother had a wealthy lover and was conflicted about her treatment, which might be illicitly subsidized. As a girl, X had a fantasy that she was a beautiful princess surrounded by rich and adoring regal parents. Was this a fantasy shared with her mother? While the mother's lavish gifts to her daughter began with the girl's adolescence, X did not consider the possibility that her mother might have been having an affair long before that time. She was not prepared to deal with the possibility that she had been an illegitimate child, with more dark, dangerous secrets. Could her mother's wealthy lover be her biological father, unconsciously her analyst? The invisible source of the seemingly wonderful yet sinister gifts bestowed upon her remained a mystery, locked in her mother's Pandora's box. The myth of Pandora's box does not encompass the partner's share in co-constructing his/her own destruction.

X preferred to distance herself from these potentially explosive issues as she prepared to leave home for college. She disengaged from incestuous objects and from what she regarded as collusion in parental corruption. Her identification with analytic values and goals and her insight into Pandora's box, however limited, were important to her further development.

Family secrets become an anxiety and guilt-ridden burden for those who share them, as well as engendering inevitable conflicts of power and control. Family secrets, associated with shame and guilt, affect the developing child. There is always concern that the secret will emerge from 'under wraps' with the possibility of reprisal, recrimination, and narcissistic mortification. There may be power associated with the threat of revealing the secret. Conflicts associated with Pandora's box coalesce with the expectable fantasies and challenges of a patient's phase of development and life situation. Although manifestly female, Pandora may be unconsciously bi-sexual and bi-parental.

In the myth, Pandora is blamed for all the ills of humanity. Pandora here represents the split-off, virtually all-bad mother, and women have been demonized as sexual and aggressive witches. In modern times, mothers have been blamed for conditions ranging from autism to schizophrenia. In the other pole of splitting, motherhood was glorified and idealized. Pandora carries hope in her box-womb. Hope, like faith and charity, evolves in the object relationship encompassing good-enough mothering of an adequately responsive infant. Hope lies in the mother's capacity to set limits upon enactment of her own infantile impulses, and to control regression in the service of her infant's development. From the perspective of developmental progression, Pandora's box refers to maternal containing and organizing functions, the infant's achievements of impulse and affect control, self regulation, and integration of psychic trauma. Abstract symbols and language require interrelated ego development and object relations, and symbols both link and shape internal and external reality (Amati Mehler, Argentieri, & Canestri, 1993; Blum, 1996). Finally, for some deeply disturbed patients, supportive, suppressive psychotherapy may be indicated, helping to close Pandora's box and safeguard ego boundaries, symbolic capacities, and sanity.

Summary

The Greek myth of Pandora's box has persisted in Western culture through the ages, with preservation of its essential features. Inextricably related to psychoanalysis, the myth is also interpreted as symbol and metaphor in the social sciences, art, and literature. The Pandora myth represents the repressed unconscious, the return of the repressed, and curiosity. In addition, in the psychoanalytic process, it represents resistance and progress. The traditional symbolic interpretation of Pandora's box as the womb and female genitalia is expanded with additional unconscious and metaphorical meanings. The Pandora myth may represent concealed and revealed personal and familial secrets, a conspiracy of silence, and universal fantasies related to secrets and secrecy. There are often layers of secrets associated with shame, guilt, and humiliation. A clinical example illuminates these meanings of the myth, as do references to art, literature, and sociology. In terms of developmental achievement, Pandora's box represents impulse control, self-regulation, and hopeful optimism.

References

Amati Mehler, J., Argentieri, S., & Canestri, J. (1993). *The Babel of the Unconscious*. New York: International Universities Press.

Blum, H. (1996). The Irma dream: self analysis and self supervision. *J. Amer. Psychoanal. Assn., 44*: 1147–1164.

Blum, H. (1996). Symbolization and its relation to psychic and external reality. *Samiksa (Journal of the Indian Psychoanalytical Society), 50*: 11–19.

Decker, H. (1991). *Freud, Dora, and Vienna 1900*. New York: The Free Press.

Freud, S. (1901). The psychopathology of everyday life. *Standard Edition, 6*.

Freud, S. (1905) Fragment of an analysis of a case of hysteria. *Standard Edition, 7*.

Freud, S. (1964) *The Letters of Sigmund Freud*. E. Freud (Ed.). New York: McGraw-Hill.

Freud, S. (1985) *The Complete Letters of Sigmund Freud to Wilhelm Fliess, 1887–1904*. J. Masson (Ed.). Cambridge, MA:Belknap Press.

Johnson, A. (1952). The genesis of antisocial acting-out in children and adults. *Psychoanalytic Quarterly, 21*: 323–334.

Malcolm, J. (1982). *Psychoanalysis: The Impossible Profession*. New York: Vintage.

Panofsky, D., & Panofsky, E. (1962). *Pandora's Box: The Changing Aspects of a Mythical Symbol*. New York: The Free Press.

Sarnoff, C. (2003). *Symbols in Structure and Function, Volume I*. Xlibris, USA.

CHAPTER TWO

Deciphering the secrets of oblivion

Fidias Cesio

Memories constitute us and configure our being. Integrating the words of biology to our psychoanalytic considerations metaphorically, we conclude that the 'genes' condense memories, the foundation of our *actual* (Cesio, 1998) and *psychic* structure.

We give the name *actual memories* to the primary repressed, in virtue of the unconscious quality of their presentation: without time, space or word, manifest in 'somatic' formations in general and, in pathology, the 'actual neuroses': lethargy (Cesio, 1958), neurasthenia, anxiety neurosis, and hypochondria, perceived by consciousness in somatic terms and in terms of action. They are deeply 'forgotten'. In the case of lethargy, the memories of the buried, tragic Oedipus complex (Cesio, 1987) are memories of 'death'. In the past, the resistance blocking these contents from becoming conscious caused them to be considered non-analysable.

The other category of memories, the psychic memories, have time, because they have passed through consciousness, and, therefore, their pathological expressions are manifested as psychoneuroses or transference neuroses.

In each memory, we find intimately interrelated components: *actual, action, psychic,* and *texts*[1]. The *actual*, unconscious, and, therefore, non-temporal, is the base of the structure; using Freud's metaphor of the memory and its components: the grain of sand on which the pearl develops.

The differentiation we draw in the composition of memories is an arbitrary analysis, a point of departure for the investigation of such a complex subject.

Although we consider that, in the unconscious, memories are non-temporal, the work of consciousness shows them to us with temporal and spatial ordering. Those that pertain to the secondarily repressed, to the unconscious ego, can be recovered by analysing free association, while those that are repressed primarily and those that are buried and have no known text, cannot be retrieved in this way, but require a *construction* (Cesio et al., 1988), which is what we do with the actual, in order to give it a text that is comprehensible and interpretable.

On the complex structure of memories

As we said, we distinguish two main fields in each memory: the *actual*, characterized by its biological, somatic presentation, and the *psychic*. The *actual* component of memory is the basic one, and in it we differentiate: A) the *buried*: the Oedipal tragedy; B) the *primarily repressed*, the actual *per se*; and C) a component of action manifested in compulsions and in acts at the service of the needs of the ego.

In all cases, we consider the existence of *texts*.

The ego *texts*, secondarily repressed, are related to the words of our language and therefore interpretable.

A) and B) can only be perceived by the senses as images without meaning, and for this reason are components of the memory that reach consciousness more easily as imaginary perceptions, provided by consciousness in its capacity as a 'perceptive organ of the psychic apparatus'. Their *texts* cannot be deciphered, since they belong to 'tongues' unknown to us.

In *The Dissolution of the Oedipus Complex* (1924), Freud tells us that the primary, incestuous, tragic complex goes down to the foundations, and is 'actual' in its 'somatic' presentation. These are the memories whose texts present the greatest difficulty for coming to consciousness, the most resisted and the most 'forgotten'. The *construction*, a kind of distant translation of the original, is the means to access them, make the original texts conscious and interpret them, converting them into 'memories' that substitute the actual and action contents of the memory.

The translation into our language of the Egyptian hieroglyphs found on the Rosetta stone – 197BC – is a *princeps* metaphor of the construction. On the stone, there is a text written in glyphs[2], another in Demotic and a third in Greek. By studying certain elements co-existing in the Greek text and the Egyptian glyphs, Champollion concluded that they were versions of the same text, meaning that he made an adequate construction and was thus able to discover the secrets of the hieroglyphic language that for thousands of years had been manifest only as glyphs. The understanding of this text gave meaning to what until then had been marks on the surface of a stone. We compare the marks on the stone to the 'actual' 'marks' on an individual's 'body' and the deciphering of the hieroglyphic text to that of the latent text behind the 'actual' by means of the 'construction'. Just as the history of the Egyptian people was constructed by virtue of the deciphering of the hieroglyphs etched all over the temples of ancient Egypt, we construct the personal and phylogenic history from the construction and analysis of the 'actual'.

The word

The memories that constitute the subject are accessible to perception by consciousness in several ways: through the senses in terms of soma, affect, act, of remembrance[3] (Bidondo, 2006) and transference words or metaphoric words. Sometimes, free association has the character of remembrance.

With analysis, the words of remembrance, by receiving signification and affect, acquire the quality of *transference words*: the acoustic image activates the linguistic sign and the word and thing representation, mobilizing the unconscious repressed and buried elements (Cesio et al. 1992). The transference words, which are full words, do not make symptoms; they are the last to make their way into consciousness, undoing the symptomatic character that the other components of memory may attain.

The actual component of memory

The genes, 'inherited' memories in the biological metaphor, constitute the human being. Of all the infinite memories, we know of those that reach consciousness, which is the 'perceptive organ of the psychic apparatus', sensitive to sensory perceptions and the affects, meaning the whole range of somatic manifestations, and to the word.

We assign a special place to the set of memories that we call the soma: we consider it the source of the drives and the foundation of the ego. It is an actual organization. We learn of it from its 'biological' or 'concrete' manifestations. As perceived by the senses, the actual or somatic offers no resistance, to the point that this same facility for being perceived is the best resistance against bringing to consciousness the text corresponding to the memory excited. It is easy to 'feel' a headache, but difficult to interpret it or find its meaning.

In the actual neuroses, particularly the tragic ones, the texts that reach our perception are similar to those of nightmares: they have an intensely tragic, incestuous connotation. This memory is beyond repression: it is buried.

Freud takes a notable step towards the understanding of the relation between the somatic components – the affect – and the psychic components of memory. He tells us that the essence of the affect is 'the repetition of some particular significant experience. This experience could only be a very early impression of a very general nature, placed in the prehistory not of the individual but of the species. To make myself more intelligible an affective state (somatic manifestation)[4] would be constructed in the same way as a hysterical attack (with its somatic manifestation) and, like it, would be the precipitate of a reminiscence[5]' (Freud, 1916, p. 396). In other words, he tells us that the affect has, in its 'construction', a latent text, while in the manifest, it is the somatic component, the anxiety, that appears. He continues: 'A hysterical attack may thus be likened to a freshly constructed individual affect, and a normal affect to the expression of a general hysteria which has become a heritage.' This means that the actual, the hysterical attack, has a latent reminiscence, while its manifestation, which we know as the conversion, is somatic. In a similar way, the affect, an actual and somatic manifestation, like the hysterical attack, manifests a latent idea, an inherited reminiscence: it is also a kind of conversion, based on an unconscious idea that is beyond time. The actual component presented as soma, when there is fluid continuity with the psychic part of the same memory because of its verbal component, is accessible to interpretation.

Beyond the burying, we conceive of another vicissitude of tragic memory: its destruction, expressed in terms of the destruction of somatic substance.

In a paper I published (1999) titled 'Jealousy, Forgetting, Homosexuality and Forgetfulness', I discuss a special type of forgetting, which involves the destruction of somatic brain substance, such as we find in the lesions of the cerebral cortex, a consequence of vascular accidents and, in particular, in Alzheimer's disease. This is the ultimate manifestation of the Oedipal tragedy, when the jealousy leads to a 'crime': a partial suicide. A manifestation that goes beyond burial, corresponding to some of the meanings of the word 'Untergang', which Freud uses to name these processes that, besides burial, also mean 'disintegration', 'destruction', and 'demolition'. These memories are lost and can never be recovered.

The psychic part of memory

This is what once had a place in consciousness and, by the repressive action of the superego, has been made unconscious and forgotten, constituting the unconscious ego. As we have seen, its foundation is the 'actual'.

Personal history, a text constructed out of the psychic components of memories, is a construction based on what has become unconscious, meaning the secondarily repressed, whose 'capitalist partner' is the 'actual' components that give it power. In consciousness, the psychic part of memories, with their ego qualities, configure thoughts, fantasies, delusions, illusions, etc. Their resistance to interpretation is due especially to their character as remembrance, meaning the actual components, particularly those corresponding to the buried tragic Oedipus complex.

The verbal component of memory is the most strongly resisted, the forgotten, and at the same time, the one that works the greatest transformations in it. In hysteria, the repression of the psychic component, the verbal text, generates the symptom, thus placing the actual component of the memory in the foreground. What we call conversion, the actual symptom, appears then as the manifestation of the resistance to making the tragic text conscious.

The action component of memory

Actions are the expression of the action component of memory; it is manifested in compulsions that express the actual dramas and, ultimately, the Oedipal tragedy, in which the ego has secondary participation. When the action is worked through by the ego, it is ascribed to the satisfaction of its conscious needs and aims.

The field of transference

It is in the field of the transference (Baranger, & Baranger, 1969) that the infinite memories constituting the patient-analyst dyad unfold. In the session, at each moment, we conceive of this synchronicity and thus interpret the psychic components of the memories, constructing and interpreting what is presented hypochondriacally and what corresponds to the Oedipal tragedy, etc. This is to say that, although we use a language that runs through time and space because its protagonists are words, on the other hand, we also intercalate memories from the two organizations, and thus operate in function of the synchronicity of their presentation.

We interpret Freud's words when he tells us that there is no transference in the actual neurosis, in the sense of the transference that we find in the analysis of the psychoneuroses. They are *actual transferences*, both non-temporal and non-spatial, that are manifested especially in the somatic terrain in neuro-vegetative-cellular-humoral terms. These transferences are based on primordial identifications: in Freud's words, the 'direct ones, previous to any object cathexis'.

The interpretation of free association, a text in the words of our language, is initially an interpretation of the elements of the psychic component of repressed or forgotten memories that we situate in the unconscious ego; but after analysing the psychic component, we find a barrier, its actual foundations, which then occupy the foreground and present greater resistance, which can only be resolved through construction and interpretation. If we cannot do this, the tragic version of the actual transference, as action, becomes dominant, leading to the 'negative therapeutic reaction'.

A clinical vignette distinguishing between the 'actual', the 'psychic', the 'word' of remembrance, the transference word, and the 'action' component

This is a dramatic-tragic case that helps us to understand what an act is when it comes into the foreground in the manifestation of a memory. In puberty, a female patient suffered a violent trauma during a pogrom in a village in Russia, where she witnessed the murder of her father in the midst of the burning down of her home. In the first interviews, she narrated this episode in a cold tone, as cold as all her associations, which we considered mostly 'remembrances'. I frequently experienced the beginning signs of lethargy in the sessions: an *actual*, tragic manifestation. At one point, when I felt that it was unbearable, I intervened, making a *construction*; I described what was happening in the session, her monotonous speech containing something tragic that was making me feel lethargic. The patient experienced terror – *affect* – and in a state of agitation, jumped up from the couch and wanted to escape from the office – *action*. When she recovered, she told me that she had seen flames in a picture of Freud – the analyst father – and very moved, went on to associate with her traumatic experience – *transference words* – words that kept me participating affectively in the analysis and interpreting her associations.

In this example, we find the components that constitute each memory. A) In the first interviews, in the words of *remembrance*, the narration of the *buried Oedipal tragedy*. B) In the lethargy, we find the *actual, somatic* manifestation. C) The *construction* mobilized the *somatic* and *action* components of the memory. D) Finally, the verbal component appeared with meaning and affect: the interpretable *transference word*.

The construction

This is the indispensable instrument to access the primarily repressed and the buried memories. The material for the construction is what provides the consciousness of what is in the transference field, the analyst's affects: for example, in the above vignette, the lethargy I felt, thoughts, memories, words, emotions, etc. We compare the construction to a dream. When it is enunciated, like the narration of a dream, it 'awakens' a latent text that, when translated and interpreted, undoes the 'forgetting' that generates the symptom of the actual neurosis.

The recognition of the existence of a text, the remembering of which makes the actual manifestation disappear, just as we observe in conversion hysteria, with the discovery of the text that is maintaining the somatic symptom, confirms the hypothesis of the existence in actual manifestations of a 'forgotten' text, a component of memory. A simple example: a patient comes to session crying, while he tells me that his father has died: word, act, and affect. When I told him that he was crying because he couldn't remember how he hated him, about which he had spoken to me more than once, a construction-interpretation, he stopped crying and began to associate about the ambivalence that united him to his 'father'.

With the construction, we can only make a kind of translation, a screen memory, something that we assume is similar to the primary text, but is never the same, since it is impossible for us to 'remember' something that never went through consciousness. It is a way of inferring the text of primarily repressed memories and of the buried memories, the actual component that appears in terms of somatic material or action.

Forgetting, remembrance, and remembering

It is indispensable that we think about memories in order to conceive of forgetting. Our work consists in salvaging their text from repression. We forget visual and auditory images, inner experiences, etc. when they are integrated into an inner experience, they have meaning and affect, constituting a text, but the word occupies a privileged place, because it is the most effective element for making a memory conscious and, consequently, rectifying a symptom. For this very reason, it is the text that presents the greatest resistance. When the road into consciousness is opened without its full meaning or lacking the corresponding affect, it is only the perception of an image, a remembrance. With analytic work, we add meaning and affect to it, making it into a memory.

When memories remain in the unconscious and it is impossible for us to 'remember' them, we say that they are forgotten. Memories present diverse degrees of resistance to becoming conscious. The actual memories present the greatest resistance, in particular those that are buried, because of their tragic incestuous nature; they are followed by the primarily repressed and, finally, the secondarily repressed, those that pertain to the unconscious ego.

As an ultimate hypothesis, we assume that 'inanimate objects' are constituted from memories whose text is totally repressed or forgotten. Freud suggests this idea in *Analysis Terminable and Interminable* (1937), when he provides us with the metaphor of the 'bedrock' as the limit between the biological and the psychic. This is the rock into which the hieroglyphs are carved, the sacred and fundamental marks that we conceive of as the 'fundamental language' from which all words and tongues derive, an unknown and 'forgotten' text; to discover it and make a memory of it requires an effort of construction like Champollion's work.

A paradox: the word of the text is privileged, in the sense of its power to make the repressed memory into a memory; however, when it is only a word image, a remembrance, it conceals and acts as a counter-cathexis, a resistance against the full word, which carries meaning and affect, becoming conscious. Also, when the affect, an actual manifestation, occupies a dominant position instead of being an integral part of the word, it is a counter-cathexis to the word coming to consciousness. With repression, the idea that occupied consciousness loses its qualities as a full word, and the notion of time and space, meaning and affect, is 'forgotten' and is memory.

Our creations are similar to those of the sculptor who has before him a rock, the unconscious foundation, the 'bedrock' in Freud's metaphor, which encloses infinite memories and tries to liberate one, represented by a human body. Michelangelo knew how to bring forth a grand personage, his Moses, from the rock, but he didn't have the poet's gift for discovering the verbal text of that memory; powerless to do so, in his desperation, he struck the statue with his hammer, shouting, 'Speak!' We too, like the sculptor before the rock, know that uncountable memories inhabit the unconscious, but we have to develop the sculptor's art in order to free them and also the poet's art, to salvage its texts from oblivion, the verbal texts in particular.

Notes

1. We define a **text** as the set of gestures, signs, and spoken or written words that express an idea.

2. Glyphs: chiselled ornamentation engraved into an object. Hieroglyph has Greek roots: hieros: sacred + glipho: to engrave.
3. A word that is a remembrance: a word image that reaches consciousness from the actual without acquiring ego properties or binding to the affect, lacking any transference or metaphoric quality, but is always actual and always repetition.
4. What is in parenthesis in this passage has been added by me.
5. Reminiscencia: 'unconscious memory'.

References

Baranger, W., & Baranger, M. (1969). La situación analítica como campo dinámico. In: *Problemas del Campo Psicoanalítico*. Buenos Aires: Kargieman.

Bidondo, A. (2007). La rememoración, un 'hablar para no recordar'. *La Peste de Tebas*. Año 11. No. 37. Ed. La Peste. Buenos Aires.

Cesio, F.(1958). El letargo. Una contribución al estudio de la reacción terapéutica negativa. *Revista de Psicoanálisis, 15*.

Cesio, F. (1960). II. Contribución al estudio de la reacción terapéutica negativa. *Revista de Psicoanálisis, 17*: 289–298.

Cesio, F. (1987). Tragedia edípica. Sepultamiento. Acto. Transferencia y repetición. *Revista de Psicoanalisis, Vol. XLIV, No. 1*.

Cesio, F. (1998). Las enfermedades actuales, patologías y 'neurosis'. *La Peste de Tebas*. Año 3. No. 7. Ed. La Peste. Buenos Aires.

Cesio, F. (1999). Celos, olvido, homosexualidad, desmemoria. *La Peste de Tebas*. Año 4. No. 11. Ed. La Peste. Buenos Aires.

Cesio, F., Dávila, M., Guido, H., & Isod, C. (1988). Las intervenciones del analista. I. La interpretación propiamente dicha y la construcción. *Revista de Psicoanalisis, Vol. XLIV*: 1217–1240.

Cesio, F., D'Alessandro, N., Elenitza, J., Hodara, S., Isod, C., & Wagner, A. (1992). *Freud y La Palabra*. Kargieman. Ed. Buenos Aires.

Freud, S. (1916–1917). Introductory lectures on psycho-analysis. Lectura 25. Anxiety. *Standard edition 16*

Freud, S. (1924). The dissolution of the Oedipus complex. *Standard Edition 19*

Freud, S. (1937). Analysis terminable and interminable. *Standard Edition 23*

CHAPTER THREE

Self formation, symbolic capacity, and spontaneity

Gemma Corradi Fiumara

1. The challenge of mentalization

The one topic which may synthetize different preoccupations in psychoanalytic research is the process of mentalization: the core of the inner vicissitudes which sustain our growth and survival. As a uniquely human phenomenon, authentic mentalization is one of the central concerns of our psychoanalytic culture. Basically, in our clinical seminars, it is often a question of reciprocal guidance and co-vision intended to attain greater familiarity with this challenging process, which is sometimes referred to in the terms ego development, self formation, psychic growth, affective and cognitive maturation, capacity of insight.

If we then ask what are the conditions for this process to take place, we will recognize that one of the principal factors is the development of our symbolic function. Unless the developing self becomes capable of symbolic competence it will remain bound to the dominance of inner states, with the sad consequence that what is psychic tends to converge with 'reality' in general, and what seems generically real must necessarily be taken into the mind – without any refinement or internalization. So tentatively articulated, this deadening condition gives the impression of an inner world of hopeless passivity that can only be 'overcome' by reactive expressions of rage – however silent, exhausting, and futile. No process of mentalization seems to take place. This condition, moreover, can only allow for re-actions but cannot empower us for actions proper.

If we cannot play with symbols, we remain victims of mental states, that is of an endless sequence of affective conditions from which we cannot take a perspectival distance, for we cannot name/think them. The development of a sense of 'play' with respect to inner conditions seems thus necessary. In fact, the increasing experience of symbolic and playful ways of somehow describing reality (inner or outer) helps us learn that our negative affects do not necessarily contaminate the world, and that what seems real does not necessarily coincide with our inner world.[1] The creation of a second-order perception (but then, only a symbolic order enables us to attain an ulterior perspective) of affect states produces the instruments for the regulation of affective mental states and for their use. In simple terms, this could be seen as the basic transition from biological reality to psychic existence.[2] Clinically speaking, we can only give what we *are* (rather than what we *have*), and this reveals the specificity of the process in the sense that only to the extent that we are proficient in mentalization we can 'confer' it to others. If we are not, it is impossible to impart this capacity to others. It is not, moreover, a sheer matter of giving and taking something, as it is rather a complex experience of sharing. We can share this capacity to the extent that it is truly ours. By sharing it with others, in fact, we lose nothing of it. And also, only those who are ready for it can ultimately share in this mutative venture.

To trust this profound transformer of behaviour, and in order to enhance mentalization in others, we must lovingly *live by* it. Mentalization is not something with which we can be enriched as if by sheer absorption; it is a way of psychic life which only develops *inside* us and that we can attempt to share with others. The mentalizing efforts that the developing person may express will be approved and encouraged to the extent to which these capacities are spontaneously active in the other members of the micro- or macro-community. By contrast, tendencies towards mentalization that members of the family fear and disapprove will determine a negative and nearly vindictive response, as in the case of parental figures that hate themselves and their offspring. Of course, parents have a primary influence on the development of mentalization as they can only 'teach' what they have previously developed in themselves. If their processes of mentalization are rudimentary, confusive, destructive, they will only be able to project these mechanisms. But then, if the processes of mentalization that they have developed are enriching and spontaneous, it is exactly these complexive attitudes that they will beneficially share with the young ones.

Perhaps the core problem hindering mentalization is the presence of some narcissistic wound, or persecutory affect, together with the pernicious conviction that we can best cope with this original 'sin' by perceiving it as being part of the external others and as not belonging to the self. If we could see this condition as a general human problem, we would more easily appreciate that most of our world resources are certainly absorbed by the costs of our psychic survival rather than of our biological sustenance.[3] And the current decline in popularity of our psychoanalytic culture could be explained in terms of this unpopular tendency to replace projection as well as the enormous costs of compensation with strenuous efforts of creative personal work – in fact, the challenge of mentalization.

It is true that our metapsychology is rooted in the paradigm of conflict while ego development is based on the capacity to generate, endure, and make good use of paradoxes, to transform contingencies that we find too absurd to survive into situations that are worth exploring for our growth. Within the suggested theme of *Symbolization, language, and psychosis*, we can thus realize that the 'talking cure' that we practice is no simple talk, chat or conversation, as it is more in the nature of a challenging interpersonal confrontation through which the mind may spring to life, and for its own good.

As in psychic growth, the mental state becomes more detached from physical reality, the infants whose caretakers provide affect-congruent and sufficiently symbolized responses actually facilitate this detachment.[4] By contrast, whenever affective difficulties prevail in the adults, or in the analysts, and they are too easily overwhelmed by the child/patient's negative affects, they will be incapable of creative mental action and only prone to reaction; they will produce realistic – unplayful, unsymbolic – expressions of emotion that not only disrupt the attempts of affect regulation but also stifle the processes of symbolization. A major opportunity is thus wasted for learning the difference between linguistic capacities and actual mental states. As is known, these repetitive failures will increase the rigidity of the equation between internal and external conditions, an equivalence that tends to dominate the inner world of individuals with deep seated personality disorders. Unless we are capable of mentalization, we will manage object relations by means of relatively rigid paradigms, which, of course, restrain development and waste unproportionate amounts of time, as if we were all ensnared in a delusion of eternity. Mentalization, moreover, does not entail standards of performance or degrees of approximation to a hypothetical perfection, for, in fact, processes of mentalization operate in the open domain of whatever forms of human creativity – from the most conspicuous to the most invisible. The analytic approach demands, in fact, an inversion of trend: from condition to mentalization, from reaction to action.

If we invoke Winnicott's suggestion that whenever the infant fails to find *himself* in the mother's mind he will find the mother instead, we could say that he will be forced to internalize the representation of the adult's state of mind as a core part of his own self.[5] But in such cases, the internalized other remains alien and unconnected to the instinctual roots of the self. When the caretaker's affective response is incongruent with the child's actual feelings, the secondary representation will be necessarily distorted. To the extent that the emotional state of the child has not been properly recognized by the adult, the developing self will feel intruded and it will only display imitative representations of affect that lack vital connections with the constitutional self. If we assume that the self as an agent arises out of the infant's perception of his presumed intentionality in the mind of the caregiver, when parental care is insensitive and misattuned, the sense of subjective agency will be blurred. This climate of confusion does not facilitate the development of an agent capable of sufficiently good construction of object relations. And, again, this danger of blurring subjective agency is in no way part of some unverifiable sophisticated theory of our psychoanalytic culture; we commonly witness that the struggle for survival is increasingly transferred from the biological level onto the psychic and symbolic domain where humans attempt to prevail upon each other symbolically and politically.

2. Compliance, conflict, and paradox

If we seriously invoke Winnicott's suggestion that 'Interpretations are useless until the patient can begin to play',[6] we shall also appreciate that playing is a symbolic concern that requires increasing abilities and constant training in the sense that a capacity to play is something most serious, comparable to playing an instrument or playing soccer. But then, if an interpretation is not useful, is it just useless or can it be harmful? As he also indicates, such 'interpretative' interventions only produce indoctrination and compliance.[7] But what is wrong with indoctrination and compliance? Nothing much, if they take place outside of analytic therapy for, after all, they seem to be the rule in most cultural contexts, including psychoanalytic institutions. In the analytic relation, however, indoctrination and compliance tend to reproduce and reinforce the cumulative trauma that has inhibited the growth of the mind; they, in fact, incline to further conflictual splittings rather than towards the creativity of metaphoric constructions and paradoxes.[8]

However minimal, attempts at naming and symbolizing, describing and connecting, or alluding to events inside one's own self and the other, are all ways of gaining some agentive capacity, some nuclear intentionality. If these capacities are not sufficiently developed, we can only settle for an expanding scenario of conflicts, and never reach the possibility of creating and enduring paradoxes. We could think of paradoxes as thoughts that seem false but are true or, by contrast, as convictions that seem true but are false; we could envisage a paradoxical experience as something that is both nourishing and toxic, facilitating and restraining – something internal that we can conceive of and endure. The proliferation of conflicts and ensuing projections is an 'enjoyable' but weakening mental style, while the capacity to think and utilize paradox is more corroborating and usable for the most disparate creative developments. Granted that we do need the famous 'sufficiently good' parent to survive and develop a mental life, we especially need the capacity to deal with the 'partially bad' parent that we must inevitably cope with. Even though the good-enough part does prevail, the truly bad part cannot be eliminated or ignored. The question is how we can deal with the ineliminable poison that comes together with the nourishment in our early formative interactions. One of the essential abilities is the development and endurance of paradoxes, of inner symbolic structures that mentally connect opposites instead of simply floundering into ever more divisive oppositional states – only usable for splitting and projection. We strive for a transition from conflictual inner states to a mentalization of these conflicts in the form of usable paradoxes. How is that for personal growth and peace of mind? This is, perhaps, the only filtering function that can help us cope with the imperfect nature of our human minds – in daily life as well as in analysis.

But why is it so essential to develop the capacity to make these distinctions between conflict and paradox? Why should we produce symbolic, theoretic inner means of creating usable distinctions rather than simply splitting unbearable affective states? In our formative vicissitudes, the psychic support that we obtain from caretakers is inevitably interwoven with adverse messages and, thus, it is vital to create inner means, however rudimentary, which may sustain these distinctions. This is as vital in early infancy as it is essential in analytic treatment, where we cannot possibly presume that absolutely *pure* psychic nourishment is provided.

Affective support and emotional corrosion are often so interwoven in our growth as to become indistinguishable, and even when their difference is discerned, it may be impossible to obtain the one without the other in the sense that in order to get affective nutrients one may *have* to take in emotional toxins[9] – perhaps even in analysis, and certainly in our globalized coexistence. For some individuals, life may ultimately feel not quite real without a high level of emotional toxicity – which we often proceed to acquire from entertainment. We are not suggesting the hypothesis of a pre-meditated destructive scheme on the part of caretakers, but simply envisaging parental figures who are prone to psychic hatred; the inchoate person may then defensively contract into an apparently invulnerable imitation of a self.

Of course splitting enables the individual to have well-defined images of others, but these are necessarily inaccurate, oversimplified, and only allow for an illusion of mentalized interpersonal exchange. The caregiver who generates such attachment disorganization typically provides contradictory information regarding her infant-directed mental attitudes: sometimes she abuses the child, while at other times she seems to deny this and even deals in affectionate manners; on the basis of contradictory and ambivalent intentions the child often faces the impossible task of anticipating the other's behaviour and consequently loses interest for *his own* personal intentionality.[10]

Given our 'universal' need for projection of whatever is unbearable, how does this interdigitate with the paramount importance of our symbolic function? The affective content of an analytic interpretation can be accepted by the patient if it is not really attributed to the analyst as an actual emotional reaction, that may almost sound as a retaliation. The patient's projection is often most powerful and concrete, while the interpretation is 'just' symbolic, 'just' talk, involving no practical consequences; this is so even though the purely symbolic texture of the interpretation requires great force, concentration, and intensity on the part of the therapist. And these reality-detached expressions are further supported by the experience of safety and non-consequentiality that in fact allows for the analytic spontaneity of growth.

An insufficient capacity to mentalize places a heavy burden on the developing ego, for in order for the self to be coherent the unbearable introjects need to be seen as parts of external objects that can be disparaged – or idealized. In order to afford some coherence the suffering subject needs 'the other – often the therapist – . . . to frighten and intimidate, to seduce and excite, to humiliate and reduce to helplessness'.[11] And of course the prospect of the other's loss signals the return of these 'extrojects' and the deterioration of coherence.

Whenever the false self deriving from compliance and impingement is externalized onto the other and controlled therein, the individual illusorily feels as an active agent who is in command, despite the fragility of the self. The heavy price paid is that in forcing the other to behave as if he were one of his own representations, the potential for a real relationship is compromised and the subject is actually preparing the way for abandonment. The projective construction of the other's mind in intimate relationships represents a coercive and distorting attitude that is resented by the partner. The eventual disruption of the relation also means a return of the projected alien self, together with consequent feelings of disorganization.[12]

A serious nurturing of a capacity for coexistence with discrepancies and for generating paradoxes is certainly more enlivening than the splitting-projecting paradigm – however 'exciting' this may be. The apparently enjoyable but deadening attitude of splitting and projecting can even be exasperated by the analytic experience of being accused of this psychic 'sin', something like being accused of not having grown enough. 'Why do you think I am here?', could or should say the patient, who is ultimately a client. 'Try to help me generate paradoxical connections whereby I can endure discrepancies', 'Empower me for actions rather than just reactions', he might wish to say.

Having to confront these difficulties, the therapist must occasionally allow herself to become the vehicle for the patient's false self. If she is to be of any use to him, she has to become what he needs her to be. Yet, if she entirely becomes that person, she can hardly be of help to him. Letting herself be used as required, yet trying to retain in her mind a clear image of the relationship that could facilitate mentalization in the patient, the analyst should be capable of hyper-mentalization, of any series of paradoxes. The internalization of the therapist's concern for representing and symbolizing any mental states ultimately enhances the patient's capacity for a similar concern towards his own experience. And, of course, the capacity for paradoxical connections should spontaneously function in the analyst so that patients may internalize a mental style, rather than just a good-enough object.

Simply said, the language which is not instrumental to the good of the other tends to become a devastating impingement; conversely, when language is hierarchized in such a way that it is an asset to respectful care, it can serve the purpose of distinguishing between representation and reality, signifier, and signified.[13]

The question of how one does recognize poison and how he can cope with it may make the individual aware to the fact that the toxic part is an inevitable component of whatever formative nourishment. Mental filters must thus be developed and attentively cared for. Otherwise, the mixture of poison and care may become compressed into something concrete and indecipherable, something like a knot that affects the whole style of life. This much-needed *filter* is a mental function that is capable of handling conflicts in the form of paradoxes, contradictions as occasions for negotiations, oppositions as opportunities for differentiation. 'Why don't you help *me* develop this filtering capacity you actually work with?', seems to tacitly ask the patient. 'This is the trick in your profession; I want it too.'

We often compassionately regret that some creatures are just somewhat rigid and lacking in spontaneity. Actually, when sufferers try to become analysands they seek helpers who are keen on following them all the way to these paralysing knots – and undo them. They seek relational experiences that will make them feel more human and not so stiff. At the opposite extreme, when one contracts into further restraints it becomes nearly impossible to detect the deadening style that is ruling the inner world. As Bion suggests, one may not survive with too many knots and will tend to explode; one may express this inclination 'by a sudden and complete silence (as if to go to an extreme as far from devastating explosion as possible), as if explosion and silence became one'[14]. And, of course, the discernment of these non-mentalized connections can be beneficially shared with patients so that they may become more themselves and less devoured by corrosive versions of their stiffened selves. Sometimes, tracing fantasies to 'end it all' helps sensitize us to what it means to endure the burden of a stiffened mental life. Patients need safe opportunities for re-thinking what is wrong as well as help in sharing the feeling of how painful it can be.

3. The deterioration of symbolic capacities

People of our days, even though not ill according to any taxonomy of mental illness based on symptoms, appear shrouded in and coerced by compensations of all kinds. And when the aspiration to evolve manages to 'vex' us, it does so only in a numb, obscure fashion: the latent kernel of our more authentic self speaks out with difficulty, as if it were inserted in a mental field overburdened by pseudo-symbolizations and thus prevented from metabolic maturation. When the analyst keeps attentively silent it is often in order to auscultate that part of the true self which cannot, or cannot yet, speak. If we think of a false self in terms of defensive, imitative expressions, we could say that the array of symbolizations borrowed from an insufficiently empathic environment are quite different from the *personal* rendition of the traumatic relational style. In fact, in the subsequent symbolic re-enactments, the subject tries to be a more active agent who is in control of the interpretation of things, whereas during the actual vicissitudes he is a helpless subject passively experiencing difficult conditions. And the analyst's silence may equally serve to avoid becoming ensnared into those highly expressive manifestations of the false self which are composing and unravelling endless 'cogent' arguments. In this connection we could recall Wittgenstein's remark to the effect that he is trying to teach us 'to pass from a piece of disguised nonsense to something that is patent nonsense'.[15]

In addressing the question of how it is that the symbolic function can even be used to destroy and confound, to the point of leading the most disparate forms of human expression into a spiral of falsification, we may recall Bion's remark that 'The human animal has not ceased to be persecuted by his mind and the thoughts usually associated with it – whatever their origin may be'.[16] An awareness of this danger is a matter of constant concern. Symbolization is, thus, often used as an all-powerful (and, hence, false) means of imitating the world and, therefore, of simply 'extracting' reality out of the subject, instead of laboriously coming to recognize it in persons and nature. As is known, paranoid, persecutory defences are hardened through the 'support' of symbolization, used in omnipotent fashion, and are thus rendered inexhaustible. For the intelligent human beings that we are, it is no longer enough to manage our mental life in such a way as to perceive threats as originating from without; it also becomes mandatory to assert, demonstrate, and justify one's inner account of the menacing 'facts'. Such defensive constructs, however, do not obviously constitute a symbolic product in its full sense. A pseudo-symbolic process which has the appearance of symbolic language but is not conducive to fuller object relations is hardly metabolic in the sense of enhancing psychic life. To be closer to the vital complexities of language, we could suggest that communication is symbolic when we have expressions that lead to richer interactions and that, insofar as this is achieved, the activity is also a truly metabolic, vital one. Pseudo-symbols are 'diabolic' in the sense that they cannot possibly be metabolic. Especially in the early phases of mentalization the symbol is a necessary metabolic element, inasmuch as the energy involved in connecting an expectation with a negative contingency (as when something goes wrong) is channelled by means of the symbol towards the formation of inner and outer reality. Thus, no vicissitude is neutral with respect to growth because any event is intensively for or against maturation.

But then, language itself – that is our symbolic domain – can also be passively imitated, taken in and pretended whenever personal creation is not sufficiently facilitated. And a deadening, false, non-metabolic language may come to feel like a poisoning inner atmosphere. Sometimes our pseudo-symbolic structures determine a toxic inner climate that seems inescapable. If there is a sufficient awareness of inner poisons, one may begin to beware of those destructive convictions that can lead to fatal behaviour. We seek therapy when cumulative inner deterioration threatens to overwhelm our sense of life's goodness. In a report concerning a narcissistic person with whom it was not easy to work analytically, Khan stresses the patient's highly expressive, articulate, incisive style of speaking and yet he goes so far as to remark that 'She was perpetually . . . 'acting into' language, which is then not symbolic discourse'.[17] We may suppose that this acting of one's illness into language may have been useful as a defensive strategy for protecting an inchoate real self in some crucial vicissitudes. But when 'acting into language' persistently continues and becomes a compulsion, it may turn into a stifling, pathological habit that deadens the mind's life. And a relational system based on pseudo-symbols cannot possibly metabolize and develop.

As is known, our linguistic potential may be suppressed by the despotic influence of a falsifying cultural normality as well as by the requirements imposed so that normality may prevail. One might even surmise that linguistic normality is linked with a latent pathology involving as much falsification as consensus, and, ultimately, deafening the mind to those inner dynamics which run counter to the prevailing illusory normality. The degradation of language can be conceptualized only in terms of a ubiquitous, never-ending perversion that benumbs inner life. As soon as there is an attempt to describe this 'killer' and its profile comes into sufficient focus, we are already in danger of being misled. Our 'forger' (or 'counterfeiter'), in fact, is never there to be recognized in any ostensive way: ever versatile, it can assume radically different attitudes from one context to the next. 'He luxuriates in crude rationality, since he always talks for effect, and has no concern for true insight' – says the psychiatrist-philosopher Jaspers. And he goes on to say: 'Descriptions might be continued interminably. They circle round a nameless power which in secret might gain the mastery over all, either in order to transform us into itself, or else in order to exclude us from life.[18]'

We are trying to combat this sense of deadness, uneasiness, disease that connotes all kinds of mental illnesses. The deadener, the killer, is the most dangerous because it cannot be identified, singled out or pinpointed. In fact, it is a style, a generalized condition, an unlivable atmosphere. Although it cannot be apprehended and scrutinized it is nonetheless a life-stifling threat. The self-propagating power of languages which crystallizes into some kind of ideology – scientific, political, epistemic – may ultimately make it impossible for us to advance to the level of speaking individuals and confines us instead to being spoken subjects, in the sense that it is 'language' which speaks through us. Such languages stiffen into a 'symbolic' frame which is of little maturational use inasmuch as it is detached from the subject's efforts at self-creation.

The painful confusion brought on by the forced coexistence of incompatible messages is aggravated by the derivatives of the archaic prevalence of symbolic equations, namely the insufficient distinction between sensations and ideas, fantasy and reality, self and not-self. When the analyst is not sufficiently aware of how difficult it can be to make contact with the depths of the true self, the relationship will be steered in such a way as to avoid the 'danger' of attempting unexpected links and connections. The 'analyst' will select the pathways which are already well known, and present no threat to the epistemology he inhabits. Within such a relationship, disapproval and threats might be expressed, for example, by withholding all articulation or by inundating with benevolence. Without implying any cognisant strategy on the part of the analyst, such policies could paralyse vital impulses. Recognizing a patient's thirst for 'a mind of his own'[19] implies a continuous struggle for inner renewal which one is not always able to sustain.

Talking himself into what he is not, the patient may privilege the experiences which are amenable to expression through the pseudo-language that prevails, at the cost of inducing an even greater discrepancy with the experiences deriving from a silenced, truer part of the self. To the extent that the false self is amenable to verbalization by means of dialogic responses, it will increasingly establish its dominance. Pseudo-symbols may acquire the stability of semantic constructions intimating who one is and should be. The work of interpretation is therapeutic not so much because the various fragments of discourse become clearer and gradually form a whole, but rather because the interpretation welcomes and grasps the unutterable upsurge within (irrepressible but not yet thinkable) and thereby permits functioning thoughts to emerge from a multitude of shapeless elements. Situations in which the subject does not know how to express a meaning which he already 'possesses' within his inner life are indeed crucial, since they constitute stages in which he is searching for a bearer of meaning which he can eventually share with others for the purpose of developing authentic consensual meanings. Distorted, abusing mirroring by the caregiver will induce emotional experiences that never feel quite true, with the consequence that words will not form the basis for the developing capacity to think: our way to a fuller humanity, including our symbolic function, is subject to deterioration and perversion.

Consistent with Winnicott's observations, the evolving subject who fails to develop the representation of an intentional self and is cumulatively absorbing the representations produced by others, will only attain a false and impersonal view of himself.[20] Distorted and out of touch with himself, he feels forever bound to 'react to' and even try to control the mental representations of himself he presumes that the other may develop; this forced waste of inner energy may forever induce a silent state of rage that is impossible to decry or conceptualize.

In analysis we create a transitional area for thoughts and feelings so that we can encourage the growth of the mind. There are moments when words and ideas may lose their symbolic function while carrying an unbelievable potency and destructiveness. We are to take patients very seriously when this occurs while at the same time avoiding entanglement with their equation of thoughts and reality.

4. Actions versus reactions

The current decline in popularity of psychoanalysis is probably due to the recognition that it is not a 'guaranteed *cure*', but rather a challenge; it is not, after all, a 'bargain' in the sense that one *acquires* nothing, but rather struggles to evolve into a more authentic, integrated self. Our business-dominated world seems to require a population only capable of reactions and compensations: it needs people who are primarily amenable to reacting-to (an enticement, a threat, a promise . . .) and only willing to compensate for holes and gaps with fillers such as territorial extensions, drugs, and 'safe' experiences of horror. And this is regularly under our eyes. Analysis, by contrast, aims at a lifestyle of creative action and spontaneity – no matter how 'small' or low-profile. As to the capacity to shape mental actions we should stress how important it is for each one of us to gradually become capable of actions proper rather than only of reactions.

Relying on a false self, one cannot possibly act but can only react, and increasingly so in the course of time. As the externally induced reactions are detached from the core of our personality, any chance of spontaneity is forever excluded. It is no wonder that such an invisible, nameless condition does induce a chronic state of unexplainable rage: as if we had been deprived and abused. In plain terms, we could say that creativity is more action then reaction, while pathology is more reaction than action. Paradoxically, having to deal with such an invisible inner destroyer, external tangible threats come to be perceived as a source of relief. When not available, they can be purchased in entertainment. The deadening compulsion to react is the sad admission that there is no agentive self and that the only way to be with others and not starve in psychic loneliness is to comply with the other by either agreeing or disagreeing, that is simply reacting to the other, as if the capacity for personal action had been definitely lost. In the extreme, both compliance and revolt come to the same psychic result as they are basically reactions. Of course, the developing person who is told 'You are worthless' may either agree and comply or disagree and fight back. And yet, sadly, his mental resources are all absorbed into a reactive process, which may come to prevail over his potential for action, intentionality, and spontaneity. If he could creatively *play* with words, he might be able to make quick turns, and, for instance, take 'stupid' as just a signifier, and not automatically react to the signified – thus remaining ready for personal action.

Interpersonal schemata are notably rigid and strictly reactive in borderline patients, as they cannot imagine that the other could have a construction of reality that is different from the one they experience as threatening and compelling. They often speak of something that just triggers a response, or of some compulsion to feel in a certain way as if they were forever dispossessed of a spontaneous capacity to act – rather than just react. Such individuals need a visible external enemy to alleviate the invisible destructive vicissitudes inside themselves. Genuine symbolization is the way to psychic visibility, while society at large only proposes items of physical visibility.

The sort of genuine symbolization that can be used for inner visibility is something that can only be subjectively developed and cannot be acquired from external sources, or imitated. This is especially hard to accept in a world in which whatever is advertised (theories, goods, affiliations, ideologies, knowledge, drugs) carries secret promises of happiness – however impossible. Everything is proposed in view of a single reaction: 'Buy it'. Personal action is not appreciated in an expanding business-like atmosphere. In this sense, then, we all buy promises, whatever they promise. Since we cannot think of inner maturation and we only expect personal transformations coming from external sources, the appropriate promise is the only thing that really counts and sells – no matter how false the promise is.

If the analyst does not prove that he can deal efficiently with the yet invisible inner destroyer of psychic life, the patient will be simply offended when the analyst does not agree to join forces in fighting the external 'enemy' that is vexing him at the moment. The inner style of life that wastes energies and destroys hope, also enforces rigidity in the sense that there cannot be creative actions, but only repetitive reactions; this inner pattern is not quite visible without the help of the analyst while any usable external source of threat is clearly visible, tangible, and nearly 'appealing' – however illusory. This innovative change of perspective, however, can only be achieved if the analyst can weave a sufficiently strong alliance with the healthier part of the self, the one that seeks therapy. In human ontogeny, whenever the caregiver is inclined to reaction rather than action, he will be too readily overwhelmed by the infant's despair and produce realistic, unplayful expressions that disrupt the development of affect regulation and symbolization. On these occasions, our opportunity to learn the difference between the symbolic expression of despair and despair itself, between representational and actual mental states is lost, and the infant is pushed back into a condition in which he is at the mercy of the unforeseeable sequence of affective states. According to Fonagy *et al.*, the capacity to modulate affect states, is closely related to mentalization in that it plays a fundamental role in the development of a sense of self and agency;

in their account affect regulation is a prelude to mentalization.[21] The incapacity for action in the parent, the incapacity to activate his thinking, only provides convenient but inadequate reactions. The inadequate caretaker can only narcissistically react if he cannot act – that is actively think. Even in the most offensive parental behaviour, therefore, we need not imagine the cunning of a scheme, but simply the incapacity for a thinking action which could generate an appropriate response. The caretakers who are not good-enough can only automatically react – with the most devastating consequences.

An ulterior anti-maturational aspect of inadequate caregiving is staged whenever the parent misrepresents the infant's state and, for instance, describes a condition of psychic exhaustion for sleepiness, when a condition of boredom is taken for fatigue, when terror is exchanged for excitement, when compliant defences are exchanged for offers of greater intimacy. These intrusive missymbolizations generated by the adult will, of course, lack vital ties with the core of the nascent personality. As Winnicott suggests, if the infant cannot find himself in the mother's mind, he finds the mother's mind inside himself, instead. The child is forced to internalize the representation of the adult's state of mind as if it were his own. But then, of course, the internalized representation is detached, is in-organic and disorganizing, one further slowing element into one's inner vicissitudes and just a clumsy way of coping with an illusion of inner cohesion. The capacity to act, and not only react, is essential in fostering psychic growth both in upbringing and analysis. It is vital to be able to play and not simply react – to whatever comes forth: threat, seduction, obfuscation. Playing is something tremendously involving and serious, as it could be playing soccer or cards. In these matters we exert our very best efforts, we exercise all of our ingenuity, we leave no depth of cunning unplumbed in our quest to win.

In analysis, whether it be a case of obsessive neurosis, character pathology or anorexia, we do have an invisible 'killer' to win, and that is a deadening style of life in the patient that ultimately excludes him from life. Unfocused, feeble attempts to overcome it are the most perverse, diminishing imitations of analysis. And, of course, the alien internalizations are dealt with by means of externalizations. By means of projective identification, the developing person strives to experience his own self as cohesive by projecting the forced introjections into external objects. If these processes are repetitive, a state a cumulative trauma ensues, and the slowness, clumsiness, rigidity of one's psychic life become a source of constant humiliation, silent rage, and violence. This traumatic style can be processed and attenuated via any supportive help in mentalization. Un-symbolized, un-shareable humiliation can be experienced as destructive of the self, as if one were developing a wish to entirely evacuate one's psychic world. The inability to personally think about one's own mental states hinders the possibility of psychic narratives which can be generated with the help of a real other or with the help of some internalized positive object. One way of conceptualizing the analytic process can be as a joint enterprise focused on the reactivation of personal and interpersonal interpretation. The project is one of reviving a deadened, imitative style of mentalization.

When the sort of affect perceived by the adult is incongruent with the actual affective state of the child, he will feel compelled to forge a distorted symbolization of his emotional motives.[22] As a consequence, one may either discard the mind or the caregiver, or else attribute to himself dispositional information that is incongruent with his actual initiative, and which falsifies his incipient view of himself. But, actually, he could do both, fluctuate between the two, suspend judgement, or endure the uncertainty. What he will certainly do is beware of his own intentionality, of his actions proper and definitely opt for a style of reactions together with the sacrifice of all spontaneity.

We might note in passing that misunderstanding of the young may be used by the adult for purposes of sexually or, even worse, mentally abusing the child: 'You are so ungrateful and unloving while I am so caring and affectionate, forever trying to teach you so much.' Psychoanalytic literature reiterately theorizes that the developing person will eventually tend to imitate his caregivers while in a constant state of anxiety anticipating further impingements, fearing any personal gestures and eventually forgetting that they may exist. A perpetual style of reactions is firmly established which is meant to permanently impede creative action.

For affect mirroring to serve as the basis of the development of the symbolic function, the caregiver should somehow indicate that he can play and that his comments or displays are not for real, are not serious reactions; the experience itself might otherwise sound like intimating 'Don't cry, or she will become upset and vindictive'.

Fonagy *et al.* describe this playful characteristic of the parent mirroring behaviour as its 'markedness'; its being put in double inverted commas to indicate a sense of pretend or a sense of playful distance.[23] An affective display that is congruent with the infant's state but lacks 'markedness' may overwhelm the infant. The playful-enough parent responds to the child's screaming with hunger as if he were saying 'Come on, it's just hunger, I'll be there in a second, and all will be well'. And when the infant is feeding he may say something like 'There is no tragedy, you see, we are doing well now'. The lack of play in parental response makes it feel as if it were the parent's own real emotion – his actual reaction – thus making the infant's emotion seem contagious, expanding, and, thus, even more dangerous. In the absence of the parental capacity to visualize his own relation to the infant and the consequent incapacity to describe it without an excess of involvement, the infant ultimately perceives a corresponding and realistic negative emotion which may expand rather than regulate the affective state, thus leading to cumulative trauma rather than containment. The same may happen in the psychoanalytic treatment when the most primitive and threatening emotions must be responded to with congruence *but without being overwhelmed* so that the patient will not be loaded with the additional fear of retaliation. And, of course, the analyst is often the instrument for externalizing unbearable parts of the self in the transference vicissitudes. As is well known, there can be extreme difficulties in simply communicating insight and understanding while also enduring the terror, confusion, torpor or shame induced by the relationship. How is that for an action?

5. The quest for spontaneity

One of the frequently debated questions is whether psychoanalysis remains sufficiently free from pressures on the analysand to comply. According to Casement, the nature of mental change achieved in this way is something similar to that of conversion, 'patients giving up one way of seeing themselves for another that is . . . transmitted to them by the analyst.[24]' And this, of course, will not encourage the spontaneity that comes from the capacity for personal action rooted in one's own resources. It is only through experiences of relational spontaneity, in the form of a mutual signalling to one another of an expansion of the experience itself, that therapeutic consensuality (rather than 'conversion') is somehow assured. In a context of persistent psychic pressure consensuality is inexorably extorted and the 'treated' subject is so intruded as to appear invariably compliant. As is known, parental figures who somehow offer the 'promise' of adult mental life may of course obtain any consensuality; as if they were forever saying, 'If you want to be something more than just an animal-like little child, then you have to . . .'

Whenever the partners involve in a playful context unexpectedly achieve a higher level of mental intensity and efficacy, the capacity to seek creative excitement is strengthened for future interactions.[25] Once an expansion of the mental range has been achieved and there is the mutual expression of having reached a higher level of psychic spontaneity, subsequent interactions will develop in a more facilitating analytic environment. These beneficial breaches in a deadening psychic climate do not in the least threaten the therapeutic setting but rather they enhance a response that is definitely personal, not a technical manoeuvre, as if it were extracted from an interpretative *repertoire*.

No matter how small a chosen pursuit and one's ability to achieve it, when they are finely matched and fitting, we have the playful experience of spontaneity. With this joy of mental efficacy we easily disregard the irrelevant difference between 'small' and 'great' achievements. It is by now generally accepted that something more than interpretation is necessary to bring about therapeutic progress.[26] This ulterior dimension comprises interactions between patient and analyst that can create and name new ways of organizing the analytic relation as well as the patient's knowledge of being with others. Not only do we value mutative interpretations that rearrange the affective history of the individual, but also special occasions of psychic contact with the analyst, occasions that may transform the relationship as well as the quality of the patient's sense of himself. Effective interpretations, in fact, do require adequate preparation that must include these ulterior levels of spontaneity. Traditional psychoanalysis insists on frequent sessions, possibly in the effort to ensure that this preparatory work does actually take place.

A major feature of these eruptions of spontaneity is that it will feel like a deep qualitative change. But then we should ask, what would a persistent lack of spontaneity feel like. We could say that boredom is worse than the psychic pain of pathology, and that renouncing the pleasures of mental efficacy determines a sense of impotence that is perhaps more devastating than trauma. As if the contrary of love were not hatred but, in fact, indifference. In a climate of indifference, what is ultimately internalized is a deadening style of mental life. If this atmosphere is not exorcized in the analytic relation, the 'therapeutic' process will then repeat the most archaic, unspoken, and unmentalizable ways of stifling the mind. Surely a 'killer' that cannot be tracked or exposed. According to Casement, the effort to overcome this sort of condition involves both parties in a process that seems to have its own unconscious wisdom and direction, if we learn to tune into it and follow it. And the clinical journey that ensues can lead us beyond anything that theory alone could have suggested or that we might consciously have chosen for a patient.[27] This new affective context can function as the milieu in which past events can be reorganized *and* mental actions can be attempted.

The possibility of being capable of mental actions is distinctly different from the repetitive style and rigidity of mental reactions. As is known, Freud suggests that the more mature levels of our mind constantly retell a story according to the schemas of our more recent experiences. He had the deep insight that memories are re-narrated in accordance with later experience, although he was perhaps not prepared to fully develop this seminal line of enquiry. Indeed, Freud's presentation of *Nachträglichkeit* is hinted in different parts of his numerous works: as early as 1896 the idea was expressed in a letter to Fliess.[28] Invoking his early concern for sexual traumas, he later argued that what is far more important is their *deferred* effect, which can only take place at a later period of growth.[29] As is known, there is abundant literature on the topic of *Nachträglichkeit*, variously referred to as 'differed effect', 'retranscription of memory', 'recategorization of experience', and 'retroactive resignification'.

Experiences of spontaneity do not correct past empathic failure by means of the analytic relation, as they do not compensate for past deficit. Rather, something new springs to life in the relation which transforms the quality, level, intensity of the bi-personal field. In this *new* light past experiences are re-categorized in the present, thus opening the way for unforeseen developments. But what is essential about it is our *new* way of perceiving inner events and thus move away from repetitive reactions. In Casement's view, beyond the well-trodden paths of analytic practice there lies that which still remains *unknown to the analyst*, and which may require a fundamental change of perspective for the analyst to be able to comprehend.[30]

Through a facilitating environment, the mind will tend to use its relational vicissitudes to create more coherence and consequent 'attempts' to spontaneity. In treatment, this will mean an opportunity to grasp the reciprocity of the relation even though it is not made quite explicit. These eruptions of spontaneity constitute undeniable psychic events that reveal an affective knowledge of the dyadic process for both patient and analyst. By contrast, whenever the analytic atmosphere is not sufficiently facilitating a profound grasp of the relation is preventively prohibited – as if it were a non-approachable, non-negotiable dimension.

Some aspects of the analytic relation are explicit and declarative, while others are indeed implicit and procedural.[31] These procedural, affective aspects of our work operate outside of conscious, literal language and are rooted in what we know but cannot yet properly think. It is like reciprocally playing with the 'unthought known'.[32] For instance, the infant 'knows' early in life what forms of affective approaches the parent will welcome or reject, as is widely described in the attachment literature. It is this new thinkable knowledge that actually transforms the relational field and makes it suitable for interpretation, in the sense of being sufficiently lively and mature for spontaneous mental action.

Notes

1. P. Fonagy, G. Gergely, E.L. Jurist, & M. Target (2002). *Affect Regulation, Mentalization, and the Development of the Self*. New York: Other Press, p. 9.
2. For a discussion of this topic see Chapter 11 (From biological life to dialogic relations) in G. Corradi Fiumara (1992). *The Symbolic Function: Psychoanalysis and the Philosophy of Language*. Oxford, UK and Cambridge, USA, pp. 154–178.
3. This point is elaborated in Chapter 2 (From philosophy to epistemophily) and in Chapter 4 (A passion for reason) of G. Corradi Fiumara (2001). *The Mind's Affective Life: A Psychoanalytic and Philosophical Inquiry*. London and New York: Brunner-Routledge, pp. 20–32 and 41–52.

4. P. Fonagy, *et al.* (2002)., *Affect Regulation, Mentalization, and the Development of the Self.* New York: Other Press, 2002, p 9.
5. D.W. Winnicott (1971). *Playing and Reality.* London: Tavistock Publications, pp. 111–115.
6. *Ibid.*, p. 51.
7. 'Interpretation outside the ripeness of the material is indoctrination and produces compliance,' *ibid.*, p. 51.
8. This thesis is discussed in G. Corradi Fiumara (1992). *The Symbolic Function*, especially in Chapter 10 (Genesis of the Symbolic Function), pp. 135–153.
9. M. Eigen, *Toxic Nourishment(1999).* London: Karnac Books, p. 1.
10. This question is discussed in P. Fonagy, *et al.* (2002). *Affect Regulation, Mentalization, and the Development of the Self*, p. 364.
11. *Ibid.*, p. 198.
12. *Ibid.*, p. 360.
13. On this topic see G. Corradi Fiumara (1990). *The Other Side of Language: A Philosophy of Listening.* London and New York: Routledge.
14. As is well known, the question of the entanglement of love and hatred, nourishment and violence, recurs throughout Bion's work. W.R. Bion (1970). *Attention and Interpretation: A Scientific Approach to Psycho-analysis and Groups.* London: Tavistock Publications, p. 12.
15. L. Wittgenstein (1988). *Philosophical Investigations.* Translated by G.E.M. Anscombe. Oxford: Basil Blackwell, p. 133e, paragraph 464.
16. W.R. Bion (1970). *Attention and Interpretation*, p. 116.
17. M. Khan (1974). *The Privacy of the Self.* New York: International Universities Press, p. 284.
18. K. Jaspers (1933). *Man in the Modern Age.* London: George Routledge and Sons, p. 196–197.
19. This particular expression is derived from R. Caper's essay (1997). A mind of one's own, *The International Journal of Psychoanalysis, 78 (2)*: pp. 265–278.
20. D.W. Winnicott (1971). *Op. cit.*, pp. 111–115.
21. P. Fonagy, et al.(2002). *Op. cit.*, pp. 4–5.
22. G. Corradi Fiumara (2001) *The Mind's Affective Life*; see paragraphs 'The problem of thinking affects', pp. 33–35, and 'The question of classification and terminology', pp. 60–63.
23. P. Fonagy, *et al.*, *op. cit.*, p. 9.
24. P. Casement (2002). *Learning from our Mistakes: Beyond Dogma in Psychoanalysis and Psychotherapy.* London and New York: Brunner-Routledge, p. xiii.

25. D.N. Stern, L.W. Sander, J.P. Nahum, *et al.(1998).* The 'something more' than interpretation. *The International Journal of Psychoanalysis, 79*: pp. 903–219.
26. This particular expression is derived from D.N. Stern, *et al., ibid.*
27. P. Casement (2002). *Learning from our Mistakes*, p. xv.
28. 'I should like to emphasise the fact that the successive registrations represent the psychic achievement of successive epochs of life. At the boundary between two such epochs a translation of the psychic material must take place.' Letter dated December 6 1986. J. Masson (Ed. and Trans.) (1985). *The Complete Letters of Sigmund Freud to Wilhelm Fliess.* Cambridge, MA: Harvard University Press, p. 207.
29. S. Freud (1898) Sexuality and the aetiology of the neuroses. *Standard Edition*, p. 281.
30. P. Casement (2002). *Learning from our Mistakes*, p. 114.
31. D.N. Stern, *et al.* (1998). The 'something more' than interpretation, pp. 903–219.
32. This particular expression and concept is derived from C. Bollas (1987). *The Shadow of the Object: Psychoanalysis of the Unthought Known.* London: Free Association Books.

CHAPTER FOUR

A language for remembering the future

Yolanda Gampel

With this book we pay tribute to the contribution and work of Jacqueline Amati Mehler, who spent her whole professional life exploring the complex reality of interpersonal and intrapersonal experience at the levels of language (1982, 1990), dream (2003), and thought (1988, 2004). Two of her major contributions were to show how emotional experience takes place in different languages and the variable relations between psychopathology and the developmental vicissitudes of the symbolic function. Together, all of her writings offer a challenging perspective on the nature of the associative process, the connection between memory and awareness, the connection between linguistic structure and the consolidation of the unconscious dynamic, and how all this happens in the encounter and communication between patient and analyst (1994, 2004).

The subject of my article will be the different intrapsychic languages we speak in, and the different ways and levels of speech we use. In this I follow the fascinating exploration of multilingualism, set out for us in its many forms and complexities by Jacqueline Amati Mehler et al. I explore the Babel of the unconscious, probe the different layers of the psyche and the different languages they speak in, as they display the harsh realities of the interpersonal and intrapsychic experiences of those who speak, think, and dream.

Nachträglichkeit (deferred action, retroactive re-signification) and feedback in open systems require a new view of the function and nature of time. We know this from psychoanalytical work. In this paper I lean on George Perec, Amos Oz, and others and their treatment of the function and nature of time in works whose subject is the experience of the self. Time in this type of novel cannot be simple: it will be synchronic, diachronic, mythical, repetitive, and circular . . . just like the Babel of different languages the unconscious speaks in.

Freud also distinguished different languages, different types of articulation: 'The dream thoughts and dream content are there for us as two representations or descriptions (*darstellungen*) of the same content in two unlike languages. Or better, the content of the dream appears as a translation, a transference, a transcription (*Übertragung*) of the dream thoughts into another means of expression, whose signs and laws of articulation it is our business to learn by comparing the original with its transposition (*Umsetzung*) into this other mode of expression.' (Freud, 1895, p. 277)

Bion, drawing on his penetrating work with psychotic patients, compares the situation of the psychoanalyst confronting a psychotic state of mind with the situation confronting an archaeologist, when earth tremors have collapsed the structures and objects of earlier eras into the strata of later ages (Bion, 1957, published 1967). According to Tustin, the state Bion terms 'psychological catastrophe' is the outcome of a 'psychological birth' which was either premature or wrongly managed.

In contrast, 'catastrophic change' is a change in the direction of growth, and not of catastrophe. The term began to achieve currency after Bion had delved into the theory of transformations. Philosophical in origin, the concept of transformation was then taken over into mathematics. Bion borrows it as a way of observing the different situations ocurring within psychoanalysis.

The chief source for the thoughts I set out here is Bion's *The Dawn of Oblivion* (1979).

Anyone familiar with the whole of Bion's work down the years can find in his *A Memoir of the Future* (1972–1979) not only all his early thinking but also a shedding of light on all his previous work by way of, as it were, a retrospective review of his theoretical and clinical experience and experiences. Most of us have asked in the past why he is so hard to understand. I would say that over the years his writings have become more penetrable and that with this later book,

Bion is attempting something new, with the object of obtaining a wider understanding of the inner language of the mind than his articles and books, with their abstract psychoanalytic theories, have succeeded in doing. *A Memoir of the Future* is intended as an interactive text, shared between author and reader. The reader is expected to react emotionally to it, as Bion Talamo put it; (1997) 'emotions first, reasoning afterwards'. Bion has always been much occupied with the way his writings present the emotions he wishes to convey to his readers. It may well be that he saw the technique he uses for this book as one to enable each individual reader to respond *evocatively*, to face up to his or her own emotions. As a result, the book is a hard read, for it touches the deepest levels of our self. Many believe that it is best read in a group, since a group has the capacity to contain the individual reader and, if it can act as and • function, has the capacity to cope with what could turn into resistance to a beginning insight.

Bion, in the voice of Em-Mature in Chapter 1, says: 'I cannot vouch for the truth of these tales which became known to me through scientific hear-say many years later. I admit responsibility for what I have experienced, but not for the distortions of scientific sense. I acknowledge dependence on sensible and experienced transcriptions; I cannot promise communication of pure non-sense without the contamination by sense. I shall not repeat my apology for having to borrow the language of experience and reason despite its inadequacy.' (1979, p.1)

In his earlier *Attention and Interpretation (1970)*, Bion already made the attempt to accommodate the schizo-paranoid position, which is stimulated by the way the book's text is presented, that is, in a fragmentary, non-linear fashion, devoid of an orderly narrative, compelling the reader to an incessant search for an island of temporary assurance. This is what Bion believes occurs during an analysis session, so that reading the book is, on one level, a sort of exercise in the movement and transitions of PS • D, a practical demonstration of what he believes happens when this movement happens. We have to face up to the fact that Bion is not in the habit of describing how he conducts his analyses. He always prefers to suggest that we each of us perform the • function, which for him constitutes the basic function of all mental apparatus. The book sets out for us, via Bion's own ideas, the structure of the mind, as based on Freud's thinking and the transformation of that thinking.

A Memoir of the Future exhibits all the phases of life, from the womb onwards. Bion confronts us with the very first thoughts. He wants to shake up what we hold as truths and give form to our intuitions. We, for our part, struggle to make sense of his idiosyncratic manner of writing, which neither the exact nor the social sciences have found acceptable. At the same time, we cannot deny that his manner of thinking exists within all of us. For the most part it comes out in the form of dreams, or as what Bion terms 'waking dream thought'. In this latter state, figures and images, which are generated moment by moment, enter our minds in subtle ways but always remain mysterious. We try to pin them down but, like every emanation of the unconscious, they come and in an instant have gone. They reappear, leave a fleeting impression, disappear and reappear again, in a thousand and one disguises.

In the *The Dawn of Oblivion* (1979), volume 3 of *A Memoir of the Future*, Bion puts on stage all phases of the personality or proto-personality. In Chapter 1, he says in the voice of Em-mature: 'This book is a psycho-embryonic attempt to write an embryo-scientific account of a journey from birth to death overwhelmed by pre-mature knowledge, experience, glory and self-intoxicating self-satisfaction. I was spared any knowledge of the courtship of my sperm with my ovum, but many years later was given to understand that my ancestors had a long and disreputable history.' (p. 10).

Body, psyche, ideas, drive, desire, reality and the real, ancestors and elements, all these are part of us, part of our life and self, even if we are not aware of them all. Remnants of the premature personality, he says, continue to exist alongside the post-mature occupier of the same soma-psyche. There develop psychosomatic reactions, somato-psychotic demands, unfamiliar elements which, on their appearance, we sometimes construe as illness, psychosis, neurosis, borderline state, and so on.

A permanent theme of Bion's thought has been the attempt to grasp abstractly the basic components of human existence, those scattered primary sensory inputs, and those disintegrated remnants that he calls the *beta* elements. He shows us how these remnants are turned into • elements by an • function. The basis for this operation occurs only between the two minds of mother and baby, of patient and analyst – He formulated the idea that the analyst's reverie transformed raw beta into alpha elements, just as a mother who decodes her infant's presymbolized communications – and when it does occur, it not only permits a reshaping of the basic building blocks of thought but also permits the method and change process themselves to be internalized.

In other words, Bion shows us that the • elements are neither something given to us nor visible but are unconscious. Accordingly, other essential factors enter the picture in order to harness the sequence of • elements to more fully formed images via the constantly operative paranoid-schizoid/depressive oscillation PS • D and the • • relationship (container/contained). To these we must add the parallel movement between 'negative capability' and the 'selected fact', the fact which, organizing a specific gestalt, confines choice to one possibility alone. (It was Keats (1952) who coined the term 'negative capability' in a letter to his brother, to name the ability to retain doubts without feeling persecuted.)

> *Em-Mature*: My earliest experiences were of something touching what I later heard was 'me'. The changes in pressure in the fluid surrounding me varied from what Me called pleasure to what Me called pain. My optic and auditory pits at the age of three or four somites received sound and light, dark and silence, not usually increasing beyond nice and nasty, but sometimes making Me feel more inanimate than animate.
>
> *Pre-mature:* Get on with it – when were you born? (Bion, 1979, p. 1)

Earlier, in his 1976 article *Emotional Turbulence,* Bion had posed the 'simple' question: When do things begin? When is a human creature born? Reply with the date of birth, and his next question would be: So, when is your personality born? When did you see light for the first time? What images do we retain from our intra-uterine odyssey? How and where the movements of the foetus are registered, the pleasure of thumb-sucking, the frustration of it? How is the birth itself imprinted on us?

Having himself passed through many transformations, and after writing the three books *Learning from Experience (1962) On Transformations (1965)*, and *Attention and Interpretation (1970)*, Bion found himself in closer acquaintance with ignorance and infinity. As a result, he was no longer using the concepts of psychotic and non-psychotic personality that characterized his early writings. Instead, he discussed the presence of a plethora of prenatal factors, generated by an emotional storm that bursts out within the personality this entire still in the absence of any containing mechanism. He talks of function, not of state. Further to this, Bion confronts us with the things we do not know and cannot grasp because they are unconscious, or which belong to the uterine period, before the physical or psychic or mental birth, all of them as multi-strata'ed as an archeological dig.

In *Inhibition, Symptom and Anxiety* (1926) Freud wrote: 'There is much more continuity between intra-uterine life and earliest infancy than the impressive Caesura of the act of birth would have us believe.' Birth is so strong a stimulus that it does not allow us to postulate for the foetus a proto-mind and proto-personality which continue developing after birth.

What we can say is that the mentalization of those primitive parts of the self is very different from the processes which psychoanalysis is supposed to probe. These primitive parts of the personality think with the body. The laws governing them are closer to neurophysiology than psychology. In other words, this is a world of gradations or levels of stimuli and not of nuanced variables of emotion.

To take us deeper into the subject, I shall introduce both contemporary writer-thinkers and a very distant school of thought, the ancient Chinese philosophy of Taoism. Tao in Chinese means 'way' or 'inner principle' and the two greatest Taoists were Lao Tseu and Tchouang Tseu, who wrote in the fourth and third centuries B.C.E. respectively. These two apprehended the tangible and the abstract, the individual and the absolute in a single intuition, which was not in any sense higher than rationality but an absolutely other spiritual stance, in which reason, defining, distinguishing, analysing reason, played no part whatsoever. Tchouang Tseu would meet with no little irony the attempts of human reason to penetrate the secrets of being.

> The wise man walks in the light of chaos and void, in the light of the darkness. He does not enforce distinctions but leaves everything in its accustomed place. This is true clarity of thought.

> I shall now say something. When I say something – do I state something? Do I not state something? I don't know. But when I asked if a statement had been made or not, then I certainly made some sort of statement. In that what I say is no different from what any other man says. So, I shall try to say something: Let us posit that 'There is a beginning'. If so, then there is 'There is no beginning yet'. If so, then there is 'There is not yet, there is no beginning yet'. Now, there is 'There is' and there is 'There is not'. If so, then there is also 'There is not yet, there is, and there is no, there is not.' If so, there is 'There is not yet, there is not yet, there is and There is no, there is no, there is not.' Thus do 'There is' and 'There is not' appear to us. I do not know which of them there is and which there is not. So, I have said that there is something. But in saying that, have I said something? Have I not said something? I don't know. (Tchouang Tseu, 1985, p. 210)

Ancient Chinese thought is an example of a thought that follows the back and forth of an individual's life between his self and his world. It is thought that is, at one and the same time, subtle and concrete. It probes into daily life, in the here and now. It is open, observational, intuitive, and practical. The distant ancestors of the Chinese, some two or three thousand years before the birth of Christ, were already talking this sort of language.

How is the breath directly connected to the mother-child relationship? In the text compiled by Zhang San Feng, *Dan Jing Mi Jue* (*Le secret du livre de cinabre*), translated with a commentary by Jean Marc Eyssalet in his book *Le Secret de la Maison des Ancêtres* (1990), 'the fetus begins life in the womb, where it breathes in and out in the rhythm of its mother. It receives breath filtered through its link-up to the mother. Little by little it grows and there opens a small gap in its middle like a channel – the navel – and then the breath acts as a form of back and forth communication. From the navel the breath passes to the kidneys, then to the prefrontal neocortex. Then to the base of the nose, where it creates the nose's two openings. In other words, when we look at a face we are looking at the root of the breath' (Eyssalet, 1990, pp. 190–195).

In understanding that the forming of the foetal nose begins with the navel and the link-up to the mother, we appreciate that the first and fundamental breath comes from the mother via the navel, passes through the kidneys and then along the spine, and so gifts man his ability to stand upright on the earth. It arrives at the point above the bridge of the nose which is the seat of man's ability to see and think clearly, and then comes down to the base of the nose to form the two nostrils, and so ensure the individual's continuity with his ancestors, namely, his breath and identity. It is a wonderful thing to have traced this path of development, even if the West finds it hard to acknowledge.

> From the moment the baby's breath communicates with his mother's, the mother's breath is in communication with the breath of heaven-earth, which in its turn is in communication with the breath of the great emptiness. Between one great orifice and the other the communication is mutual. There is no separation, no barrier. (*ibid.*, p. 199).

This is absolute freedom and, simultaneously, the creation of a living field. Field breathing without separation. This is for what the Taoists yearn, to reach a state where the human brain is healed of its hot, sick current state, in which it constructs a world from an infinity of objects which only drag us down with their weight. Not knowing what to do with all these objects, we occupy ourselves in setting them up in opposition to each other. In other words, free breath, free of separations, begins with the root of things.

Fundamentally, we are not being invited to take on new knowledge and information, but to learn to read dynamically what we already know, although in a fragmented, disordered manner, and then set our new reading in a broader perspective. Only thus can we achieve a qualitative transformation.

Not all of what occurs within a mother's body is under her psyche's control. Today we critically confuse the individual personality and volitional psychological elements, forgetting that there is a basic natural structure which causes people to act in the way they do. This structure exercises a special effect on women during pregnancy, when there takes place, at an exceptionally rapid rate, a comprehensive alteration and development of living tissue. The rate of development is unparalleled. This is truly nature at work. That is, there is a form of unity between the individual nature of each of us and the nature of the whole. This does not deny individual fate, however. Interlinked as we are all via an intimate nature, we nonetheless all come with our own destiny.

In the Taoist *Dan Jing Mi Jue,* the breathing personality stems from a cosmic context, from a state of which we have no awareness but which carries our own awareness: 'The fetus opens the womb and exits. The umbilical cord is cut. He sets foot on the ground (the earth as opposed to heaven, he finds support), there comes a single cry!' In the traditional view, the self's first self-expression is to quit the mother and find support on the earth. This is the start of an intimate cosmic dialogue between earth and heaven. Standing on the earth, we cry to heaven. The cry travels through the air. The precondition for the voice's shout to the heavens is the self's finding support and a firm foothold on earth! (Eyssalet, 1990, pp. 408–410)

Today, embryology and neuroscience research talk in just this sort of language. In the central nervous system, every complex mental operation also involves the basic structures, among them the brain stem, the hypothalamus, the thalamus, the hippocampus, and the limbic system. In other words, no complex cortical functioning is possible by deploying sophisticated activity networks alone. It always entails simultaneous activity on all other levels, including the most archaic. Moreover, the archaic levels let us hear the levels of the foetus as it begins to become a body within the maternal body, almost in continuity with nature. It is clear that, by applying Bion's theories, Taoist thinking can serve as a most useful counterpart to modern brain sciences research.

> Our world divides into facts because we so divide it. (Susanne Langer)

It can happen that explanation and interpretation, rather than bring us closer, take us further away from the heart of a matter and muddle us up into the bargain. I started this exploration with Bion because for me he deals with the basics, the origins of things. Then I brought in Taoist thought, more to widen our perspective than to supply explanation. To my mind, in order to recognize ourselves in the vast complexity in which we live, we need common sense and a broad and lucid vision. Phenomena and facts, everything that has form and shape, can change. To talk about phenomena and their meaning, I once again call a writer to my assistance, this time Amos Oz, in his novel, *A Tale of Love and Darkness,* one theme of which is the numerous possible forms any phenomenon selected for study can assume.

Grandma died in the bath.

Her heart attack is a fact.

But the truth is that my grandmother died from an excess of hygiene, not a heart attack. Facts have the tendency to obscure the truth. It was cleanliness that killed her. Although the motto of her life in Jerusalem, 'the Levant is full of germs', may testify to an earlier, deeper truth than the demon of hygiene, a truth that was repressed, and invisible.

After all Grandma Shlomit came from north-eastern Europe, where there were just as many germs as there were in Jerusalem, not to mention all sort of noxious things

Menace? Or perhaps the truth is that it was not the menace of the Levant that made my grandmother mortify and purify her body with those boiling-hot ablutions morning, noon and night every day that she lived in Jerusalem but rather its seductive sensual charms, and her own body, and the powerful attraction of those teeming markets that made her breathing tight and her knees weak with the abundance of unfamiliar vegetables, fruit, spicy cheeses, pungent odors, guttural foods that so tormented and excited her, and those lustful hands that groped and burrowed into the most intimate recesses of fruit and vegetables, the chillis and spicy olives and the nudity of all that ripe, bare red meat, dripping blood, hanging shamelessly naked from the butchers' hooks, and the dizzying array of spices, herbs and powders, all the multicolored lascivious lures of that pungent, highly-seasoned world, not to mention the penetrating aromas of freshly-roasted, cardamom-flavored coffee, and the glass containers full of colorful drinks with lumps of ice or slices of lemon in them, and those powerfully-built, deeply tanned, hirsute market porters, naked to the waist, the muscles of their backs rippling with effort under their hot skin that gleamed as rivulets of perspiration ran down in the sun. Perhaps all Grandma's cult of cleanliness was nothing more nor less than a hermetic sterile space suit? An antiseptic chastity belt that she had voluntarily buckled on, since her first day here, and secured with seven locks, destroying all the keys?

> Or maybe it was neither the hygiene nor her desires nor her fear of her desires that killed her but her constant secret anger at this fear, a suppressed, malignant anger, like an unlaced boil, anger at her own body, at her own longings, and also a deeper anger, at the very revulsion these longings gave rise to, a murky, poisonous anger, directed both at the prisoner and at her jailor, years and years of secret mourning for the ceaseless passage of desolate time and the shriveling of her body and the desires of her body, the desires, laundered and cleaned and scraped and disinfected and boiled a thousand times, for that Levant, filthy, sweaty, bestial, exciting to the point of swooning, but swarming with germs. (Oz, 2005, pp. 32–33)

From the depths of the psyche Bion raises up its primordial elements, making them observable in the form of group behaviour. He presents a concept of group life as one level of mental activity within the individual. Other levels find expression in physical processes. The effect of all these together can be frightening and threatening. He proposes that we have to regard all the stages of bodily development, not excepting the foetal stage, not excepting even the embryonic (pre-foetal) stage, and including, too, the weeks and months leading up to a birth, as all represented in the structure of the self.

Once again I call a writer to aid me, this time George Perec. His play, *Under the Potatoes*, offers an eccentric answer to the question: What has mankind managed to make with vegetables? The dialogue is Ionesco-like in its absurdity and elusiveness:

> *L'Homme: Des examples! Mais il y en a cent, il y en a mille! Ernest qui vend son droit pour des lentilles et Archimède qui incendie Alexandrie avec. Et les haricots-rames, et les carottes des prospecteurs! Et les choux-fleurs! Vous saviez que les choux-fleurs étaient utilisés par les anciens pour combattre les défaillances de la mémoire?*

At first glance, the speaker seems to have everthing garbled, in particular he mixes Bible stories, such as the selling of a birthright for a mess of potage with the burning down of the library at Alexandria and Archimedes. I point out only a few of the weird pairings, for instance, climbing beans and oil-prospecting carrots. These activate a series of associations taken from vernacular figures of speech, such as: *Des haricots! Vous n'aurez rien du tout.* (You won't get anything.) or *C'est la fin des haricots* (All hope is gone) or *Les carrots sont cuites* (All is lost. We've been done). And so on. On one level, the linguistic and verbal level, this garbled dialogue seems to be describing a fraught sequence of developments, whose stages can be summarized thus: waiving or betraying one's birthright, conflagration, destruction, defection, and loss of memory, in other words the main phases of Perec's biography. The parents handing over their son to someone else; his father dying in a prisoner-of-war camp; his mother perishing in a Nazi furnace. The young boy, surviving the Holocaust, experiencing this double disappearance as abandonment, subsequently totally represses the memory of parents and childhood, thus defecting from his allegiance to Judaism in general and from a particularly horrible past. (Shnitzer, 2004)

Perec recounts his inner journey through a dialogue between different times in the memory of humanity. Bion recounts for us the adult's inner journey through an endless dialogue, with all its phases and left-over parts. We are not always ready to listen to all the figures pushing themselves into this dialogue. Is the adult, whether happy with life or fed up with it, ready to listen to the voice of the six year old who did not go out to play enough or who did not play with him, as he tells how he felt deprived and that others had more?

Perec and Bion, in similar and at the same time different modes, give us the distinctive flavour and taste of remembering, of the passage of memory from absence to a particular kind of presence. Each person reads in his own way the trace of his past, which governs his future possibilities. For the readers of Perec and Bion and their ilk, memory is what is absent from the here and now and, thus, what has to be inferred.

To talk about the inner encounters between different ages, the best way is to bring in another author. David Grossman writes in his latest book, *Lion Honey*:

> Look at him: a man among men, but hiding inside a little boy with a sweet-tooth (how disturbing and touching the gulf between the magnificently developed body and the slightly childish, slightly undeveloped mind). He walks along eating and licking until he reaches home and Mum and Dad, and gives them the

honey: 'And they ate,' apparently directly from his hands. What a wonderful, sensuous thing to do! (Grossman, 2006)

Back to Bion:

Eight years: That is not how it seems to me looking at it from my side of the barrier.
Leonard: Shut up both of you and look at this drawing.
Eight years: Not bad – what is it?
Twenty-four years: Open your eyes and you will see it is darkness of the womb.
Milton: The formless infinite – the void.
Em: The light is too intense.
Twelve years: It is eye. Be not afraid. And 'e did 'it 'is eye. And Em was afraid. Ha, ha, ha!
Em: What a dreadful oscillation of pressure!
Thirty years: Who is talking words you don't understand now?
Em: Caught in a web of whirling waters.
Leonard: Hair! Water! If you only looked you would 'see what-I-mean', but –
Forty years: No – only hair, water, words –
Forty-two years: No; if you listened you would only hear 'repetition compulsion' psycho-ese.
P.A.: Psycho-analysis?
Em: Stop! Stop! I can't bear it. I am blinded, deafened!
Krishna: I told you so; wait till you are Arjuna.
Em: It's quieter now. Gametes quarrelling. Post-natals at it again. Give me Silence. 'Shape nothing lips.' 'Be shelled eyes.' Stoma – you at the other end – keep closed. 'A sealed tube'? That can't be right. Suck! What?
Four somites: Come on, wake up! Think! (Chap. 3)

This last section from the *The Dawn of Oblivion* touches on the mind's historical dimension, which can be linked to the search for historical truth, but without putting the emphasis on any one particular necessary narrative. It describes how, by accentuating the many possible dimensions, the same components can be arranged in a variety of sequences, each one producing another vertex. This is only one of the acute clinical observations that Bion tries to convey in the book. It is a book that the reader cannot read without applying his own mind and life to it and that is something that the analyst, too, must be aware of in every analysis session. Furthermore, the observer's concepts are liable to both interfere with and contribute to his observation of things. In other words, every analyst has to know how to identify which parts of mental activity belong to him and which to his patient. According to Bion common sense will show how valid these observations of his are.

Are we capable of unravelling the tangle of emotions and images of different kinds? That is what Bion's *A Memoir of the Future* is about • the life of the foetus, violence, vitality, all the tangle of experiences we pass through and which are imprinted on us as extremism and violence, brutality, wearying repetitions of a single behaviour pattern. All of these are our lot. Sometimes, we can be trapped in one fixated thought to the point of not even hearing all the other possibilities open to us.

Derrida (1967,19) asks: 'What is a text?' He answers, leaning on Freud's metaphor of the 'mystic writing pad', 'that in so far as the temporality of the text is historical and not linear, that is to say, that the text can be read backwards, upwards or downwards, or permanently modified after it has been written down (like a dream), the interpretation is bound by the laws of the trace.' For Derrida, the notion of memory traces connected with the concept of difference, but more specifically with its homonym derived from the verb '*différer*' ('to defer, to delay'). *Différance*, with an 'a', is after the event, (*nachträglichkeit*) and related to 'postponement'. Life must be conceived of as a trace before being determined as a presence. The essence of life (no thing) is a *difference.*

> To live is to be other. To feel is impossible if we feel as we felt yesterday: to feel today the same as yesterday is to not feel it is to recall today what we felt yesterday. It is to be the living skeleton of what yesterday was our life, the living skeleton of something lost, never to return. (Pessoa, *The Book of Disquiet, 1988*)

If we agree with this quotation from Pessoa, every day we encounter ourselves afresh. Familiar but unfamiliar, somewhat strange. Tomorrow there will be someone else. And what we shall look at tomorrow will be woven, constructed, and assembled from a new point of view. To bring transference into the equation, it does not convey merely the happenings and relationships of the past, reconstructed in the now of an analysis session: it is day after day a new minting.

Do we have the courage to live in the awareness that Pessoa proposes? Live in the knowledge of our ignorance? Converse with the unfamiliar and strange we encounter in ourselves? (First and foremost via our dreams. Even a dream, the moment you wake up, is gone, evaporated and repression is already at work. A dream, that product of the unconscious and the unknown, remains strangeness even to its own dreamer.)

Strangeness and otherness can be inhibiting, the other being threatened by the strange and the uncanny and the strange being threatened by the uncanny other. Psychoanalysis is curative but more importantly it is a path to the potentialities of unfolding and growth. It is also an ethic. When we re-encounter childhood and beyond, and the lost time of all the yearnings and longings, and all this remaking and reshaping of time, then the whole mental economy undergoes change, all the ability to work through things and learn from them expands. It is like finding joy, like the sensation of a child finding a new game. The question, however, that has to be asked about joy is: is it illusion or disillusion?

The 62-year-old T.A. walks into my consulting room: Well, here's your patient back again but there's no point in me being here, I'm off. Life is hard, miserable, there isn't a jot of happiness or cheer in me (what is he talking about if not joy?). He tells me what he did on his holiday, all the excursions and outings, and then asks me if there is any point in his going tomorrow to something he has tickets for or going on a trip he had planned for the upcoming Holy Days. What's the point? Ecclesiastes was right: it's all vanity and vainness. What is this so-called 'joy of life'?

Into this flow of words and moodiness, I insert, I think, that joy is evidently a matter of moments here and there, that he can find it playing with his grandchild, contemplating a marvellous view, in words from someone that suddenly make the heart overflow. I don't say this all at once but slip it in, as I can, into his outpouring.

Of course, from moment to moment he's on his feet and heading for the door because what is this stuff called psychotherapy and what is he doing here and what good does it do him to talk about it all? Of course, he stays the full 50 minutes and even steals a few extra. Afterwards, as I walk with him to the door of my house, he tells me with enthusiasm and joy of the stunning scenes and views he saw in the two places he visited over the summer. Inside, I am smiling as we go down the steps because there is joy. I give him a smile and say goodbye and that he has, after all, found moments of joy, to which he rejoins: No, it was all a mistake.

So what can we say, that the power of the encounter, of speech, of the past, of my freedom that they together have fashioned a moment of joy?

Or perhaps we can explain it in different terms? Can we not see it as an example of Jacqueline A. Melher's 'psycho-archeology', those so-called 'underground precursors' of speech which become manifest through a series of paralinguistic elements, that ever-growing complex network of polysensorial associations which make possible the transition from the concrete to the abstract, from the bodily to the mental?

Or visualizing my patient on an altogether metaphorical level, could we not say that his moment of joy is an effect of language, of the capacity to symbolize? That, even if within him are so many unborn, overwhelmingly premature foetuses of personality, the spawn of emotional storms, which, in the absence of any containing mechanism, seem to be psychotic, to not want to wake up and think. But it seems he has encountered a container.

References

Amati Mehler, J. (1982). A clinical contribution to the understanding of alterations in the capacity to achieve knowledge. *Riv. di Psicoanal., XXVIII 46.*

Amati Mehler, J. (1988). Polylinguisme et polyglottisme dans la dimension intrapsychique. *Rev. Franc. Psychanal., 2.*

Amati Mehler, J. (1994). Further considerations on love, impotence and male sexuality. *Canadian Journal of Psychoanalysis, 2.*

Amati Mehler, J. (1998). Son et parole: psycho-archéologie du langage. C'est le ton qui fait la chanson. *Journal de la psychanalyse de l'enfant, 23, Les liens.*

Amati Mehler, J. (2003). Les rêves: hier et auhourd'hui. In: A. Nakov (Ed.), *Le rêve dans la pratique psychanalytique*. Paris: Dunod.

Amati Mehler, J. (2004). Immigration, loss and memory. In: *Lost Childhood and the Language of Exile*. J. Szekacs-Weisz & I. Ward (Eds.), Imago MPLC and Freud Museum Publications.

Amati Mehler, J. (2004). Mélancolie: folie, génie ou tristesse? Les vicissitudes de l'identification et de la formation du moi. *Rev. franç. Psychanal., 4.*

Amati Mehler, J., Argentieri, S., & Canestri, J. (1990). *La Babele dell'Inconscio: Lingua madre e lingua straniere nella dimensione psicoanalitica*. Milano: Cortina.

Amati Mehler, J., Argentieri, S., & Canestri, J. (1993). *The Babel of the Unconscious: Mother Tongue and Foreign Languages in the Psychoanalytic Dimension*. Madison, CT: International Universities Press.

Bion, W.R. (1962). *Learning from Experience*. London: Heinemann.

Bion, W.R. (1966). Catastrophic change. *Scientific Bulletin of the British Psychoanalytical Society, 5*.

Bion, W.R. (1970). *Attention and Interpretation*. London: Heinemann.

Bion, W.R. (1972–1979). *A Memoir of the Future*. London: Karnac Books, 1991. Book 3, *The Dawn of Oblivion* (1979). Perthshire: Clunie Press.

Bion, W.R. (1976). *Emotional Turbulence*. In: P. Hortocolis (Ed.), *Borderline Personality Disorders*. New York: International University Press.

Bion Talamo, P. (1997). The clinical relevance of A Memoir of the Future. *Journal of Melanie Klein and Object Relations, 15:2*: 235–242.

Derrida, J. (1966). Freud et la scène de l'écriture. *Tel quell, 26*.

Derrida, J. (1979). *L'écriture et la différence*. Paris: Seuil.

Eyssalet, J.M. (1990). *Le Secret de la Maison des Ancêtres*. Paris: Guy Tredaniel Editeur.

Freud, S. (1895). Project for a scientific psychology. *Standard Edition, 4* (1950): 277.

Freud, S. (1914). On narcissism: an introduction. *Standard Edition, 14*.

Freud, S. (1919). The 'uncanny'. *Standard Edition, 17*.

Freud, S. (1923). The ego and the id. *Standard Edition, 19*.

Freud, S. (1926). Inhibition, syptoms and anxiety. *Standard Edition, 20*.

Grossman, D. (2006). *Lion's Honey: The Myth of Samson*. Israel: Yediot Ha'akhronot.

Keats, John (1952) Letters, edited by M.B. Forman. London: Oxford University Press.

Langer Susanne (1942) *Philosophy in a New Key: A Study in the Symbolism of Reason, Rite, and Art*, Charles Scribner's Son New York 1973 (Originally Published in 1953).

Lao Tse (1967). *Tao-To king: le livre de la voie et de la vertu*. Paris: Gallimard.

Oz, A. (2005). *A Tale of Love and Darkness*. London: Vintage.

Perec, G. (1981). *Theatre 1, La poche parmentier precede de l'augmentation*. Paris: Hachette.

Pessoa, F. (1988). *Le livre de L'intranquillité*. France: C Bourgeois.

Shnitzer, D. (2004). *Epilog to the translation of Perec's' Theatre 1*: 155–166. Tel-Aviv: Riesling Publication.

Tustin, F. (1981). Psychological birth and psychological catastrophe. In: J.S. Grotstein (Ed.), *Do I Dare Disturb the Universe?* Césura Press, Britain.

Tchouang Tseu. (1985). *Oeuvres complètes*. Translated by Liou Kia-hway. Paris: Gallimard.

CHAPTER FIVE

Symbolization and psychosis: the mediating function of images in individual psychoanalytic psychodrama

Alain Gibeault

> The word 'image' is in bad repute because we have thoughtlessly believed that a design was a tracing, a copy, a second thing, and that the mental image was such a design, belonging among our private bric-a-brac. But in fact it is nothing of the kind, then neither the design nor the painting belongs to the in-itself any more than the image does. They are the inside of the outside and the outside of the inside, which the duplicity of feeling [*le sentir*] makes possible and without which we would never understand the quasi presence and imminent visibility which make up the whole problem of the imaginary.
>
> Merleau-Ponty, 1964, p. 296

In Freud's theory of thinking, mental images are intermediaries; they lie somewhere between unconscious thing-presentations and the word-presentations which play an important role in bringing unconscious processes to consciousness. If we take as our starting-point Freud's *Studies on Hysteria*, the psychoanalytic process is marked by the need to substitute words for acts so as to allow repressed memories to be abreacted. This postulate led Freud (1893a) to emphasize the *motor* aspect of language, which encourages the discharge of affect through memory recall – the price to be paid, however, being less than what the appropriate initial response (crying, seeking revenge, etc.) would have entailed.

From that point of view, language is a constituent element of secondary processes and of bringing phenomena to consciousness, because thing-presentations have less to do with images than with 'thoughts' or 'ideas' about things, even though they have lost the sheer sensory vividness of perception. Also, these presentations participate in an associative process with other presentations, thereby forming a thought process, which by definition has no particular *quality* attached to it. Hence the need to have recourse to word-presentations in order to restore to thing-presentations the sensory vividness they have lost.

Freud (1923b), however, did not exclude the possibility that thing-presentations may well become conscious directly, as we find for example in dream images and in hallucinations. He goes on to point out, nonetheless, that this kind of non-verbal thinking is at best rudimentary, because 'it is of course difficult for the dream-work to find a means for representing abstract thoughts' (1923b, p. 130).

Verbal thinking is by far the best instrument for the analytical experience because it means that all parts of the mental apparatus can be accessed at any point by thought processes. As Freud (1950a [1887–1902]) points out, the impartial nature of language means that the two demands of the pleasure-unpleasure principle – the tendency to avoid presentations that evoke unpleasure and the tendency to stop at presentations that evoke pleasure, those that have to do with purposive ideas – can be put on hold. It was that particular property of speech which led Freud to the hypothesis that insofar as word-presentations are a process of hypercathexis of thing-presentations, they 'make it possible for the primary process to be succeeded by the secondary process' (Freud, 1915e, p. 202), thus allowing the preconscious system to emerge.

However, in *An Outline of Psychoanalysis*, Freud (1940a [1938]) insists on the fact that speech is not by itself the sole characteristic of the preconscious system, even though it is one of the latter's essential features. 'The inside of the ego, which comprises above all the thought-processes, has the quality of being preconscious. [. . .] It would not be correct, however, to think that connection with the mnemic residues of speech is a necessary precondition of the preconscious state. On the contrary, that state is independent of a connection with them [. . .]' (op.cit., p. 162). We have, therefore, to postulate the organization of pre-verbal thought, antedating the acquisition of speech and corresponding to the binding of free energy; this could be understood in terms of a process of binding dealt with by the preconscious before speech appears. That hypothesis is perfectly consistent with the idea that thought is originally unconscious and has to do with the sense impressions left by objects.

It must be said that the hypothesis of the existence of an unconscious implies that some kind of thought process precedes the advent of speech, something that is infra-linguistic, something that from time to time Freud likens to Kant's thing-in-itself. The issue here as regards a theory of thinking is a correlative of the meaning of the concept of thing-presentations in Freud's writings. In many of these, indeed, thing-presentations are thought of as a being mere *reproductions* of things in the sense in which that term is employed in empiricist psychology; the concept of memory-images and memory-traces tends to support that view. To an empiricist, an image is simply a carbon copy of the real world, a reproduction of reality, and as such sufficient in itself for the purposes of knowledge. That empirical tradition was challenged by the intellectualist theory, according to which the construction of meaning is a feature of the mind and is part of language as a living phenomenon.

In *The Unconscious*, Freud (1915e) rejects both of these solutions – which belong to long-established philosophical traditions – and defines thing-presentations as consisting in 'the cathexes, if not of the direct memory-images of the thing, at least of remoter memory-traces derived from these' (1915e, p. 201). In so defining the concept, Freud was referring to all that he had already worked out as to his notion of what he called the psychical apparatus, in particular as regards the dichotomy between perception and memory and the sequence of memory systems: in the spatial structure of the mind, representations are connected together according to quite distinct types of association, whence the idea that they can be less meaningful in themselves than the network of which they form a part. From that point of view, thing-presentations are less a direct duplication of the object, a fixed image, than a process corresponding to the transcription in various parts of the mind of certain aspects of the object relating to instinctual drive cathexis.

The idea of thing-presentations can go some way to explaining the difference between cathected external objects and those which correspond to the processes of introjection and projection involving such objects: it corresponds to the mind's attempts to internalize and recover memory traces. Those attempts have to do with depicting the object in such a way as to lay the foundations for fantasy creation rooted in the kind of cathexis that precedes both the perception of the object and the advent of speech. It is this hallucinatory work that precedes perception which, in the end, characterizes our psychoanalytic view of the problematic issues concerning representation: the 'psychic representation of the (instinctual) drive'. The point here is the dialectic confrontation between cathexis and the kind of depiction that places thing-presentations between sensations (hallucination of wish-fulfilment) and perception (object hallucination). Word-presentation connects with and develops the kind of reflex movement that gives rise to autoerotic gratification, while sustaining the inherent impetus of this 'motor-image'.

From this point of view, the difference between sensation and perception becomes all the more important when we look at thing-presentations, because the 'thing' is initially presented through affect and can never be fully *depicted* nor fully *verbalized* by any adequate means of expression. As unconscious representations emerge into consciousness, the affective dimension – which, for Freud (1915e, p. 178) corresponds to processes of discharge, the final manifestations of which are perceived as sensations – prevents repression from being completely overcome whether through speech or the near-hallucinatory recall of certain memories.

It is worth mentioning at this point that, though remembering was initially considered to play a major role in the process by which phenomena become conscious, Freud ended up – in *Constructions in Analysis* (1937d) – by calling into question the importance of recollection simply through words and emphasizing the significance of images and their hallucinatory recall. His clinical experience led him to insist upon the 'truth of construction' (1937d, p. 266) and its validation by 'true hallucinations [that] occasionally occurred in the case of other patients who were certainly not psychotic' (*ibid.*, p. 267) as opposed to the work of recollection and reconstruction as guarantees of historical truth.

In this context, Freud added that 'perhaps it may be a general characteristic of hallucinations to which sufficient attention has not hitherto been paid that in them something that has been experienced in infancy and then forgotten returns – something that the child has seen or heard at a time when he could still hardly speak' (*ibid.*, p. 267). In putting forward that hypothesis, Freud seems to be suggesting that hallucinatory recall in the course of psychoanalytic treatment could be understood as bearing witness to the importance of something becoming conscious thanks to the significant role played by images and pre-verbal thoughts. In that remarkable paper, Freud himself draws a parallel between hallucinations, delusions, constructions in analysis, and historical truth brought back from the past. He, therefore, felt intuitively that working with psychotic patients would require making use of images as a way of getting back in touch with primitive sensations and pre-verbal thought.

From this point of view, images come somewhere between things and words, implying that we pay attention not only to their 'containing virtuality', which helps the individual to find a way to the object, but also to their 'power to astound' (Tisseron, 1989), which could entrap the individual in near-hallucinatory fascination or even in psychotic hallucinations. Tisseron goes on to say, quite appositely, that when it is impossible to imagine a given situation, this may give rise to some kind of action – but, then again, when it is impossible to imagine a given situation as actually having occurred, the individual may well want to bring it about in order to be able to imagine it, i.e. to symbolize it by means of an image (Tisseron, *op.cit.*). In other words, when patients are in search of the reciprocity of desire, we should be in a position to offer them the *reciprocity of an image*.

This re-evaluation of thinking by means of images lies at the heart of discussions concerning how things become figurable through the psychoanalytic process and on the importance of topographical and formal regression (Botella & Botella, 2004); it becomes all the more important, indeed, when we work with patients who do not have at their disposal this capacity for formal and topographical regression, which is necessary if temporal regression, in the psychoanalytic sense of the term, is to take place.

Duparc (2005) has emphasized the relevance of contemporary thinking about mental images in psychoanalytic circles. He too underlines its status as an intermediary in the activity of representation 'between, on the one hand, the perceived image that is close to action and to the situation in reality that it attempts to reproduce and, on the other, the poetical or rhetorical image with its multiple transformations which we find in language'. Duparc adds: 'This intermediate status accounts for the positive role of images in bringing thinking back to life – images connect thinking with the body, with the affects and with the drives'; it accounts also for 'the possibility of fixations, where trauma has impeded drawing up representations that are necessary for the fantasy construction of the individual, of his or her personal Oedipus complex and family romance'.

Photos 'make my head spin'

Individual psychoanalytic psychodrama offers a setting which is conducive to developing and promoting thinking with the help of images as a way of breaking free of 'still shots' or 'pictures' that are stereotyped and repetitive; it opens on to a *movement* of images that lays the foundation for constructing both narrative and history. With the support of a psychodrama play watched by the play director, it becomes possible to create the necessary space for processes of symbolization to take place: the capacity to play with images, representations, and language.

The particular form of psychotherapy represented by individual psychodrama introduces a variation in setting and technique based on play. The paradox of analytic psychodrama is that it systematically prescribes, in the form of play, something that is otherwise regarded as an obstacle to the development of the analytic process – in particular, the lateralization of the transference and motor or verbal action. The fact that this action can take place in a context of play prevents it from becoming a resistance of the kind characteristic of these defences, in the form of acting-out as such, so that it instead becomes a preferential means of working through for patients unable to tolerate a transference relationship structured around a single analyst. While both the mainspring of the process in psychodrama – namely, the transference – and its aim are those of classical psychoanalytic treatment, it is the setting that differs.

Analytic psychodrama, in accordance with the theories developed in the 1950s by Serge Lebovici, René Diatkine, and Evelyne

Kestemberg (Lebovici, Diatkine, & Kestemberg, 1969–1970; Kestemberg & Jeammet, 1987), and more recently by Jean Gillibert (1985) and Philippe Jeammet (Jeammet & Kestemberg, 1981), establishes economic and topographical conditions whereby interpretations can be heard without being experienced as intrusive, and can thus be introjected. This kind of psychodrama centres on a single patient and involves a group of therapists comprising the leader, who is responsible for interpreting, and not less than four co-therapists – two of each sex – as potential actors. Each weekly session lasts about half an hour.

A recent extract from Mr A's psychodrama[1] will allow me to illustrate this function of images in psychoanalytic treatment, whereby body and mind, sensation and perception, representation and affect can be re-integrated. Trapped between a possible tendency to commit suicide and a delusional outcome, Mr A, in the ten years his psychodrama has lasted, has done a significant amount of work, to such an extent indeed that he can now own his instinctual drives and acquire the capacity to distinguish between thinking and doing. He used to be overwhelmed by anxiety over non-differentiation between himself and the primitive maternal imago; the paternal transference has helped and supported him in his desire to integrate a paternal line of descent. After reading Gérard Haddad's book *How I was adopted by Lacan*, Mr A managed to express in play his fantasy of being adopted by the play director and the psychodrama team: his 'new family', in other words.

It was in this context that he was able to express for the first time and in a very eloquent manner his relationship to images. He was talking about a visit to a photography exhibition.

When I, as the play director, asked Mr A to suggest a theme, he thought deeply for a good few moments, his arms folded, then looked at me for the first time since the beginning of the session.

Mr A: Well, okay, why not, er, I'm not really sure, but at the Fnac [*a specialist retail store*] there's an exhibition of photos about St Petersburg . . . There could be Mme Enguerand and . . . er, me, for example.

AG: Right. So, Mme Enguerand will be. . . ?

Mr A: She's a lady I happened to see there.

AG: So you're both watching [*Mr A: That's right*] the photo exhibition [*Mr A: That's right*] about St Petersburg [*Mr A: That's right*]. Okay, that's fine. [*The actors take their places*]

AE: Oh, I didn't know there were 'white nights'[2] in St Petersburg, that's a really strange phenomenon, in St Petersburg, white nights, do you know how that comes about?

Mr A: I knew that they existed, but not in that sense.

AE: What sense were you thinking about then?

Mr A: Well, anyway, we passed by each other a moment or so ago and you moved [*AE: Oh?*] and I said to myself 'What on earth is she doing?'

AE: What did I appear to be doing?

Mr A: Well, making the sign of the cross (*he laughs*).

AE: So maybe I was inspired by these Russian churches and landscapes.

Mr A: No, there's no church there (*he is still laughing*).

AE: That's right, there is no church, it's . . .

Mr A: There's no church, that's all there is to it.

AE: So I would have prostrated myself before that there? No, you must have dreamt that I was making the sign of the cross.

Mr A: Okay, then, I may have invented that.

AE: Yes, I think so, that must be it. Maybe I was a bit agitated, I really do think these photos are beautiful, they are thrilling, with their magnificent colours, the impression of 'white nights' – but do you have 'white' ['*sleepless*'] nights?

Mr A: Because there's more of a contrast.

AE: Yes, it's a very particular kind of colour, that milky-white space there.

Mr A: My understanding was that it was a clear night, anyway . . .

AE: And when we use the term 'white' night, what about that?

Mr A: Yes.

AE: Does it happen to you from time to time?

Mr A: When you can't sleep.

AE: Yes. [*silence*] Anyway, the sun doesn't look as though it's setting there, does it?

Mr A: Hmmm. [*silence*]

AE: That must really be quite strange, in fact, it seems they dance all night long in St Petersburg, they're always coming and going.

Mr A: But there, nobody was there, just the sea, and the sea was frozen over.

In that sequence, Mr A talks about the excitement aroused in him by the sight of the photos of St Petersburg, represented by the 'madness' of the female visitor who made the sign of the cross. The image of the white/sleepless night points to his incapacity to cope with that excitement, which prevents him from falling asleep, while the image of the frozen sea represents a counter-cathexis of that excitement/excitation. Mr A goes on to make an association to the upsetting feelings which the sight of the photos evoked in him.

AE: And you, what do you do? Do you like photography? Do you visit photo exhibitions?
Mr A: Yes, I like photography, I do.
AE: And you are . . .
Mr A: But I mustn't see too many of them.
AE: Oh!
Mr A: It's like paintings.
AE: They make your head spin.
Mr A: You can say that again, that's exactly right.
AE: So you think it could be dangerous?
Mr A: Well, no, but they do make my head spin.
AE: Spins round. [*Mr A: Hmm*] They make your head spin . . .
Mr A: I soon have enough of it.
AE: Yes, it can tire you out. A short while ago, I was a bit agitated, you thought I was making the sign of the cross, it gets me all keyed up with excitement, maybe that's what you feel is dangerous?
Mr A: Well, yes, maybe, because afterwards I don't know what to do about . . .
AE: You have to hurry up and do something about it!
Mr A: It all fades away.
AE: It makes me . . .
Mr A: Or else it stays inside your head and that's all there is to it.

The scene ends with Mr A recalling the photos his father used to take, and he makes an immediate link to the 'slaps' he would receive when as a young boy he wanted to see his father's photos. In the ensuing discussion between Mr A and me [A.G.], he talks of his inhibition as regards doing any painting himself; I interpret this to him as 'the fear that it might make his head spin, because there could be too much pleasure'.

With a significant degree of insight about himself, Mr A then associates to the relationship between pleasure and annihilation anxiety:

> *Mr A:* Yes, because when . . . That happened to me when there were things I did and I understood, well, they . . . Well, it's as though they annihilated me, I couldn't go any further because, well, yes, that's it, because it's linked to pleasure . . . it kind of overflows!

I point out that psychodrama is a form of play and that it is possible to share pleasure without feeling that it is overflowing; it is not the same thing as used to happen when he was a boy, playing war games with his father when 'all of a sudden it turned into something that wasn't a game anymore'. After a moment's silence, Mr A says: 'Yes, murder. . .' I continue: 'Yes, murder, so we stop playing and say to ourselves "I'm never going to play any more".'

Thanks to the support Mr A draws from the play director and the other team members, he can evoke the ins and outs of images in their two-fold polarity: mental image and actual picture, thus linking the function of quasi-hallucinatory non-differentiation to the containing function. For Mr A, an image had to be a carbon copy of what was actually real, thus leaving little room for its evocative potentiality and the dimension of affect – because, otherwise, the risk would be that he might find all too quickly that his head was spinning, that he was 'full up' or even 'annihilated'. The words the patient uses to describe the photographs at the St Petersburg exhibition are quite impressive; the sight of an image is rapidly transformed into a source of anxiety about non-differentiation, from which he can free himself only by switching off – just like a dreamer who, by wakening up, triumphs over the images of a nightmare. Murielle Gagnebin (2003) wrote on this point of the *shadow of the image*. 'Confronting shadows *inside* the image may lead to various dangers, including that of exuding an alarming and stupendous pain that comes close to annihilating all meaning and all awareness.' (p. 10) The risk then is that one finds oneself with 'an image that will never again have the slightest shadow' (*ibid.*), one that has no 'depth'.

On this point, Laurie Laufer, (2005) has described with some considerable talent what, in cases of traumatic loss, images carry with them: 'In the case of trauma, there may sometimes be a *freeze-frame* (a still picture), and that freezing may be due to terror or fascination, which brings about a complete paralysis. All affects are frozen, the individual can no longer be 'moved' – in other words, experience his or her drive-related body, in particular through language' (italics added). Laufer goes on: 'What is an image without movement – the eyes that look at it are either blinded or seized hold of.' (see also: Laufer, 2006) It could also be the stare of the Medusa – a look that petrifies. The only solution comes through 'working at looking', which involves the possibility of 'closing one's eyes' and making contact with the invisible aspect which lies at the edge of the visible world. In a nightmare he had some time ago now, Mr A dreamt that he 'was a surgeon, that a patient was lying on the operating table and that the operation consisted in removing the patient's eyelids'. What better way to represent the conditions required for 'working at looking', with the need to introduce a movement of continuity and discontinuity, opening and closing the eyes, in order for an image to have depth of field, distance, and the necessary space between what is being looked at and the person doing the looking?

'Working at looking' is one way to describe the hallucinatory dimension that attempts not only, of course, to ensure identity of perception but also to draw all *movement* in the direction of identity of thought. Without this temporal dimension, an image is no more than pure sensation which blinds and burns: that is what Laufer calls the 'melancholic freeze-frame'. From this point of view, a distinction must be drawn between the status of the image in pathological hallucinations and in the hallucinatory dimension concerning the quality of that movement. Furthermore, the *movement* of the image which opens on to the dimension of representation and history is not the same thing as *mobility*, which leaves the image in a non-historical repetition in the service of sense-data.

Here, then, is the foundation of the functional opposition between perception and memory that Freud borrowed from Breuer to describe the succession of psychic systems. Perception does indeed appear *in the place* of a memory trace; the two cannot exist *at the same time* (Freud, 1925). Simultaneity is never absolute. Where they do coexist

– i.e. in schizophrenia – it is a matter of a topographic split and not a regression: Gillibert (1977) correctly notes that in this case, there is, on the one hand, a memory trace in the form of word cathexis, and, on the other, perception, as the obliteration of this trace, in another place and at the same time. This perception no longer corresponds to a perceptual 'experience', but takes the form of a 'sensation', of an affect of fright that reflects the terror inspired by the hallucinatory image. 'Word-presentations' will henceforth constitute a form of inert protection from this terrifying 'sensation'.

Repression is a true correlate of object loss, and of the elaboration of this loss as not being permanent; the permanence of the object guarantees its appearance/disappearance and the symbolic substitutions of its reappearance. It is when the loss is experienced as final, as in psychosis, that fixity substitutes for permanence, mobility for movement, and the juxtaposition of opposites for contradiction. Thinking in terms of opposition is tantamount to losing the dimension of psychic conflict, which can be understood only in terms of difference. The aim of working with psychotic patients is, precisely, to encourage the transition from *splitting* of the ego, which is imprisoned in the juxtaposition of opposites, to the dimension of conflict based on *contradiction*.

These ideas are illustrated by the working of the Mystic Writing Pad, used by Freud as a metaphor of psychic functioning. Consciousness is possible only by virtue of unconscious cathexis, just as the writing on the waxed paper depends on contact with the wax slab; at the same time, however, it is because this contact is not permanent that the system *Pcpt.-Cs.* can renew itself: 'If we imagine one hand writing upon the surface of the Mystic Writing Pad while another periodically raises its covering-sheet from the wax slab, we shall have a concrete representation of the way in which I tried to picture the functioning of the perceptual apparatus of our mind' (Freud, 1925a, p. 232).

This reference to the periodic raising of the sheets shows that the dimension of temporality must be introduced in order to account for the structure of the psychic apparatus and to overcome the difficulties inherent in optical or photographic models, in which *simultaneous* performance of the functions of perception (succession) and memory (permanence) is not possible. As Derrida (1967, p. 334) rightly points out, 'the traces therefore create sufficient space for their inscription only by allowing themselves the time needed for their erasure.' The dynamic element must be restored if we are not to be locked into a representation of the psychic apparatus based on Cartesian space and time, characterized by the mutual externality of the parts. We will thus be in a better position to acknowledge what is at stake as regards space and time in the way the mind works, in both neurosis and psychosis. The dimension of psychic conflict presupposes that there is neither permanent contact nor discontinuity between psychic systems – no pure perception, and no pure memory. On a certain level, Freud's neo-Kantianism causes the differentiation of the psychic apparatus resulting from the work of the drive to be lost: the diversity of the systems cannot be reduced to the mere opposition of positive and negative.

The role of primal repression, which according to Freud (1915) allows the drive to be bound to a representation – by the sole mechanism of countercathexis – can be understood in these terms. This is because its aim is to contain the tendency towards absolute discharge of the excitation and to defend against the hallucination of satisfaction by the creation of a fantasy process and the constitution of primal fantasies. At the same time, this attachment lies at the root of the 'power of the compulsion to repeat' and 'the attractions exerted by the unconscious prototypes' mentioned by Freud (1926, p. 159) in connection with id resistance.

This is because primal repression is responsible for the primitive 'inertia' of the psyche that, in return, permits the 'illumination' of consciousness and openness to the world. Perception is possible only because full presence is always exposed to the risk of vanishing into memory; perception presupposes mourning for absolute presence, and indeed its negation, failing which it is likely to be mere hallucination. The Unconscious is the 'index' of this negativity, whose present manifestation is a negative process – namely, resistance, auto-eroticism, and the absolute discharge of tensions. Yet this negativity has an underlying *raison d'être* that is no longer negative but positive, because it allows consciousness to appear and to exist, and the judgement of existence to be performed.

Considered thus, the work of the analysis with Mr A shows clearly that access to the hallucinatory dimension will be possible only once the 'murder' of the object has been processed and its potential representation constructed in the mind. The philosopher Marie-José Mondzain (2002) puts it very eloquently in her description of the outcome of the mind's attempts at processing: 'What cannot be represented must expect symbolization to come only from vision itself' (p. 120). Until now, Mr A has experienced psychodrama as something that will help him recover his capacity to see, to envision; the task is not yet over, but this session has highlighted the patient's ability to understand what is at stake, in the light of his increased capacity to look and be looked at as a self that can cathect, as well as be cathected by the object. This in turn makes possible the process of differentiation between self and other, and gives access to the structural workings of the mind.

'What do I see in paintings?'

In the following session, Mr A started off by saying:

> 'That last session made me feel much better. I think it's because I mentioned the word "murder".'

That gave us the opportunity of thinking together about the difference between fantasy and reality: we can talk about murder without actually killing anyone. Mr A's relief was an indication of his capacity to experience hatred without fearing that he would destroy either himself or his object. At that point, the way was therefore open for differentiating between *orgasmic* pleasure – which increases in intensity, then subsides – and *transitional* pleasure, which enables access to de-sexualized thinking and sublimation. For Winnicott (1971), the experience of transitionnality does not have a 'climax' and is quite different from 'phenomena that have instinctual backing, where the orgiastic element plays an essential part, and where satisfactions are closely linked with climax' (p.98). That was also in Freud's mind when (1924) he discussed satisfaction as being linked not to the discharge of a *quantity* of excitation but to its *qualitative* dimension related to rhythm. From that point of view, sublimation has to do with the possibility of organizing the thought processes that Freud described in his *Project for a Scientific Psychology* (1950c [1895]) as involving the use of small quantities of energy; in this way, there arises the possibility of taking pleasure in something that is not specifically linked to the discharge of a quantity of excitation, following the principle of inertia, but to the preservation of some degree of tension, in accordance with the principle of constancy.

Mr A is henceforth able to think about the way his mind works. As he reflects on his desire to paint and on the difficulties he encounters with that, he tries to understand what he sees when he looks at a painting; for the very first time since he began psychodrama, he is able to recall a hallucinatory experience that took place while he was still a child, one which in all possibility proved decisive for his traumatic vision of the world.

Mr A: Well, I can't say that I really believe in light, but. . . [*silence*]. Anyway, in fact, when I look at the painting, that's what I see, and I wonder why I see that.

AG: Perhaps we could have a play of some sort around that idea? How would you set the scene?

Mr A: Well, there'd be me and somebody else, and, well, no, no-one will represent the painting.

AG: So there are two of you looking at two paintings? Or both of you at just the one?

Mr A: Yes, that's about right.

AG: Who'll be the other person?

Mr A: Mme Villarino.

AG: Okay, Mme Villarino.

[*The play begins with the two actors*]

MV: Well then?

Mr A: Yes, well, it's as though there were, let's see, a tremendous light in the painting.

MV: Well, I'd say, anyway, in your eyes there's something shining, so much luminosity that it lights up the painting and illuminates you as well.

Mr A: I don't know why, but the 'zenith' comes into my mind.

MV: Zenith?

Mr A: Once you've. . .

MV: Well, yes, you see the saints, they always have a bright halo of light.

Mr A: Yes.

MV: Is that how you see the painting?

Mr A: At my first communion, I don't remember what it's called . . .

MV: Go on. . .

Mr A: Well, there was a head with. . .

MV: With your name on it, the day of your first communion [*she moves her hands as though to indicate a religious image*]

Mr A: Hmmm.

MV: Yes.

Mr A: Hmmm.

MV: You were there, you gave. . . The day you received communion, you were aglow, in a state of grace.

Mr A: No, no.

MV: No? You don't think that's right?

Mr A: No, not now, not now, no, no! [*makes as though to push aside a memory tinged with disillusionment*]

MV: But. . .

Mr A: No, well. . .

MV: Mind you. . .

Mr A: I don't believe in anything.

MV: That painting over there, it's true that when we look at that painting, we really feel moved.

Mr A: It's the body that receives something, that's all.

MV: Grace.

Mr A: No.

MV: It moves you deep inside, doesn't it?

Mr A: Hmmm.

MV: Sometimes it makes things clearer for me, I don't quite know how to put it, as though I were coming out of a thick fog!

Mr A: Yes, it's a pleasure to be able to see that.

MV: Well, it's more than just pleasure; er, I, well, no, I change, I'm no longer the same person.

Mr A: Yes, but afterwards it disappears, it fades away.

MV: No, no, with me it hangs on; with you it fades away at once?

Mr A: It's not like something that remains for a very long time.

MV: But it does last, because afterwards I think about it, I remember it! But not you? It fades away immediately? And afterwards you don't remember it?

Mr A: Huh? [*he coughs*] Yes, yes. . . I . . . yes, yes.

MV: You're not very convinced, are you?

Mr A: Well . . . [*silence*] No, but it's like the day I saw the Blessed Virgin.

MV: Really? You saw the Blessed Virgin?

Mr A: Really.

MV: Well! What was *that* like? Was it at your communion?

Mr A: No.

MV: No? Well then, how did you see her?

Mr A: They were going to show a film called *Bernadette Soubirous.*

MV: Yes, okay, and then?

Mr A: Well, I saw her through the hole in the roof [*he laughs*].

MV: And then she. . . [*MV stretches out her arms, as though in invitation or preparing to hold something*] She . . .

Mr A: Like for the film, everybody was waiting, becoming more and more impatient. [*He moves his arms about a lot*]

MV: And was there a light? [*They are talking together animatedly, their hands gesticulating, their voices full of expressive intonations*]

Mr A: Oh yes, yes! When I told the priest that – but it wasn't very long ago that I did tell him, when I went to Sardinia, because somebody in Marie's [*his current woman friend*] family is a priest, and he asked 'Didn't she say anything to you?'

MV: Well, then, what did she say to you?

Mr A: Not very much.

MV: But what did she say, after all you did see her.

Mr A: [*silence*]

MV: She didn't say anything to you?

Mr A: No, no.

MV: Why? Did the whole thing scare you?

Mr A: Oh no! I wasn't scared, no, not at all, but she didn't say anything.

MV: Well then, I didn't know things like that could happen! You're, well, you're lucky to be able to be all lit up like that, because, for me, it's only when I'm in a museum that I see that kind of light, sometimes I feel as though I've been caught up in something. . .

Mr A: [*interrupting her and speaking in a much louder voice*] No, I, well, anyway, what do I see in the paintings?

MV: Yes, it's like the Blessed Virgin.

Mr A: But maybe I can see something else.

MV: Yes? What do you see?

Mr A: Well, I don't really know, but I'm able to see something else [*he clears his throat noisily*].

MV: There, look there at that painting, the one just facing us [*cf. Fig. 1*]

Mr A: Hmmm.

MV: Well, what do *you* see? What's that, can you see?

Mr A: [*in a very lively tone of voice*] The blue bit there?

MV: Yes. Can you see anything in that?

Mr A: Well, what I see there is, er, a vagina.

MV: Ah! Well, you're quite right – it is quite an enormous vagina in fact [*Mr A coughs*], but. . .

Mr A: Well, it's always enormous.

Figure 1: Irena Dedicova, "Promontory", 1982, (66x49cm)

MV: But, wait a minute, the vagina, then. . . What's that? There's something inside.

Mr A: Yes, but I don't know what it's called.

MV: But what is it? Because there is something, isn't there, right in the middle of the vagina? What is it? What can you see?

Mr A: It's. . .

MV: Anyway, that vagina isn't empty.

Mr A: Hmmm.

MV: It's something that seems to be going back inside or maybe something that's coming out, I can't quite see.

[*Silence*]

Mr A: That? [*a questioning note in his voice*]

MV: What can *you* see?

Mr A: Well, yes, yes, I can see a phallus.

MV: So it's going in. Mind you, when you say enormous I could perhaps see a baby coming out, that's where it comes out, isn't it?

Mr A: Yes, well, you can't see a thing.

MV: Okay.

Mr A: When you come out, I mean.

MV: Completely blinded.

Mr A: I don't know anything about that.

MV: Mind you, I imagine you can see light, a white light.

Mr A: Coming out of the hole, you're, well, dazzled.

MV: That's right, dazzled!

AG: Okay, then.

[*AG and Mr A sit down*]

Mr A: Well, that makes me think of being born.

AG: Can we be born without being dazzled, blinded by the light?

Mr A: Well, anyway, I was blinded by, well, by the I hate I felt towards my father at that time!

AG: But at the same time, it's a matter not only of hate but also of love, you're now able to represent to yourself what happened in the past, when you were completely blinded, in the midst of your delusion, for example, and you're capable of understanding something of your own personal history. A person with his or her history, that means History with a capital 'H' [*Mr A had begun the session by mentioning that he had just bought a book called 'The Individual and History'*]. And

> as far as you are concerned, it means you in your own history [*Mr A: Yes*], in the history that we have been able to share together here and through which you have followed your own path. I think it's very important to be much less blinded than used to be the case [*Mr A: Yes*], so that relationships become possible without having to think about murder; and it becomes possible, too, to take leave of each other without that implying a complete void, emptiness . . . You see, you have had a deeply emotional experience there, one which is shared by all human beings. I think that today, thanks to all the work we have been doing together, you can put words on your past and understand your own history – and, as a result, be in a better position to imagine life.

The session ends with an evocation of the difficulties Mr A encounters in his love life, which are now seen to involve castration anxiety and a kind of inhibition that could be called neurotic. The session highlights Mr A's ability to process conflict and his trust in the transference, which enables him to talk for the first time about his hallucinations.

The question arises as to whether the evocation of his hallucinatory vision of the Virgin Mary, involving identification with Bernadette Soubirous, the young girl from Lourdes, is a reference back to Mr A's primary psychotic experience, in much the same way as Freud described projection in paranoia through his study of Daniel Paul Schreber. If there is no possibility of creating a break in the hallucination/perception pattern corresponding to a process of negative hallucination, projection can be made only on to external reality, with the ensuing confusion between inside and outside that corresponds to positive pathological hallucination.

Mr A finds apt words to describe what vision involves: 'It's the body that receives something'/'Maybe I can see something else'. And in fact, when he looks at the landscape painting in the psychodrama room, he sees first of all a vagina; thinking by means of images remains sexualized and functions as a symbolic equation. However, he goes on to talk of birth and the dazzling impact brought about by the overwhelming presence of the object – which, of course, may also evoke its overwhelming absence. There is the image of a tunnel at the end of which a powerful white light is dazzling – in much the same way as patients coming out of a deep coma describe their near-death experience.

Paul-Claude Racamier (1987) described the psychotic catastrophe in the same terms as those used by Mr A; he saw in it the fantasy of self-procreation that is marked more by sensory feeling than by representation: 'What to me seems both obvious and highly significant is that the activation of that 'fantasy' [of self-procreation] brings about an extremely rare modification in the individual's state of mind. It constitutes what I would call a *blank psychic event* (and I do mean *psychic*). Blank[3] something that lights up as in a flash of lightning, creating an explosion all around, and blinds you. I may as well say it now: that psychic event corresponds exactly to the primal catastrophe. And thus we have in the history of a delusion a process that is different from and more precise than a simple decathexis. Of course, it does require massive denial – but there's more to it than just denial: there is the constitution and activation of this fantasy which is extraordinarily *seductive* in nature. And I say that all the more because self-procreation is directly related to *narcissistic seduction*. Any person who reaches that particular dimension will be exposed to the 'blank' event, both fascinating and terrible, which will empty everything out of his mind, and the only way to recover from it is via the creation of a delusion.' (p. 38)

Piera Aulagnier (1985) compares the hallucinatory experience to the feeling of a hand clinging on to a rock that is falling endlessly into nothingness, as though caught up in a breathtaking whirlwind. The only solution is to generate delusional images, especially those of persecutors chasing you, in order to avoid sinking down into a free-fall without representations.

Mr A understood that his psychotic crisis had to do with hatred; he was able to put that into words because he had recovered a capacity for love through his cathexis of psychodrama. The intensity of this is indicated by the creative cathexis to which it gave rise both in Mr A and in every member of the psychodrama team. The work of symbolization is truly one of co-creation between patient and analyst in what Winnicott (1951) called 'an intermediate area of experience', as embodied by the psychodrama stage. Although Mr A has not yet taken up painting again, he is giving himself the means to understand in depth the reasons for his inhibition both as regards artistic activity and in his love life.

Symbolization and the synergy of sensations

Thanks to the work we did together in psychodrama, Mr A was thus able to work through his 'aesthetic conflict' – a conflict described by Meltzer (1988, p. 22) as the experience of the overwhelming presence of the object, the mother's beauty, which cannot be assimilated by the child if there is too great a distance between the 'outside of the "beautiful" mother, available to the senses' and 'the enigmatic inside which must be construed by creative imagination'. As Meltzer rightly points out, the child 'has, after all, come into a strange country where he knows neither the language nor the customary non-verbal cues and communications. The mother is enigmatic to him; she wears the Gioconda smile most of the time, and the music of her voice keeps shifting from major to minor key' (*ibid.*).

Painting and music here again correspond, thus accounting for Mr A's experience of having been unable to cope with his mother's 'ambiguous messages', so that he had been forced into psychotic confusion and the impossibility of integrating any kind of creativity, be it intellectual, emotional or artistic. The need here, in Bion's terms, was to transform beta-elements corresponding to intrusive sensations that are impossible to process into alpha-elements that can be worked over in thought, dreams and fantasy. This is in line with the description given by Laplanche (1987), in the context of his generalized seduction theory, of the child's need to make sense of the mother's enigmatic messages.

In an earlier session, before the summer holiday break, Mr A had spoken for the first time of a memory of being, as a child, completely submerged by incomprehensible feelings and sensations when he was in the presence of his parents. As he thought about why he linked the idea of separation to that of emptiness, he began to wonder if he had perhaps been abandoned early on in life. When I asked him at what age this could have occurred, he replied: 'When I was four years old', then corrected himself, saying: 'I don't remember when I was four, but before then, while I was still in my pushchair, there was complete silence; my parents were present, but without saying anything. They were quarrelling, and I couldn't understand what was going on – it was just *soundless words*.' He went on to explain that the argument was over the rent that their landlord was demanding, because Mr A's father had not paid it. Mr A added: 'I'm a bit like that nowadays.'

It was his inability to integrate all these sensations that led Mr A to establish relationships with other people based exclusively on being either too absent or too present, just as in the image of himself as an infant in his pushchair, unable to understand 'soundless words'. That was Mr A's somewhat strange way of describing 'wordless sounds', an incomprehensible noise equivalent to 'soundless words', the destructive silence emanating from the parental couple who, because of their quarrelling, were unable to do anything other than de-cathect and disregard what their child was going through emotionally.

That memory of a child in distress, unable to take on board his parents' auditory messages, had led Mr A to over-cathect visual images to the point where he became hallucinated. But what about his other senses? In one of his recent sessions, Mr A began to think about why he felt invaded by the word *'rance'* [rancid, stale]. That gave him the opportunity of becoming aware of his rejection of all sensoriality, since the word *rance* evoked that of *l'errance* [restless wandering, roaming] and hence its homophone *'lait rance'* [rancid milk], the smell, taste, and colour of which he had never been able to tolerate. He chose to play the word 'rancid', moving from words to things and representing, for the very first time, his primary relationship with his mother based on smell and physical contact. After saying, 'My mother gave off a bad smell', Mr A associated insightfully to his own drive-related feelings:

> 'At one point, I gave off a rancid smell'
> then: 'I spoil everything'
> and: 'As soon as I touch anything. . . . Humph!'

As an infant at the breast, he had rejected his mother because of those tactile, olfactory, and gustatory sensations that he had experienced as bad and destructive.

In the course of that play, the patient again spoke of the bad smells coming from his father, who used to 'fart' – in older days, this used to be looked upon as an indication of manliness, albeit in a destructive fashion, because bodily wind (or 'gas', as they say in American English) evoked the gas chambers of the Nazi death camps. Mr A's father and grandfather had both been collaborationists during World War II; that fact had led Mr A to reject any kind of masculine identification other than sadistic. By dramatizing in this way the bad smells emanating from both of his parents, Mr A was giving himself the means to understand, in a more emotional sense, that the primal scene had destructive – because anal-sadistic – connotations for him.

After this discussion with the play director on the polysemous nature of the word 'rancid', Mr A became aware of his rejection of his body and its sensations, as well as of the parental objects who had left him completely unprepared for discovering the world around him, for experiencing it and thinking about it.

Mr A: Er. . . [*silence*] I don't know . . . [*silence*] Well, yes, I don't know why. But if I think now of the way my father used to fart, it makes me think of the way you said 'gas', *pffffffft* [*he makes a face*], well, anyway, afterwards it's still a massacre and I'm right in the midst of it.

AG: I think that what you're saying is that we all have a body [*Mr A: 'Yes'*] and that sensations and smells, well, they're part of it.

Mr A: Yes. Yes. Yes.

AG: And there's a part of you that wanted to get rid of these sensations and smells.

Mr A: Yes, well, I mean, no smells, what would that mean? Nothing.

AG: It would be nothing.

Mr A: No body at all.

AG: No body, that's right.

Mr A: A person who doesn't give off a smell. [*silence*]

AG: There's a saying: 'odourless, colourless, and tasteless' [*i.e. completely bland*].

Mr A: That's right, yes. So you couldn't see the person.

AG: You couldn't see him.

Mr A: Or smell him.

AG: No body, as we said.

Mr A: No taste either.

AG: That makes me think . . .

Mr A: [*interrupting*] Oh, yes, that would follow on from the sacrifice . . .

AG: Yes.

Mr A: Last week.

AG: That's right. The body was to be sacrificed. Yet, as you yourself put it, our body is what makes life possible, makes

> existence possible [*Mr A: 'Yes'*], lets you feel things [*Mr A: 'Yes'*], and share things too – especially in a love relationship [*Mr A: 'Hmm'*]. You were asking me about love relationships.

Mr A then associated to the scent of flowers, suggesting that we play out a scene about 'good smells'. The 'flower' theme had already come up in a session some years previously, following on from his first transference dream: *He was bringing me an enormous bunch of sweet-smelling, colourful flowers, so big that I disappeared from sight behind it.*

That highly condensed dream bears witness to the fact that Mr A was able to dramatize the inverted or negative form of the Oedipus complex by projecting the feminine position on to the analyst, while still representing the anxiety he felt when faced with the devouring 'flower/woman/vagina'. The flower theme, representing as it does the female sex, gave us the opportunity of thinking about his fear of *touching* the woman/flower in case he would be sucked in, and about his need to keep these flowers at a safe distance by restricting himself to simply *smelling* their scent. In the transference dream, the sweet-smelling flowers could of course be touched – but they did, nonetheless, carry the threat of making other people (or Mr A himself) disappear from sight.

In the more recent session, Mr A was able to gain a deeper understanding of the origins of his rejection of the female body through the negative memory of breastfeeding – 'the milk made me ill'; thanks to this, he was more able to envisage a relationship with the object that did not immediately prove disruptive as far as narcissism was concerned. The scent of the flowers – their frag*rance* [cf. *ranc*id] – can, as he put it, intoxicate and 'disorientate'; he was, however, now able to evoke the 'smell of musk' and 'vaginal discharge' without feeling disgusted. Flowers could henceforth evoke the image of women who were no longer an immediate source of anxiety and destructiveness. At the end of that session, Mr A said to my three female colleagues who had played the part of the flowers: 'You can smell them, look at them . . . and touch them too', thereby evidencing a significant change in his psychic economy. He can touch without 'spoiling' everything, just as he was 'touched' by the transference experience of psychodrama without feeling 'overwhelmed' by the presence of a threateningly intrusive object.

We can imagine that the subjective re-appropriation of his own body and its sensations will allow him to leave room for his wish to paint and for his desire to fall in love with a woman without being overwhelmed by anxieties that are impossible to put into words. The eyes of a painter can go beyond the opposition between dazzling light and total darkness, insofar as the vision of colour correspondingly brings with it the whole range of sensations, be they olfactory, gustatory, tactile, auditory or visual, within the synergy that Bion (1962) called 'the consensuality of the breast'. The integration of the sensory self can therefore give richness and depth to the work of vision, thereby facilitating the processing of non-verbal primitive anxieties and integrating them with castration anxiety.

Conclusion

The creativity of Mr A's mind is both the equivalent of a psychological birth, in which the visual dimension is no longer anxiety-provoking on condition that various sensations be brought together, and the emergence of the kind of auto-eroticism that includes the object and representations of it. In her discussion of the French writer Colette, Julia Kristeva (2002) emphasizes in a particularly apposite way what is at stake in this mutually-supportive role played by the senses in our perception of the world. 'Every flower is a bunch of coenaesthesias: seen, heard, smelled, eaten, caressed, it invites all the senses to communicate and to contaminate one another as it comes close: "I do better than see the tulip recover its senses: I hear the iris opening out" (Colette, 1924, p. 95). And all these sensations come together to sharpen the way we look at the secret of floral rhythms.' (Kristeva, 2002, p. 282). In his famous poem of that title, Baudelaire also insists on the 'correspondences' between sensations, these 'forests of symbols' where 'scents, colours and sounds answer one another'.

The therapeutic strategy and interpretative tactics in the treatment of psychotic patients aim to encourage symbol formation; these patients have often lost all possibility of differentiating between a symbol and the object that is symbolized, between past and present, between paternal and maternal imagos. Psychotic anxiety means that the individual has to deal with the non-representable conflict of being simultaneously the one who devours and the object that is devoured; an external and internal setting, therefore, has to be offered to these patients so that they can introject interpretations more easily. In psychodrama, the play director, with his or her third-party role as mediator, can help the patient to break free of anxiety concerning non-differentiation and to acquire the capacity to play with representations, images and words – a capacity that, as Winnicott suggested, lies at the very root of the process of symbolization.

Notes

1. For a more detailed presentation of the early stages and evolution of Mr A's psychodrama up to the present sessions, see Gibeault (2002, 2004a, 2004b) and Gagnebin-De M'Uzan (2003). The psychodrama team is at present composed of: Play director – Alain Gibeault (A.G.); psychodramatists – Clément Bonnet (C.B.), Anne Enguerand (A.E.), Murielle Gagnebin (M.G.), Monique Israël (M.I.), Marina Loukomskaïa (M.L.), Pierre Mattar (P.M.), Laurent Muldworf (L.M.), Brigitte Reed-Duvaille (B.R.D.), and Martha Villarino (M.V.). From time to time, with Mr A's consent, foreign colleagues may be present at the psychodrama sessions, although in a non-participant capacity. In this first session, a Russian colleague, Andrey Rossokhin was present, a factor that clearly contributed to the choice of theme.
2. This is the literal translation of the French '*nuits blanches*', with the word '*blanc*' referring to the colour 'white', as in the actual photograph; the expression '*nuits blanches*' also means 'sleepless nights' as will become clear in the following paragraphs. (Translator's note)
3. Here again, the word used in French is '*blanc*', carrying this time the meaning of 'blank'. (Translator's note)

References

Aulagnier, P. (1985). Le retrait dans l'hallucination : un équivalent du retrait autistique? *Lieux de l'enfance*, *3*: 149–164.

Bion, W.R. (1962). *Learning from Experience*. London: William Heinemann. [Reprinted London: Karnac Books.]

Botella, C., & Botella, S. (2001). *La figurabilité psychique*. Lausanne: Delachaux et Niestlé. [*The Work of Psychic Figurability*. London: Routledge, 2004.]

Colette (1924). Fleurs: aventures quotidiennes. In: *Œuvres, Vol III*, Bibliothèque de la Pléiade. Paris: Gallimard, 1991.

Derrida, J. (1967). Freud et la scène de l'écriture. In: *L'écriture et la différence* (pp. 293–340). Paris: Seuil. [Freud and the Scene of Writing. In: *Writing and Difference*. Translated by Alan Bass. University of Chicago Press, 1978]

Duparc, F. (2005). De l'image à l'idéologie. Unpublished paper read to the Symposium on Image, psychoanalysis, society, Albi (France), 11 June 2005.

Freud, S. (1893a). With Breuer, J. On the psychical mechanism of hysterical phenomena: preliminary communication. *Standard Edition, 2*: 3.

Freuds, S. (1915). The unconscious. *Standard Edition, 14*: 161.

Freud, S. (1923b). *The ego and the id. Standard Edition, 19*: 3.

Freud, S. (1924c). The economic problem of masochism. *Standard Edition, 19*: 159.

Freud, S. (1925 [1924]). A note upon the 'mystic writing-pad'. *Standard Edition, 19*: 227.

Freud, S. (1926d [1925]). *Inhibitions, symptoms and anxiety. Standard Edition, 20*: 87.

Freud, S. (1937d). Constructions in analysis. *Standard Edition, 23*: 257.

Freud, S. (1940a [1938]). *An outline of psychoanalysis. Standard Edition, 23*: 141.

Freud, S. (1950a [1887–1902]). *Project for a scientific psychology. Standard Edition*: 295.

Gagnebin, M. (2002). L'image et ses ombres: polysémie et polyvalence. In: M. Gagnebin (Ed.), *L'ombre de l'image. De la falsification à l'infigurable* (pp. 7–16). Paris: Champ-Vallon (pp. 7–16).

Gagnebin – De M'Uzan (2003). Pouvoirs du psychodrame sur la mutation des puissances tutélaires. *Psychanalyse et Psychose, 3*: 61–70.

Gibeault, A. (2002). De l'auto-engendrement à la scène primitive. De l'élaboration de la psychose par le psychodrame. *Psychanalyse et Psychose, 3*: 129–143.

Gibeault, A. (2004a). Omnipotence et finitude: le sexuel et la création chez Monsieur A. *Psychanalyse et Psychose, 4*: 135–150.

Gibeault, A. (2004b). Therapeutic strategy and interpretative tactics in psychosis. *Psychoanalysis in Europe, Bulletin of the European Psychoanalytic Federation, 58*: 92–105.

Gillibert, J. (1977). De l'auto-érotisme. *Revue Française de Psychanalyse, 41 (5–6)*: 774–949.

Gillibert, J. (1985). *Le Psychodrame de la psychanalyse*. Paris: Champ Vallon.

Jeammet, P., & Kestemberg, E. (1981). Le Psychodrame psychanalytique. Technique, spécificité, indications. *Psychothérapies, 2*: 85–92.

Kestemberg, E., & Jeammet, P. (1987). *Le Psychodrame psychanalytique*. Paris: Presses Universitaires de France.

Kristeva, J. (2002). *Le génie féminin, Tome III: Colette*. Paris: Fayard. [*Colette: Female Genius, Vol. 3*. Translated by Jane Marie Todd. Columbia University Press, 2004.]

Laplanche, J. (1987). *Nouveaux fondements pour la psychanalyse*. Paris: PUF. [*New Foundations for Psychoanalysis*. Translated by David Macey. Cambridge, MA: Basil Blackwell, 1989.]

Laufer, L. (2005). De l'irreprésentable à l'hallucinatoire. Unpublished paper read to the Symposium on Image, psychoanalysis, society, Albi (France), 11 June 2005.

Laufer, L. (2006). *L'énigme du deuil*. Paris, Presses Universitaires de France, 217p.

Lebovici, S., Diatkine, R., & Kestemberg, E. (1969–1970). Bilan de dix ans de pratique psychodramatique chez l'enfant et l'adolescent. *Bulletin de psychologie, 285, XXIII, 13–16*: 839–888.

Meltzer, D. (1988). The aesthetic conflict: its place in the development process. In: D. Meltzer & M. H. Williams, *The Apprehension of Beauty: The Role of Aesthetic Conflict in Development, Art and Violence*. Strathclyde, Perthshire: Clunie Press.

Merleau-Ponty, M. (1964). *L'œil et l'esprit*. Paris: Gallimard. [Eye and Mind. In: James M. Edie (Ed.), *The Primacy of Perception and Other Essays on Phenomenological Psychology: The Philosophy of Art, History and Politics* Evanston, IL: Northwestern, 1964. Also in: Thomas Baldwin (Ed.), *Basic Writings* (pp. 290–324) London and New York: Routledge, 2004.]

Mondzain, M.J. (2002). *Le commerce des regards*. Paris: Seuil.

Racamier, P.C. (1987). De la dépossession du moi à la possession délirante ou: A la recherche du nouveau monde. *Les Cahiers du Centre de psychanalyse et de psychothérapie, 14 (La solution délirante I)*: 29–50.

Tisseron, S. (1989). Des mots et des images: le rôle des images dans la cure. *Revue Française de Psychanalyse, T.53, 6*: 1993–1997.

Winnicott, D.W. (1953). Transitional objects and transitional phenomena *International Journal of Psychoanalysis, 34*: 89–97. Also in: D.W. Winnicott, *Collected Papers: Through Paediatrics to Psycho-Analysis*. London: Tavistock Publications; New York: Basic Books, 1958; London: Hogarth Press and the Institute of Psychoanalysis, 1975; London: Institute of Psychoanalysis and Karnac Books, 1992. Brunner/Mazel, 1992.

Winnicott, D.W. (1971). *Playing and Reality*. London: Tavistock Publications.

(Translated from the French by David Alcorn)

CHAPTER SIX

'White Psychoses': silence and delusions

Adolfo Pazzagli

Introduction

In psychoanalytical literature and in communication among analysts the term 'psychosis' is, albeit with some important exceptions, more frequently used than those more strictly psychiatric terms which refer to a specific set of symptoms, to illnesses, to 'disorders' in DSM III and IV. A number of factors probably explain this use of a more general, but also less precise, term. First, it expresses a level of seriousness; of interpersonal, emotional, and practical involvement; and of the sense of reality of the person who suffers from it – an altered mode of psychic operation which is not necessarily linked to specific symptoms. The term 'psychosis' thus does not correspond to a psychiatric diagnosis, which is based on scholarly convention as well as natural observation, as, for example, with 'schizophrenia'.

'Psychosis' also more effectively designates the sort of observation characteristic of psychoanalysis, which seeks to discern the specific communicative value of each symptom and sees a risk in the grouping together of these (but only some of these – the others are neglected!) to form a single picture. For such a picture can end up being considered a 'natural' pathological phenomenon, something cut off from the person, his personal history, and his context. This sort of simplification is useful for a great deal of psychiatric treatment and for epidemiological and therapeutic research, but tends to conceal the individual, the singular, the specific. In psychoanalysis, moreover, one cannot avoid reference to something mental which is stable and organized, which lies behind the symptoms, in the 'psychic apparatus', following Freud, incorporating, as with bodily systems, a variety of functional, structural, and organizational aspects. The search for something stable underlying symptoms impels one to discern structured and organized features related to a psychotic mode of mental operation rather than to identify the symptoms of more or less specific illnesses. One should, finally, bear in mind that psychoanalysts are better able than others to discern more nuanced symptomological patterns, which may elude more short-term observation conducted with qualitatively different, more objectivizing methods, such as that of psychiatry. The term 'psychosis', therefore, indicates both a level and a type of stable structural operation within a personality, which are not only linked to a serious limitation of the person's sense of self-fulfillment and capacity to find pleasure in relationships, but also to a dramatic limitation of their freedom. This sort of situation may, in turn, be linked to symptoms specific to such psychiatric illnesses as schizophrenia. It may, however, be linked to symptoms of other illnesses as well or even to 'hyposymptomatic' conditions which are either largely free of common symptoms or – what is rather common – show few and indistinct symptoms.

The term 'psychosis', then, covers a vast area which includes cases showing specific and readily identifiable symptoms but also many other cases which do not constitute distinct clinical phenomena. In the area of psychoses one encounters a specific quality and an operational level with identifiable characteristics but, most likely, at the same time anxieties, defences, structures, and even forms of mental organization which are heterogeneous.

Many have written of these 'psychotic' modes and levels of operation in the terms noted above as features that are commonly encountered in correct and in-depth analyses conducted on patients with serious problems.

For a survey, for the methodological approach to the subject, and for clinical cases, see Amati Mehler (2000). In particular, in this paper the author considers the clinical implications of contemporary theories that imply the co-existence of different levels of narcissistic and psychotic psychic functioning, but also of non-differentiated areas of mental functioning in severe patients. Amati supports with apt clinical material the contention that classical theories must be changed but not the classical analytic setting, and that traditional criteria of non-analysability are often the product of ideology or socio-economic issues rather than strictly psychoanalytical considerations and criteria.

The problem seen from the perspective of descriptive psychopathology

The existence of 'psychoses' exhibiting few, or only slight, symptoms of full-blown cases has been central to the work of numerous psychopathologists and has, with time, emerged as fundamental in the context of various studies, in the case of schizophrenia for example, to the point of identifying clinical forms based on precisely the characteristics presented above. Examples include Kahlbaum's 'heboidophrenia' (Kahlbaum, 1890), Bleuler's 'schizophrenia simplex' and 'latent schizophrenia' (Bleuler, 1911), Blankenburg's 'subapophanic' schizophrenias (Blankenburg, 1991), what Kimura Bin has described as 'schizophrenia sine schizophrenia' (Kimura Bin, 1992), and so-called 'negative schizophrenia' (Andreassen, 1982).

If one wishes to speak of core and periphery, one needs to have an idea (if only a very general one!) of what one's subject is, of what, according to a certain line of reasoning, stands at the centre of the issue. Is it possible, for example, nowadays to define exactly what we mean by 'schizophrenic pathology'? Currently the answer to that question can only be 'no', and this has been considered 'the scandal of psychiatry': its taking as pivotal a domain, schizophrenia, but without actually being able to trace its boundaries. The problem is so glaring that some years ago Mario Maj proposed replacing the diagnosis of schizophrenia with that of 'idiopathic non-affective psychosis' (Maj, 1998), thus accepting both its heterogeneity and the absence of precise criteria and pathognomic symptoms, and turning, as psychoanalysts often do, to the general term 'psychosis'. If, nonetheless, we attempt to extract a set of fixed coordinates common to the scientific discussion of idiopathic non-affective psychoses (whether or not we wish to call them forms of schizophrenia) as a whole, we find that over the years at least three core concepts, three referential schemes, have emerged as constants:

1. A core which we may call 'schizoid', and which to some extent overlaps with the popular notion of 'social inadequacy'; of being eccentric; unpredictable; incapable of grasping contexts; modulating behaviour in response to one's immediate *milieu*; or creating a rapport with others; phenomena ultimately linked with a fragile awareness (even sensorial) of one's own Self. This core may be a precursor to the full-blown pathology (pre-psychotic state), the primary feature of many clinical conditions (hyposymptomatic forms of schizophrenia, strictly speaking), or a condition lingering after an acute phase (residual schizophrenia, schizophrenic defect). Recent studies have revealed a close correlation between the presence of these characteristics prior to the onset of full-blown schizophrenia and an unhappy prognosis (Parnas & Bovet, 1991; Cutting & Sheperd, 1987, 1989).
2. A series of psychotic symptoms whose presence is neither exclusive to, nor inevitable in, cases of schizophrenia (Carpenter et al., 1973; Mellor, 1982; Maj, 1998). It is these, however, which are taken to be diagnostic, which are often considered 'iron-clad' and which, in accordance with the currently prevailing psychiatric orientation, give this disorder its medical respectability.
3. A series of symptoms belonging to other pathologies, which are now prominent in the literature (Prince et al., 1994), but which had already been thoroughly described (and at times emphasized) by European psychopathologists in the remote, as well as recent, past (Garrabé, 1992; Berrios & Beer, 1994). Their symptoms recall many other pathologies that are entirely distinct from schizophrenia: affective disorders; anxiety disorders; obsessive-compulsive disorders; panic-attack disorders; eating disorders; personality disorders; substance addiction. These symptoms may make themselves felt before and after a period of full-blown schizophrenia. It is probable, for example, that a given patient who suffers from a generalized anxiety and/or obsessive-compulsive disorder before the appearance of a symptomatically full-blown schizophrenic psychosis will, when the psychotic episode has passed, experience the return of those same symptoms, to such an extent as to constitute a clinical case of

> obsessive-compulsive disorder or generalized anxiety disorder. Object relations theory equips psychoanalysis to fully grasp these phenomena, as has – since its inception – the antilocalizationalist stance of Freud, and as has its reference, in the field of neuropsychology, to Jackson.

The notion thus presents itself that there exist psychoses with underlying psychotic structures but with few or no apparent symptoms of psychosis; a part of the literature in French calls these 'white psychoses' (*psychoses blanches*). The choice of the term 'white psychosis' avoids the problems, connected to the history of psychiatric nosography, raised by the word 'psychosis' as indicating the seriousness of the affliction and a more or less deep rift dividing the sufferer from some segment of reality, and as indicating a primitive (in a primarily ontogenetic sense) mode of mental operation and of constructing one's own subjective experience (Garrabé, 1997; Green,1969, 1990).

Hyposymptomatic psychoses, psychoanalysis, and the onset of delusions

Psychoanalytical technique changes as patients who come for analysis change and as the training of psychoanalysts becomes more sophisticated. In 1984 Gaddini noted an increase in the number of these cases, writing, for example, '. . . in fact psychoanalysis . . . distanced itself at its inception from psychosis only to find today that its progress has led it to the verge of an encounter with psychosis. I believe that this development was not guided by patients, but, on the contrary, that patients are guided by the development of psychoanalysis'. This very strong statement was shaped in part by his marked emphasis on the centrality of psychoanalysis combined with his scepticism concerning the observational capabilities of psychiatry, but it includes a plain truth in indicating the role of psychoanalysis, which is not exclusive but is fundamental. The other leading role has been played by the growing number of hyposymptomatic psychiatric patients, cases posing difficult, delicate, and even paradoxical diagnostic and therapeutic problems.

This 'paradoxical' notion of 'psychotic' operational levels, mental structures or mental areas (other metaphoric formulations are possible) which manifest themselves without, or with only occasional, symptoms can, though under extreme circumstances, be exemplified paradigmatically, and its problems can be formulated, through reference to delusional symptoms. If, however, we consider delusions not as a 'category', a symptom that may be present or absent, but as a 'dimension' varying in implications and extension (Strauss, 1969; Kendler et al., 1983; Zapparoli, 1967; Pazzagli, 1997). Paula Heimann, in a discussion of paranoid states (1955), attempted to gauge the scale of these symptoms according to their duration and implications, concluding, in her own words:

> Psychopathology of everyday life abounds in examples of paranoid delusions. We are all apt to feel at times that it always rains when we have planned to spend a day out of doors, that the bus going in the opposite direction to ours comes first, that some unfortunate experience we have had was directly due to somebody's ill-will or at least to fate's. Usually, however, this type of paranoid delusion is easily corrected. [. . .] Following this type of thought we come to discern a rising scale of severity in delusional attitudes. There is the momentary reaction – 'Damn that fool!' Ascending the scale, there is the mood which may persist for some hours – 'I knew everything would go wrong with me to-day, and it has!' Neither of these leads as yet to harmful consequences; both are entirely compatible with sound mental health. Next in severity might be a paranoid state lasting for days or weeks or more. Delusions can thus, according to this view, constitute the core of a position of the personality, with potentially extreme consequences.
>
> Finally, there is the psychosis in which the person's life is totally determined by his belief in a persecution, the delusion having become permanent, and the focus of a rigid system . . . To say that transient paranoid delusions are found in every analysis is only repeating the observation that they form part of the psychopathology of everyday life.

This long excerpt nicely illustrates the psychoanalytic position that places the meaning of everyday actions and emotions within a continuum (whereby, one might say, between a 'white psychosis' and a full-blown 'black psychosis' stretch infinite gradations of grey corresponding to degrees of health and illness). At the same time, the passage cited also nicely illustrates the complexity of these symptoms and the great difficulty in fully understanding their origin, and here psychotic hyposymptomology offers some important clues.

With these considerations in mind, psychoanalytical treatment of hyposymptomatic patients, who suffer from 'white psychoses' or have 'a psychotic character', as defined by Frosch (1960, 1970), may shed some light on the psychological process behind the inception, construction, and operation of delusions, and the inverse process behind their destructuring and even disappearance through transformation into narratives. Concerning the former, the appearance of delusions on the basis of highly disturbed and poorly organized personalities, it is important to note that the structuring of a delusion is a very complex – albeit pathological – mental operation. The difference between something related to delusional truth and a narrative, together with the possibility that analysis can help change the former into the latter, are effectively illustrated by two dreams with analogous contents dreamt some years apart by a patient in the course of psychoanalytic treatment.

Clinical vignette

B. is a 24-year-old, single workman from a small provincial village. He has an identical twin; the two brothers were separated only a few days after birth, and B. remained at home with his parents, whereas his brother was raised by an aunt and uncle who lived in the country not far from the parents' home, where the brothers were reunited at around the age of fifteen.

He requested analysis about two years after an attempt at independence from his family (taking a job far from home) had led to an acute psychotic crisis, both hallucinatory and delusional, and to hospitalization. Recovery from this episode was followed by an accentuation of obsessive symptoms and, above all, by a feeling of emptiness and solitude, a suffering that could not be put into words, all of which led him to seek analysis. The seriousness of certain symptoms, the patient's suffering, and, at the same time, his ability to experience all of this as something taking place in his own internal world and to express these feelings with a richness of language that contrasted with his social origins and cultural level, convinced the analyst that the patient's proposal of analysis could be accepted.

For B., psychoanalytical treatment meant leaving home and taking a job, which this time he managed to accomplish in a few months. He began analysis, with three weekly sessions, about a year after the first meeting, due to financial problems, while working as a porter in a hotel. The material he brought to these sessions was very rich and highly stimulating from many points of view. One of the first dreams reported in analysis, about a year from the beginning (session 142): 'I was at home with my family, or rather I think there was just me and my parents, and that's all. Well, at some point Mom comes in, and Dad says he's discovered a new position for making love, so they try it out right then and there. I tried to watch but I could hardly see anything ... My brother comes in – my twin brother – and demanded that I explain it all to him ... I didn't want to but I saw it as my fault because I couldn't explain it. In fact it's always been that way.' This dream seems to present a sort of primary scene in the form of a sensorial, photographic impression that the patient is not able to develop and narrate. The patient cannot explain but only look on, so that the dream – leaving aside this 'signalling' of an ability to perceive only in an 'imitative' way (Gaddini, 1969) in certain primitive, emotionally fraught areas – seems to bear no unconscious meanings to be uncovered and in this exhibits analogies with delusions. There is, however, an indication of the goal towards which the patient feels that he and the analyst should move: the formation of representations of perceptions that can be recounted. This lack of the ability to narrate appears to be linked to the absence of a part of the self which has been separated from him and projected upon his twin, with whom it has gone away, a loss the patient feels is his own fault. Living at home with his mother, he in fact seems never to have developed the ability to leave her and, thus, to have his own representation of the world and of events. All of this is reawakened in analysis, with an analyst whom he cannot tell, but only show, certain aspects of his life and of the sexuality of his parents.

A fragment of a dream dreamt after some years of analysis (session 418): 'I was with a cousin picking grapes at my aunt and uncle's [the ones who had raised his twin brother] and the vines were high, some on the ground and some with ladders ... The ones with ladders needed more work . . . Dad tells me to climb the ladders, and I said, "Right, Dad. Tonight we mount!"' (Note: the verb used, *montare* ['mount'], can very idiomatically express the action either of climbing [e.g. a ladder] or of [a male] having sexual intercourse.) This dream is in some ways analogous to that just examined. It is concerned, however, with the dreamer's own sexuality as well as that of his parents, and this is not presented by means of direct, sensory data but through representations that are even further removed from perception, admitting the use of allusive constructions ('Tonight we mount!'). The second dream is more strongly permeated by elements of the secondary process, with a marked modification of the characteristics of remembering with respect to the first dream.

Another fragment from a dream had in the same week of analysis seems to illustrate a mechanism underlying this change: 'I'm in a part of the hotel [B. still works as a porter in a hotel] that's as big as the rest of the hotel but where I'd never been and which I didn't think existed, and I find lots of valuable objects, heavy silver forks and spoons covered by a lot of dust . . . Nobody knows about this stuff and I'm thinking of stealing some of it . . . I take a fair amount of these forks . . . In comes Beppe (a colleague who has often represented his twin brother), and we find ourselves having to sweep and clean the whole place . . . and I like it, I'm happy to do it, but Beppe tells me just to get it over with'.

Leaving aside various other meanings (for example, the discovery of an unknown twin part of himself), which nonetheless emerge in a very rich analysis, dreaming 'objects covered by dust' seems to indicate the function of time and of repression in the very formation of a normal psychic life. In that sense the Freudian 'model' of revealing repressed material corresponds to this mental mechanism. Freud himself (1927), however, used another fundamental model, that characterized by denial, the splitting of the Self, and the emergence of remote material barely modified by condensation and displacement. These two models present different conceptions of perceptions and memory, and of their organization. A lack of the 'dust of time' can lead to the formation of a delusion as a saturated historical truth. 'Sweeping away the dust' (lifting repression) increases one's knowledge of oneself and one's history, but without ever making this knowledge absolute, complete: on the contrary, it leaves it 'unsaturated', a point that Freud emphasized as a limitation of memory in his late works, for example in *Moses and Monotheism* (1939) and *Constructions in Analysis* (1937). But this very limit is, perhaps, a characteristic that signals the possibility of formulating 'narratives'; here memory is the ability to construct memories and not a pristine archive, as seems to be the case with the nucleus of historical truth behind delusions. This sort of nucleus seems never entirely to overcome the characteristic of leaving a stable record in an archive. Alongside the narrative component there is always a more or less sizeable element of 'acting out'; perhaps it is this portion that accounts for P. Heimann's assertion that day-to-day life is full of delusions, and for the impossibility of representing events completely through narrative, since this process is always accompanied by an element of acting out, according to Morris (1993), for whom representation and acting out are two different but interacting means of bringing the past into the present.

At the end of adolescence B. had been designated clinically 'psychotic', though the observations record only muted symptoms. This came about with his abrupt separation from his mother, but then the situation stabilized with the prevalence of obsessive symptoms. The structural improvement indicated by the dreams was accompanied, paradoxically it would seem, by the appearance of paranoid states, which did not require hospitalization or psychiatric treatment but did necessitate a lengthy and difficult analysis. The psychoanalyst was accused, alternately, of separating him from his hometown and his family but also of driving him to return to them, given the suffering his thirst for money was causing B., 'forcing' him into homosexual prostitution and drug abuse. The psychoanalyst was likewise violently accused of wishing to separate him from his twin brother but at the same time of not being able to make him self-sufficient and thus leaving him painfully frustrated by his feminine ties to his mother and submission to his father, and by an unmanly inability to overcome his anguish and make it on his own. Bitter accusations and forms of acting out (occasional drug abuse and prostitution, suicide threats, automobile accidents, and threatening telephone calls in the night) characterize the period following the work described above with a marked improvement coming only after many months.

This case illustrates the existence of aspects of the mind dominated by sensory memories but seemingly incapable of narrating their content. Analysis did not 'interpret' but did facilitate the construction of different levels of meaning. It consequently seems that the very existence of these levels makes it possible to learn from experience and to recount experiences but also – as if in opposition to all of this – to fashion delusions, understood as very primitive and sensorially vivid experiential content which can be expressed through 'acting out' (Bion, 1965) but not narrated in the sense noted above. These clinical phenomena and these experiences can emerge and be observed only if more mature aspects coexist with them and act as a 'background' to these psychopathological figures. Where these healthier components are lacking, in personalities that are very seriously deficient in that respect, they cannot 'emerge', nor, therefore, take shape, leaving the subject in a psychotic condition but without – or with few, indistinct, and unstable – 'productive' or 'positive' symptoms, which are primarily delusional. In this sense the genuine pathology can emerge only against the background of healthier workings, without which the condition remains asymptomatic or hyposymptomatic, being less organized.

The considerations we have briefly presented confirm, in specifically psychoanalytical terms, something that has already been noted and stressed, the possibility that a 'continuum' stretches between the extremes of normality and full-blown and entirely manifest schizophrenia. They also highlight the fact that organizing full-blown pathologies necessitates some sort of structure, immature or incomplete though it may be, since otherwise there can be none of those symptoms which bring anguish but also provide useful, though primitive, defences.

Psychotic symptoms, symptomological silence, and psychoanalytic process

It can be no surprise, in the light of these considerations, that a delusion should appear in a patient in analysis for other reasons (see Pazzagli, 1997) or, conversely, that work with patients considered 'psychotic' according to the criteria noted above should go on for long periods in the absence or near-absence of psychiatric symptoms.

In the course of thirty years, the author has had two patients in analysis and eight others in psychoanalytic psychotherapy, each of whom had been diagnosed as schizophrenic by expert and, on the whole, reliable psychiatrists, though of differing orientations. With each of these patients there were long stretches of sessions characterized by accounts of everyday life, of work done, of persons encountered, and of conversations had. The dominant feature of these accounts may be obsessive boredom or narcissistic disdain and may even be tinged with a hysterical seductiveness, features which seem to be those prevalent in the patient's relations with external or internal objects, which are regularly brought to light by therapy. The story told in these sessions is in any case flat, colourless, its life apparently sapped, its purpose to display the normality of the things done, the conversations had, etc. The patient seems to wish to certify that he is healthy and in touch with reality, seeking confirmation from the therapist to whom he has come for treatment but to whom he also brings material attesting to the contrary. Content aside, the story does bring 'inanities' (Racamier, 1980) to the sessions, the attribution of this to external reality, along the lines of: 'I did this ... that ... Everything you people do ... So what of it? The world is empty all the same...' '... and I'll make you experience it', one might add. Such 'normal' periods recall borderline organizations, but without the 'stable instability' connected to the latter's distances and separations, being dominated, on the contrary, by a sense of the world's immutable, rigid lifelessness. Though disappointing, these periods may, especially at the outset of treatment, ease one's mind, but then, quite frankly, they become boring, irritating, repetitive – perhaps one could say 'claustrophobia-inducing', revealing the patient's need to adhere to hard reality due to the anguish aroused by the prospect of psychotic breakdowns and of involving the therapist in that anguish.

Another clinical vignette

A patient about forty years of age was in psychoanalytical psychotherapy, rather than analysis, both because he refused to accept the requisite commitment and because, as his rigid, controlled, and wary attitude led one to suppose, he feared that with time analysis might have exposed elements he wished to keep hidden but which had not emerged in his recent history. Actually there had been, during his student years, a period of acute crisis described only as a 'nervous breakdown' but highly susceptible to interpretation as psychotic. His subsequent life had been characterized by tiredness, symptoms of hypochondria that, according to the patient, made it impossible to work in some periods, which his colleagues interpreted as spells of laziness and of hostility towards them, since they would have to take up the slack. This led to tension, strife, and – for this patient – failures, which, in turn, made him even more 'listless and lazy'. Otherwise, he had a conventional family life (wife and children), though this normality was generally accompanied by a dulled emotional life. Psychotherapy was undertaken – after the failure of numerous prescription drug treatments for 'nervous breakdown', 'neuroses', obsessive disorders, hypochondria, and the like – by a very reluctant patient. The therapist too began with some trepidation, but was at first, as noted above for other such cases, reassured and then bored by a patient who, ever punctual and formally respectful of the rules of the setting, confined himself from the outset to narrating in a monotonous, controlled, and obsessive manner the ins and outs of his normal activities.

Several months into the treatment, however, the patient began occasionally skipping sessions, excusing his absences on the grounds that he 'didn't feel well' due to unspecified physical ailments. Upon his return, the patient brusquely stated that he had not been able to come, that he had had to make a journey, emphasizing the *not having been able to* or the *having to go away* but never offering any further explanation. After a number of such occasions, finally, when he had again returned with the same justification, the therapist told him that he had been wondering, and would therefore ask him, what he meant when he said that he 'had had to go away', that he 'had had to' miss sessions. Jumping to his feet and shouting, the patient accused the analyst of knowing everything and pretending not to know, of being in league with his persecutors. In the course of that and subsequent sessions, these persecutors proved to be individuals he did not, and could not, identify, but 'extraterrestrial beings' who terrified him by virtue of their being indistinguishable from normal persons; so much so that when his state of mind and his anguish indicated the presence of these persecutors, he was stricken with a terror compounded by his inability to tell friend from foe. He was thus driven to flight, sometimes great distances and even across the continent. During the session following his first outburst of paranoia, he violently ransacked the desk and bookshelves in the office in search of the microphones and tape recorder that were doubtless hidden there in order to record the sessions and his accounts. Confronted with the interpretation that he was trying to remove from the doctor's office/head his story, now made intolerable by the fear that it should come back to haunt him when he was well again, he took a knife from his pocket and began fidgeting with it, with the all-too-clear suggestion of a threat. Suddenly, he planted it in the desktop, then he pulled it out and left. He skipped some sessions, but the analyst learned that his family too had noticed his delusional state and that a psychiatrist who had previously been consulted now suggested that this was a schizophrenic disorder, yet the patient refused drug treatment. He nonetheless resumed regular attendance, as dull and monotonous as ever. The 'stormy weather', as he called it, had, however, left its mark, and it was now possible to begin working on his taking refuge in a posture of 'normality', of submission, and, at the same time, of protest, assumed in order to pass for a proper adult, to escape the panic induced by not being able to distinguish earthlings from aliens, friends from enemies, the good from the bad. As work continued there were two more crises, which the patient recounted on his return without any particular difficulties. The first drove him to flee northward, all the way to Scandinavia; the tale of his terrors, largely nocturnal, of fiords that darkly and ominously plunged into the sea and of only sporadic lights in the darkness, signalling a possible haven but also the potential presence of his unrecognizable persecutors, was taken in by the therapist but essentially as symptoms of an illness, of 'madness', especially because in fact Norway had appeared to the therapist himself, in a recent and happy vacation, as a green land with clear skies and a blue sea. The second crisis sent the patient to Turkey, and his account brought to the sessions the nightmares and the perceived threats that hounded his travels across the plains of Cappadocia, which concealed subterranean cities inhabited, in his mind, by mysterious and hostile characters. These states of mind led the therapist to experience analogous nightmares of persecution in a land not known directly to him, the atavistic terrors ('Mother! The Turks are coming!') of our South, but at the same time led him to examine the knife mark still on the desktop, which was seen to run perpendicular to the (imaginary) line that had joined patient and doctor . . . 'a separating rather than a killing knife, then', the therapist thought. Not knowing how to tell friends from foes, the good from the bad, was again made explicit and was completed, as emerged in the long period of work that followed, with the confusion between the loving mother who cared for him as a child and the mother who wanted him all to herself, even if that meant having him ill; between the analyst who treated him and the one who recorded the sessions with his accounts of his crises and of his terrors in order to save them and perhaps to blackmail him or keep him in his care and never let him go. This work put an end to his flights, which never recurred even after treatment had ended. The patient did revert to an analogous 'neurotic' or quasi-neurotic state, but this was much attenuated, much less serious, and more controlled than that which he had experienced previously, also with far fewer inhibitions and a greatly enhanced performance on the job.

Work continued because the analyst/psychotherapist had the chance to not cease thinking and day-dreaming about even the most destructive and dangerous behaviour of the patient and to put together the two parts: the 'normal' adult, conformist in his realism but emotionally stunted, and the dangerous madman; fitting them together through the 'construction' (Freud, 1936) of a story common to both. This tale, taking its cue from the early-childhood origins of his behaviour, explained its violence and drama, but taking them in benignly, allowing them to manifest themselves in their relationship to him, their eloquence no longer blocked by his illness. Treatment gave the patient the framework of a stable setting, whose very existence, whose limitations with respect to the pair, whose guarantee of a welcome, confirmed the presence of libidinal, object-oriented aspects tied to the mind in opposition to the omnipotence of grandiose, fusional, and narcissistic aspects.

The opportunity/ability to bring together different aspects of the patient, the external, factual reality 'reified' and the delusion, and to use both in order to grasp the personal, overall sense of the patient's contrasting parts, testing them through the therapeutic relationship in progress, through transference, and even tracing them back to their remote origins in early childhood, and thus to a world which is at once real and fabulous (of the 'Once upon a time. . .' sort) came first to the analyst and then to the pair. A potential space was thus opened for the pair – though with great difficulty and under the constant threat of destruction – which made communication possible between two different areas, as is recommended for the psychoanalytical treatment of psychoses by Boyer & Giovacchini (1967, 1980), by Feinsilver (1983) and by Benedetti (1991).

Conclusions

Winnicott (1953) has written that from the inception of life a human being is occupied with the problem of relating what is perceived objectively to what is perceived subjectively, and that the intermediate area is precisely that situated between primary creativity and fact-based objective perception. Just this area is lacking in psychotics, even a- or hyposymptomatic psychotics, who fail to make this distinction and in whom the two realms appear to be either rigidly separate or jumbled one with the other. Rigid separation, if maintained, leads to the presence of symptom-free psychotic modes of operation ('white psychoses'); jumbling manifests itself through the presence of a psychotic profile completed by confusion as to what is actually happening and, readily enough, by delusions as well. The latter are invariably also attempts at healing, as Freud pointed out in his day, in *Neurosis and Psychosis* (1924, p. 151) for example: 'In regard to the genesis of delusions, a fire number of analyses have thought us that the delusion is found applied like a patch over the place where originally a rent had appeared in the ego's relation to the external world'

The coexistence of these two functional modes, which are so deeply divided one from the other, explains why a person, psychotic or schizophrenic though they may be, is capable of perceiving reality in its most evident, hardest, and most strongly shared characteristics. If this condition is stable, it becomes that of the white psychoses. At the same time, however, the psychotic is not capable of making external and internal reality coexist, of giving meaning as well as a definition to *realia*. The patient's behaviour, then, shows that he is either compelled to adhere rigidly and forcibly to hard, shared reality or to break with that reality and inject it with content from his internal world, which is unconscious, usually indistinct, not susceptible to narration, but which at times forms the basis of delusions. This is why the patient can only oppose his psychotic experiences, whether delusional or not, through a strict adherence to reality, which is consequently experienced and recounted in a flat, cold, stereotypical, and impersonal fashion with none of the filtering or enrichment that comes from feelings or emotional ties. It seems that only psychoanalysis, where possible, or a psychoanalytical stance, despite the difference of setting, in forms of psychoanalytical psychotherapy, again where possible, can offer the opportunity for a structural change, if only a partial one, in this psychotic organization. Even at the expense, at times, of bringing about an apparent worsening of the symptomatic picture with the appearance of delusions, which are at the same time potential threats to the treatment and forms of communication essential to bringing about change.

References

Amati Mehler, J. (2000). Psicoanalisi: teoria e tecnica oggi. *Psicoanalisi 4 (1)*: 39–58.

Andreasen, N.C. (1982) Negative symptoms in schizophrenia: definition and reliability. *Arch Gen Psychiatry, 39(7)*: 784–788 (1982).

Benedetti, G. (1991). *Paziente e terapeuta nell'esperienza psicotica*. Torino, Boringhieri.

Berrios, G.E., & Beer, D. (1994). The notion of a unitary psychosis: a conceptual history. *History of Psychiatry, 5*: 13–36.

Bion, W.R. (1965). *Transformations:Change from Learning to Growth*. London: William Heinemann Medical Books Limited.

Blankenburg, W. (1991). *La perte de l'évidènce naturelle*. Paris: PUF.

Bleuler, E. (1911). *Dementia paecox oder Gruppe der Schizophrenien*. Wien: F. Denticke.

Boyer, L.B., & Giovacchini, P.L. (1967) *Psychoanalytic Treatment of Characterological and Schizophrenic Disorders*. New York: Aronson.

Boyer, L.B., & Giovacchini, P.L. (1980). *Psychoanalytic Treatment of Characterological, Borderline, and Schizophrenic Disorders*. New York: Aronson.

Carpenter, W.T., Strauss, J.J., & Muleh, S. (1973). Are there pathognomonic symptoms of schizophrenia? *Arch Gen Psy, 28*: 847–852.

Cutting, J. Sheperd, M. (Eds.) (1987). *The clinical roots of Schizophrenia*. New York: Cambridge University Press, 1987.

Cutting, J., Dunne, F. (1989). Subjective experience of schizophrenia. *Schizophrenia Bulletin 15*: 217–231.

Feinsilver, D. (1983). Application of Pao's theories to the case study of the use and misuse of medication. Psychoanalytic Inquiry, 3: 125–145.

Freud, S. (1924). Neurosis and psychosis. *Standard Edition, 19* (pp. 149–153). London: The Hogarth Press and the Institute of Psychoanalysis, 1960.

Freud, S. (1927). Fetishism. *Standard Edition, 21* (pp. 149–158). London: The Hogarth Press and the Institute of Psychoanalysis.

Freud, S. (1937). *Constructions in analysis. Standard Edition, 23* (pp. 257–269). London: The Hogarth Press and the Institute of Psychoanalysis, 1964.

Freud, S. (1939). Moses and monotheism: three essays. *Standard Edition, 23* (pp. 7–140). The Hogarth Press and the Institute of Psychoanalysis.

Frosch, J.P. (1960). Psychotic character. *J. Am. Psychoanal. Ass., 8*: 544–551.

Frosch J.P. (1970). Psychoanalytic considerations of the psychotic character.. *J. Am. Psychoanal. Ass., 18*: 24–50.

Gaddini, E. (1969). On Imitation. *International Journal of Psychoanalysis,* 50: 475–84.

Gaddini, E. (1984). Se e come sono cambiati i nostri pazienti sino ai nostri giorni. *Riv. Psicoanal. 30 (4)*: 560–580.

Garrabé J. (1977). *Le Concept de psychose.* Paris: Masson.

Green, A. (1969) La nosographie psychanalytique des psychoses. In: C. Laurin C. & P. Doucet (Eds.), *Problématique de la psychose.* Amsterdam: I Excerpta Medica Foundation.

Green, A. (1990). *La folie privée. Psychoanalyse d cas-limites.* Paris: Gallimard.

Heimann, P. (1955). A combination of defence mechanisms in paranoid states. In: *New Directions in Psycho-Analysis* London: Tavistock Publications.

Kahlbaum, K.L. (1890). Über Eboidophrenie. *Allm Reitschz für Psych, 46*: 44–65.

Kendler, K.S., Glazer, W.M., & Morgenstern, H. (1983). Dimensions of Delusional Experience. *Am. J. Psychiatry, 140, 466–499*

Kimura, Bin (1992) *Ecrits de psychopathologie phénoménologique.* Presses Universitaire de France.

Maj, M. (1998). Critique of the DSM IV operational criteria for schizophrenia. *Br J Psy, 172*: 458–460.

Mellor, C.S. (1982). The present status of first-rank symptoms. *Br J Psychiatry, 140*: 423–424.

Morris, H. (1993). Narrative representation: narrative enactment and the psychoanalytic construction of the history. *Int. J. PsychoAnal.,*74: 33–54.

Parnas, J., & Bovet, P. (1991). Autism in schizophrenia revisited. *Comprehensive Psy, 32*: 7–21.

Pazzagli, A. (1997). Deliri, costruzioni e verità. *Psicoanalisi 1, 1,* 89–100.

Prince, M. & Phelan, M. (1994). Invisible schizophrenia: a postal survey of the incidence and management of new cases of schizophrenia in primary care. *J. Mental Health* 3: 91–98.

Racamier, P.C. (1980). *Les Schizophrènes*. Paris: Payot.
Strauss, J.S. (1969). Hallucinations and delusions as points on continua function. *Arch: Gen.Psychiatry 21, 581–586.*
Winnicott, D.W. (1971). *Playing and Reality*. London: Tavistock Publications.
Zapparoli, G.C. (1967). *Psicoanalisi del delirio*. Milano: Bompiani.

CHAPTER SEVEN

When actions speak louder than words

Fred Pine

This book reflects Jacqueline Amati Mehler's interest in language and symbolization. In my contribution to it, I shall describe a particular clinical phenomenon wherein, at least at the outset, effective symbolization is not possible. Words, though available, are psychically useless. In the specific region of vulnerability, 'actions speak louder than words'.

I shall start with an example, the first in which I became aware of the phenomenon. Mr A came to me seeking analysis at age 57, shortly after retiring. He had been very successful in his profession, money was now no issue, and his time was entirely his own. He was married and had two grown children who were out of the home. In his first presentation of himself, he said he just wanted to expand his self understanding to 'appreciate how I work'. And, while overall that did remain his guiding relationship to his analysis, it also rapidly became clear that he had a mood disorder, with rapid swings between high and low, that had always been a burden to him.

Mr A threw himself into the analytic work with diligence and high interest. He endeavoured to speak freely, and he was alert and interested when I spoke. 'I'm getting familiar with the (interior) landscape' was one of his frequent statements. It was not intellectualized but seemed quite genuine. And in fact, time would show that he achieved considerable self understanding and made significant gains in his functioning.

Several months into the treatment, a new phenomenon began to emerge. Mr A would be speaking, and I would be listening and saying something when I had something to say. But then he would begin to fade out. It was as though he were running out of gas. His speech would slow, get less certain, become fumbling, sputtering, and his voice volume would reduce almost to a whisper; gradually he would stop speaking altogether. When I asked what seemed to be going on, this man who ordinarily readily looked inwards and came up with observations, would only say that he did not know, but that he just could not speak. It took perhaps a half dozen repetitions of this event before I thought I noticed that it always followed my making an interpretation in the transference. I mentioned this to him, saying something like, 'You seem to fade out whenever I bring myself into the session.' His response was immediate and clear. 'Oh, now I know what it's about. You become my father; I'm reminded of his presence. And whenever he was present we (his mother, sisters, and himself) had to focus all our attention on him. We would be propping him up, and I would feel I was wiping myself out.' This clear and simple statement, so easily offered by Mr A, turned out to capture a powerful and central experience of his life.

I had known his father's history from the initial consultation sessions, though I had not known this pattern of family interaction. When his father was a nine-year-old boy, he was in an automobile accident in which every other member of his family was killed, though he escaped uninjured. He spent the rest of his life living as a bereft and traumatized man, and the family he later created with his wife always focused on holding him up. Now I learned that, in the patient's experience, this meant obliterating himself.

The striking point, however, was that my patient's immediate and clear understanding of the phenomenon had absolutely no impact upon it. His reaction to transference interpretations remained the same and, talk about it though we might (as was attempted in subsequent sessions, both within the transference and within the life), he would fade out for the remainder of the session.

I had of course made transference interpretations from the outset, but this phenomenon had not appeared. Our eventual understanding was that I had simply not mattered enough to him at the outset for me to be able to produce such an effect. But as I came to matter, I became the vulnerable transference-object father who 'needed' to talk about himself and have all of the attention centred upon himself.

Why does something get repeated? In this case it was the patient's apparent 'obliteration' (in the face of a transference interpretation) that got repeated. We are certainly familiar with repetition in analyses. Significant phenomena seem to reappear in endless guises, to sneak through every side door. The concept 'working through' refers in significant part to the necessity of doing just this kind of repetitive work. Repetition is usually powered by wishes, on the one hand, or internalized object relations that are repeated in by-now-fruitless efforts after mastery – a turning of passive into active. What we saw with Mr A was certainly more like the latter – an object relational pattern of childhood was internalized, carried, and repeated. This is the common history of the strain trauma (Kris, 1956) of childhood, in my view the most common and widespread source of repetition in human functioning. Interactions that might be painful but that would not have a lasting impact if they occurred rarely or just once in a while, become traumatic by their steady repetition day in and day out. Turning passive to active, the person plays this out on others, or elicits it from others – in either case making it happen, though generally without awareness of so doing.

But this did not seem to be the case with Mr A or the other patients whom I shall describe. His experience continued to be a passive one; something was to him and he was reacting as he always had. He/we could locate no experience of his *making* it happen. While, of course, he was interpreting the situation in his own historically dominated way, this view of what was going on, putting responsibility back into the patient, was essentially formulaic and academic, bearing little relation to the patient's inner state and experience. Perhaps a sufficient level of agency, or self formation, or ego function – choose your concept – has to be attained before a person can truly internalize an object relationship and turn it around actively. Mr A had certainly achieved all of those things, but not (I believe) in the region of this particular interaction. It remained as an experience of passive obliteration.

Over time, this changed. After multiple experiences of the kind described and with no progress through apparent understanding, at one point I told him that it was not necessary to bring myself into what I say and that I would not. I kept to this agreement for about six months, during which time his father's vulnerability and the patient's self-obliteration was often the centre of our work. Then, on one occasion, I told him in advance that I would like to say something about him and me, and asked whether he thought he could tolerate it. He thought he could; he did; and we were on our way. Gradually, and again with occasional pre-warnings at first, it became possible to work in the transference without detrimental impact, often while also looking at this very fact and its history between us. I believe that my action of taking myself out of the sessions, respecting his vulnerability, and then bringing myself back in only with his permission (thus giving him a measure of control) made the difference. We never had to change the basic understanding of the phenomenon that he told me with his initial 'oh, now I know what it is about'. But a revised experience (between us in this instance) had to take place, permitting some kind of internal alteration, perhaps a sense of active control, before Mr A could function differently. In all of this, 'actions' were central – first my 'action' of putting myself in the centre (as the patient experienced it) by making an interpretation in the transference, and then my action (made explicit) of avoiding such interpretations; it was never the specific content that mattered.

In brief contrast, and to highlight the difference, I think of another patient who faded out in an apparently similar way, but clearly did so as part of an internal defensive process whenever she spoke too vigorously of sexuality, aggression, or autonomy. The fading out, here, was to counteract her sense of vigour and excitement. Words, in the form of interpretations, were the only necessary tool in working with this.

Having identified this phenomenon with Mr A (and I have no idea how many times I might have missed seeing it in my prior analytic work before coming to think of it as a significant phenomenon), I have come to see it periodically in the work. My experience is that it generally comes as a surprise to me, with a feeling of 'oh, that's the same thing again!' And what is that 'same thing'? Some aspect of the analyst's ordinary way of working becomes retraumatizing for a particular patient. The phenomenon is not reported in the initial consultations, and in fact does not occur at the outset, but, as with Mr A, only when the analyst becomes intrapsychically important enough to the patient. And, in each instance, though the understanding was clear and virtually immediate, it had no effect unless, ultimately, there was a behavioural change in the analyst. (Of course, it could always be argued that the understanding was incomplete and that fuller understanding would achieve the goal without any change in the analyst's behaviour. My inclination is to see that view as a product of excessive loyalty to a theory of technique, and missing a valuable fact about the patient's inner life.)

Now a second instance. When Ms B, a 27-year-old professional dancer, came to her first appointment, she also made clear that she was seeking an intensive treatment, and was fully receptive when, after a few consultation sessions, I suggested an analysis. She was talented at dance, but seemed to have considerably less success at it than she might have, in significant part because of relationship difficulties that seemed to befall her (although we eventually came to understand how her particular responses in certain triggering situations heightened these difficulties). But her principal reason for coming was based on her internal suffering – states of guilt and self hate that were overwhelming and disorganizing.

I shall not describe the analysis in any detail, wishing to focus only on the phenomenon that parallels the one already described in Mr A. This patient , too, was committed to the analytic work, had a strong attachment to the analyst, and was receptive to interpretation, though discerning about what she accepted and what she did not. Once again, the phenomenon I wish to describe appeared only when we were well into the work, at a time when my importance in the intrapsychic life of the patient had developed more fully. And once again, the phenomenon appeared in the form of interventions by the analyst that, although quite ordinary in analytic functioning, were experienced as retraumatizing by the patient. They were clearly transference manifestations, but again aroused feelings of passive victimization. And finally, and again, though the patient could tell me exactly what was going on in the transference, and what it was repeating, the understanding had no effect on the experience of traumatic re-victimization. After a while (including some analytic work that went nowhere), I chose here, as before, to alter my behavior, and this made all the difference. In this instance, the alteration was permanent as there was no loss to the work in the altered behaviour (as there would have been with Mr A had I remained unable to interpret in the transference).

One bit of background. The form of my interpretive interventions generally reflects the degree of confidence I have in what I am saying. So, when I have only a general sense of understanding (but for whatever reason it seems to me an intervention is appropriate), I may begin with a 'perhaps' or 'do you think it could be that . . .' But, at the other end of the scale, when I feel the evidence is strong and I have considerable confidence in what I am saying, my whole delivery reflects it; sometimes I may even begin with an alerting comment like, 'Oh! I see what's happening,' and then offer the interpretation I have in mind. I find that most analysands react well to these gradations and, with the stronger statements, are still able to disagree but more often find them clarifying and organizing. Not so for Ms B.

At some point in the work, strong interpretations enraged this patient. This reaction burst upon the analytic scene at one point, quite evidently something new that had not been present earlier. Before I had even become clear that it was precisely the convincingly stated interpretations that produced this effect, the patient told me just that, along with an explanation. But she did it within her rage reaction so that, while it clarified the situation for me, it hardly had the modulated quality of an 'insight'. It was known in her gut, and she threw the explanation at me to get me to stop. And what did she tell me? That I was backing her into a corner, controlling her, telling her what to think; that I gave her no room for her own thoughts and feelings, no room for her to participate in figuring things out, and that it was exactly what her parents did to her when they told her what to think and feel and what not to think and feel.

I had known about this aspect of her relationship with her parents, but now I came to know it more vividly as she fully re-experienced the rage (that she could not express with them) during the sessions. All of this was useful but, once seen, I could not see how it would continue to be useful for me to act in ways that the patient felt as controlling and that produced rage. Like with Mr A, Ms B felt this as something being done to her, not as something she could usefully see as evoked by her or even experientially interpreted by her. It was too real and immediate.

I want to emphasize that this was her personal reaction based on personal history; other patients have had no difficulty altering, rejecting, or ignoring even, interpretations that are given with conviction, and more often find them, as stated already, clarifying and organizing. So one could say this was a transference response. But, as with Mr A, knowing about it, and subsequently working on it together, had no effect on how any later strong statements by me were received. In fact, like with Mr A, I changed my behaviour, not giving this degree of certainty to my voice tone or sentence construction. It did not seem necessary to do so, and for Ms B it was tactless and destructive. So it dropped out of my repertoire with her, though the fact of the experience with her parents did not drop out. Actions again spoke louder than words – both my 'action' of speaking with certainty (and again, it was never the content of what I said that produced the rage; just the tone of conviction) and my action of no longer doing so.

One cannot help noticing that in both patients described thus far the experience that touched off the disorganization or rage was one that produced a sense of there being no room for an autonomous self. Mr A had to put his 'self' aside to prop up his father, an experience that was recreated in the session when I put myself forwards (in his experience) as needing the focus of attention on me. Ms B felt no breathing room for her own self as her thoughts and feelings were controlled by her parents or by me. The same general inner situation is seen in the third patient that I shall describe, though, of course, in totally individualized ways.

Mr C was 33 years old when he came seeking treatment. While his initial expectation was that he would enter psychotherapy two times a week, within a few weeks he responded receptively to my proposal for a full analysis, and we began. Although he was a respected scholar and teaching intellectual history in a local university, he nonetheless felt considerably unsettled about his career wishes; and, in fact, a career in psychology and psychoanalysis had been one of the things that had attracted his interest over the years. His marriage of some ten years was in trouble, with his idealized wife quite unreliable in her relatedness. And he suffered severe bouts of depression.

With the perspective of time and the work done in the analysis, I can now say the following about Mr C's history and psychological functioning as backdrop to the particular aspect of the analysis that I shall address here. Starting in his childhood (and this already appears in memories), and flourishing by his teens, Mr C seems to have begun to function in automaton-like ways with respect to others – setting his needs aside, almost 'obeying' the needs and suggestions of others, and drawing whatever scraps of self-esteem he could from any signs of affection he received in return. How this evolved is unclear, though there were some indications that it had to do both with trauma in his relation to his mother in early infancy (which seemed in the transference to produce shaky self-boundaries) and specific aspects of his relationship to his father; but I need not go more into this historical material for my purposes here.

Suffice it to say, however, that this automaton tendency played itself out in the analysis in numerous ways. While it could even have been somewhere in his ready receptivity to my suggestion for analysis, an opposite factor seems more likely to have been operative – that is, his genuine suffering, his wish for help, and especially his deep satisfaction in the attention to his real fullness as a person (quite the opposite of the automaton) that analysis could give. This whole state became progressively more clear, however, in the analytic sessions through the disruptions that a failure to attend to him as a person would produce. On numerous occasions, my silence when Mr C wanted (though not known to me at the time, I would now say *needed*) a response, would produce a sense of helpless despair that often took multiple sessions to set right again. Thus, it was the opposite side of the automaton tendency that became more significantly active in the transference as time went on – the disruption produced by the experience of failed attention to his sense of self (again, the analyst's 'action'), an inability to settle for 'scraps' of attention and the self-esteem it produced in bits. These incidents of my failure to respond were a heavy weight on the analysis for a long time. Although we talked about these moments and seemed to understand them in important ways, and although he always recovered after a few sessions, they seemed to me more retraumatizing than anything else, although it was not always clear how to avoid them. Then Mr C brought in one way.

At one point, and I come now to my point of focus here, Mr C spontaneously and compellingly stated his need for something different. He had asked me a question and, sensing my hesitation in responding directly, he said: 'That's a real question and I need you to answer it. I'm perfectly willing to analyse why I asked and my response to your answer, but first I need an answer.' Given the history just described, of both the disruptive failures to respond in the analysis and the history of his automaton behaviour with others, organized around meeting their perceived needs, I thought of this request as an important progressive step and one which, in any event, I saw no real reason to refuse. In the whole subsequent history of the analysis, Mr C would ask questions periodically and never asked one that I felt was inappropriately intrusive; he often asked questions about my professional life, which fitted with his regrets about not having pursued a career in psychoanalysis. In most instances I would answer directly and simply and our work would go on. At first, I would carefully try to analyse 'why (he) asked the question and his response to my answer' (as he had offered to do) but, after a while that seemed to me to become ritualistic – as though for me to prove that we were properly 'analysing' – and it dropped away except on occasion when some enquiry seemed to me relevant.

At the moment of the patient's statement that he needed me to answer and would be entirely open to analysing afterwards, I said: 'I'm willing to try that and see how it goes. It's not what I am used to (and in fact he had asked before, without my responding) but let's see what comes of it.' So I answered whatever that question was and, as noted, perhaps rather self-consciously made a point of 'analysing' the question and his reaction to my answer, until that came to seem ritualistic.

In what sense is this about 'actions speaking louder than words'? After all, I did use words in answering Mr C's questions. But I believe that it was not my words that mattered, but my action of answering, and therefore of reversing what he already knew was my more usual tendency to wait (after a question) and see what became of the question itself. Once again, therefore, we have a situation where the ordinary actions of the analyst (this time, delaying and analysing in response to a question; previously, interpreting in the transference with Mr A and making a strong and convinced interpretation with Ms B) stepped into a once-traumatizing situation and led to a repeat of the sense of trauma. And once again, I want to point out, that the traumatic damage was experienced as an injury to the autonomy of the self, of the whole person and his/her sense of agency.

I would like to offer a number of comments at the clinical level about these phenomena. While analytic tact ordinarily is sufficient to ensure that the patient can feel adequately (and not intrusively) attended to, in the reported patients, violations of these experiences through the analytic process itself became central. Although I list the core phenomena simply (being in the centre of attention, not being controlled, being responded to), in no instance did the patients I am referring to have clear words for them when we began the analysis. They emerged and became formulated through experiences in the analyst-patient interchange at a time when the analyst had grown in importance in the patient's intrapsychic life. In that sense they are iatrogenic experiences, since the analytic process puts issues of attention, response, and control so much at the centre; but they are also clearly transference experiences, reflecting individual history as refracted through the analytic process.

I do not regard such experiences as universals, though perhaps tactlessness could evoke them in anyone. It is for such patients in particular, as I understand my experience with them, that empathic failure (Kohut, 1984) becomes a central issue in analysis – failure signalled precisely by the rage/disintegration response to an experience of the analyst's violation of the particular wish/need. 'Empathic failure', in this sense, is not a 'mistake' of the analyst but is rather a phenomenon inevitably present for those patients who have high vulnerability in the listening and talking in relationship and process as it goes on between patient and analyst. Although one should certainly not aim to produce such failures (and need not, for they will surely occur spontaneously), it is nonetheless true that a very considerable part of the actual work of the analysis takes place in relation to these very 'failures' – coming to be able to recognize and understand their meaning to the patient, to know their history in the life story, and to alter them in the analytic interchange.

Similarly, though in reverse, I have also noted (in clinical work not reported here) that for some patients one or another aspect of average expectable analytic listening and tact may provide a central, reorganizing new object relationship experience that contrasts sharply with personal history and moves the analysis forward in surprising and individualized ways – enabling the patient to articulate, often for the first time, some experienced deficit in the parental provision. I am thinking of one patient's feeling heard for the first time and another's discovering reliability (non-loss) of the other through the analyst's regular appearance at sessions. These are not things we 'do' for the patient; they are what the patient finds in what we *are*. We could not prevent them should we wish to, because they reflect longings or need states that the patient unknowingly carries into the transference. Here again, it is the analyst's stance, experienced by the patient as an action (listening, reliably showing up for sessions), that has a powerful, often unnoticed, and therefore potentially 'unanalysed' effect (though in the two instances given we came to understand the effects quite well).

The patient's specific experience of need (to be heard, confirmed, given the centre, not be intruded upon) is not equivalent to a need for nonspecific care, concern, or empathy (though gratification of the specific need can often be 'found' in the nonspecific good-enough care that analysis provides). Despite all due care and concern, specific violations of what the patient feels he or she needs will nonetheless occur, and will occur again and again since that is so much a reflection of how the patient is constructed. The analytic process, even when carried out with optimal sensitivity on the part of the analyst, will create violations of the specific needs felt by these patients. It is not as though some wished-for 'perfect' technique can avoid them; these are the phenomena the patient brings, and in a good analysis the patient will find a way to experience them, then to work on them, and eventually to work them through to some degree.

And finally, though the emergence of such phenomena is central and significant, I do not find that it shifts the whole nature of the work – say, to a more self psychological model (Goldberg, 1978). In the three patients I have described, as well as in others with similar phenomena in the analysis, the treatments were many-sided, complex, with different foci at different times, but with the here-reported phenomena of special note for this paper.

I would also like to raise a few questions about these clinical phenomena at a more theoretical level. The patients I have described retain a sense of acute pain in relation to something they experience as a fault or deficiency in their relationships, ordinarily to their parents. Because the pain is so acutely felt when something in the analysis touches it in the wrong way, I think of it as a 'raw wound'. Why is history carried this way in some patients? Let us say, as an example, that a parent regularly views a child with disdain. *Why is it that one person will internalize the object relationship and re-enact it with others, treating the others with disdain, or, alternatively, will actively evoke disdain from others, while some (parallel to the patients reported here) will carry the painful sense of disdain as a raw wound, a wound that can be painfully exacerbated at a wrong touch?* One speculation is that it takes a certain degree of formation and differentiation of a self to internalize and then repeat an early relationship, and lacking that, the experience is carried as a subjective sense of wound. This suggestion points to different degrees of psychological activity. Thus, the internalization and enactment of old object relationships ordinarily involve some cognitive restructuring of the experience, some inner processing, and a turn from passivity to activity. Not so the direct continuance of the sense of injury and vulnerability. This is not to say that such experiences do not undergo alteration and secondary elaboration over time. They do get endowed with 'meaning' – they are 'explained' via fantasy and idiosyncratic connection – but the sense of being a victim of experiences at the hands of the primary caretakers and, later, others, retains affective centrality and power.

I suggest a link of such phenomena to psychic mechanisms with which we are very familiar – and the mechanism is trauma or, more particularly, strain trauma (Kris, 1956). For the experienced impact of the parental failure (by not doing or wrongly doing, as the case may be) leaves the child with an inner experience of aloneness, or invadedness, or cast-asideness, or worthlessness that is beyond what can be mastered. (Though attempts at mastery through participation, as in Mr A's self-obliteration and Mr C's automaton behaviour, may appear.) My emphasis is on strain trauma (rather than shock trauma – Kris, 1956), of course, because the assumption is that these situations reflect ongoing patterns of caretaker-child interaction. I assume that single instances of such relatedness are not likely to have sufficient shock power to create trauma but that the additive effect (over years of childhood development) of repetitive forms of humiliating or under-acknowledging or controlling or invading relatedness adds up to an intensity of experience that is not mastered – hence, the continuation of the 'raw wound' state.

Given this description, I find no problem in seeing such phenomena as 'subjective states of self' and as *primary units of mental life*, in Kernberg's (1976) sense. An experience of self and object linked by some affect is laid down in memory in some form as a 'unit' that ever after operates intrapsychically, organizing the way experiences are understood and disorganizing the person when the repetition of the trauma gets to be too great. Given the patient's vulnerability in the analytic process because of his or her exposure and because of the inequality of the relationship, it is not surprising that there are experiences of the repetition of the childhood strain trauma – the moments of experienced failure in the analytic relationship I have described – moments that, optimally, become foci of the analytic work. That is, these subjective states are neither epiphenomenal nor secondary to something else but are directly recorded experiences that become organizers; and when the strain trauma has been great enough, they become organizers of a considerable segment of mental life. They then become foci for fantasy formation, self-definition, wish, defensive flight, and interpersonal vulnerability; in short, they enter into the sphere of conflict. As Sandler (1981) has suggested, just as the child has primary needs for safety and care beyond the domain of sexuality, so too there are primary needs for recognition, confirmation, and respect for boundaries – which, when provided, go almost unnoticed but which, when violated, become highly visible in psychic life.

In conclusion, I have described a group of patients, different in multiple ways from one another, who nonetheless each show a specific vulnerability to incursions upon their autonomous self. In this area, while they can describe and understand the origins of the vulnerability, this understanding does not permit them to withstand even displaced and metaphoric 'repetitions' of the 'incursion' (i.e. in the transference). Altered behaviour of the analyst, in the instances described, was the chosen (and effective) path to working through. The phenomenon was looked at in terms of the insufficiency of symbolic representation (language) in achieving mastery, and the necessity for experiential correction alongside of it. While all of this can be viewed simply as an exercise in analytic tact, that view covers over the opportunity to formulate a significant psychological phenomenon.

References

Goldberg, A. (1978). *The Psychology of the Self: A Casebook*. New York: International Universities Press.

Kernberg, O. (1976). *Object Relations Theory and Clinical Psychoanalysis*. New York: Aronson.

Kohut, H. (1984). *How Does Analysis Cure?* Chicago: University of Chicago Press.

Kris, E. (1956). The recovery of childhood memories in psychoanalysis. *Psychoanalytic Study of the Child* , *11*: 54–88.

Sandler, J. (1981). Unconscious wishes and human relationships. *Contemporary Psychoanalysis, 17*: 180–196.

CHAPTER EIGHT

Reflections on listening to and speaking with the patient during analysis

Ana-Maria Rizzuto

Introduction

To honour Jacqueline Amati Mehler's contributions to psychoanalyis, I wish to share my reflections about listening to and speaking with my patients.

The complexities of being a patient and an analyst

For my patients, I am the analyst they have chosen under the urgency of psychic suffering and the conflicted hope of finding alleviation of pain and meaning for confusing symptoms, derailed intentions or an unfulfilled life. The analysand's acceptance of starting analysis with me has multiple sources. At the conscious level, the analysand relies on the appraisal of my aptness to help and on the recommendations of whoever provided the contact with me. At the dynamic level, unconscious transferences related to remembered and forgotten objects of the past are already at work, while overt and repressed wishes for understanding, communication, love, and erotic satisfaction compete with fears of rejection, humiliation, and failure. The conjunction of conscious and unconscious hopes, wishes, and fears prompt the analysand to arrive at the first analytic hour with trembling expectations about what will happen between us.

I, in turn, have evaluated the patient's strengths and pathology and have reached the conclusion that such person, regardless of predicted difficulties, can benefit from analysis. To arrive at my decision, I have created, consciously and unconsciously, a working model (Greenson, 1960) of the patient's character structure, developmental problems, and probable course of the analysis. Such evaluation includes impressions about the analysand's primary objects, conflicts, dominant defences, and developmental vicissitudes and their impact on the patient's life. I am aware that there are already in me some transferential links to the analysand as well as to some of the patient's internal objects (Racker,1957), and people in his/her life as well as to people in my life.

We both accept the analytic setting and agree about our respective commitments. The patient is to say what comes to mind as freely as possible. I am to listen to what he or she is saying *to me* to assist my analysand to find *personal meaning* in his/her words and affective experiences. The analysand will comply or rebel against saying what comes to mind while at the same time s/he will be making hesitant attempts to communicate emerging desires and needs *to me*, even if they appear wrapped in a defended form. As Brenner (1999) suggests the patient's words represent unavoidable compromise formations between conflicting and competing motives. Such are the words that the patient directs to us. Yet, the words unconsciously organized by the analysand as a compromise formation never fail to address the person of the analyst in the *hope* (Rizzuto, 2004) of achieving meaningful emotional contact and of communicating, even if in an obscure and defended manner, what the patient needs the analyst to know. The patient's words always carry with them *an emotional petition* to be heard as the person who says them. How do we manage to listen to such complex words and hear the analysand *in* them? We know from Corradi Fiumara (1990) that 'an individual can speak only if he is listened to' (pp. 1–2). The continuation of the analysis and its later termination depends on the patient experiencing that we do listen.

I believe that the completion of a successful analysis enables the patient to listen to his/her inner reality and to be capable of clarifying personal meanings by self-analysis. In this respect, even from the beginning, I strive to help the patient to listen to expressed and secret feelings, experiences, desires, words, and actions to recognize them and him/herself in them until they become personally meaningful. I *hope* that the deep emotional engagement (Rizzuto) resulting from our verbalized and enacted involvement and explorations would help my analysand revisit in *our* present the loved and hated objects of the past, the conflicts with them, and the critical moments of self-development that have contributed to his/her being a particular object for others in the present, including the analysand as an object for him/herself. I *wish* that at the time of termination the patient would have been able to be self-accepting and capable of taking charge of the psychic transformative process that unavoidable life changes require of all of us.

The question now is how to do it. How do I, how do we listen? How do we speak to achieve our aims? The complexity of the task exceeds neat descriptions. In talking about it, we can only take a segment at the time: transference, countertransference, resistance, defences, empathy, free floating attention, free association, and so on. Nonetheless, when we sit on the analytic chair, listening and ready to talk when necessary, all these things, each one of them so complex, are present simultaneously from the beginning. The patient is for us a composite of himself and our model of him plus our countertransferences. The analyst is herself plus all the appraisals, transferences, and models of her that the patient bestows upon her person. So, who is speaking to and with whom when we listen and talk in analysis? How do we manage to listen and hear a patient that comes wrapped in so many layers of psychic clothing from transferences to desires? How do we manage to speak as analysts when we too see the patient under the filter of our working models and transferences?

Waugh (1976), cites Roman Jakobson, the linguist, as saying 'we speak to be heard and need to be heard in order to be understood' and concludes with him that 'the whole structure of language is built on this evident fact' (p. 26). The 'evident fact'of human spoken language becomes remarkably complex in analysis. Who listens when the analyst listens? And to whom does he listen? On the other side of the dialogue: Who speaks when the patient speaks and to whom does s/he speak? What are the patient's conscious and unconscious intentions when speaking to the analyst? And what are the analyst's conscious and unconscious intentions when talking to the analysand?

Psychoanalytic literature on listening

The psychoanalytic literature on listening frequently focuses on the *content* of the processes the analyst listens for and to: the form of transference (Freud, Gill, Kohut), specific defences (Gray, Bush), unconscious derivatives (Freud, Arlow), subjective experience (Schwaber), words and language of the patient's verbalizations (Makari and Shapiro) to name only a few. Other works refer to the mode of listening: free floating attention (Freud), empathically (Ornsteins), through reverie (Bion, Ogden), intersubjectively (Stolorow & Atwood), interpersonally (Levenson), under the light of social constructivism (Hoffman), and other variations. Few say explicitly that the analyst listens *to the patient*, the whole patient, in all his/her complexities, dynamic processes, fantasies, wishes, feelings, words, intentions, etc. I believe that we need a theoretical and technical approach of listening *to the analysand as a single and unique person* to give a foundation to the contents and modes of listening listed above. Such approach focuses on the way the analyst listens to the whole patient *in* the patient's productions as well as in the manner the analyst addresses the patient as *his/her* interlocutor in analytic exchanges.

Listening to the analysand as a unified being, a single functioning mind, leads to the recent debate about the mind as a self or as a conglomerate of selves. Mitchel (1993) discusses singular and multiple selves and concludes that the concept of multiple selves facilitates understanding the different ways in which people know themselves and create different versions of themselves according to the relationships they are involved in, what he calls a multiplicity of selves-in-relation. Lachmann (1996) favours the notion of a single self: 'When the self is thought of as an *overarching hypothetical construct*, an independent center for initiating, organizing, and integrating experience and motivation, it provides an umbrella that covers the interplay, the cooperation and competition among the patient's motivational systems. . . . Multiple selves then become a question of specifying the relevant motivational systems in competition and cooperation' (p. 611, my italics). There is a conceptual difficulty in describing a *hypothetical construct*, that is, a concept, as a centre for actual *initiative* on the patient's part. Meissner (1993) understands the self as

> a supraordinate and *structural* construct with the tripartite entities as component substructural systems . . . the self-system is equivalent to the total person, including and expressing the total human personality. In this sense, the self includes but is not equivalent to the subjective self; it is synonymous with the self-as-agent. The self-system in this sense is not synonymous with the self-representation since representational entities cannot serve as sources of operations or agency. In the psychoanalytic process, *the self-as-agent is the responsible actor* in the engagement in the therapeutic alliance and in the function of self-analysis. (p. 459, my italics)

I favour the notion of a single *structural* self conceived as the total person, as the agent of all actions initiated by the individual, be they conscious, preconscious, or conscious. My clinical experience with all patients, but in particular with psychotic and borderline patients, has convinced me that even the most disturbed individuals have a notion that they are a single person. Today, multiple personality disorder is understood as the result of profound dissociative processes (Klufi,1992) resulting from unbearable trauma. The conclusion follows that I favour listening to the total person *in* any partial manifestation s/he brings to the analyst. By partial manifestation, I mean any of the elements that configure the analytic process be it transference, defence, dream, fantasy, words, gestures, and so on. It is the person, as the unconscious and conscious agent of any of those manifestations that needs to be heard and understood by the listening analyst. The patient talks to me as the total actual and historical person s/he is and who *hopes* that I, the analyst, will listen and respond not as a psychoanalytic technician but as a flesh and blood being capable of becoming engaged with the words and feelings addressed to me. I must practice neutrality (Hoffer,1985) to achieve a balanced listening to the patient in all communications. My neutrality, however, also implies that my affective disposition remains in finely attuned empathic contact (Buie,1981) with the analysand's desires and fears. Who is the listening analyst? The analyst is a person, an agent self, who has committed his/her professional life to analytic work. The psychic and personal life of the analyst is broader than the analytic commitment. The capacity to carry out an analysis is a learned ability obtained after a rigorous training and persistent disciplined participation in the treatment of patients under supervision. Analytic education has many levels: theoretical, technical, and, most specifically, the progressive exercise of learning how to use oneself and one's perceptive competence, from conceptual and affective to verbal and gestural to grasp the communications from the analysand and, also, the analyst's internal responses to them. The analyst, however, has only his/her own self to perceive, register, understand, and give meaning to what the analysand is saying and doing during the hour. It is inevitable that the already present evaluation of the patient's pathology and predicaments organized as a 'working model' of the patient and the analyst's own preferences and conflicts will act as partial filters to capture the patient's communications and their motivational sources. Yet, the listening and speaking analyst *must* use his own self to listen. There is no other tool available to him/her. We hear the patient only in the way each of us, with our peculiar dispositions, can hear that particular analysand. It is never perfect hearing but it is very frequently good enough for the patient to feel listened to, particularly when the patient realizes that we, the person we are, do *intend* to listen to the analysand in the best way we can. What, then, could make the difference in our listening, that would permit the patient to feel heard, understood, and be able to continue the frequently painful transformative exploration of his/her own psychic life? Furthermore, what could make such a difference when our multiple theoretical and technical approaches and modes of listening or attending to associative contents seem to be doing things so differently, and, yet, patients of analysts of different convictions seem to feel understood and do improve? What common denominators may bring about somewhat similar results from such divergent array of analytic stances?

I have pondered over this question for a long time not only as a theoretical issue but also as a way of understanding my own psychoanalytic listening and the words that I address to the analysand in my efforts to advance the analytic process and the patient's improvement. I have come to the conclusion that the analyst's *affectively committed disposition and dedicated intention* to hear and understand a person deemed *unique* and the mode in which we listen and speak to the analysand as *an autonomous adult self* hold the key to articulate a response about such common denominators.

The analytic interlocutors

A disposition implies customary moods and attitudes towards others and the way of acting with them. The analyst's disposition to being and talking with the patient is highly original and similar to the transference love it may elicit, it 'is one for which there is no model in real life' (Freud, 1915, p. 166). The analyst's mode of listening, talking, relating, and engaging the patient in the analytic process has only partial antecedents in other relationships, including those that give rise to positive transferences. The patient has never before encountered a person with the disposition to commit all his or her capacities to listen and to dialogue in order *exclusively* to attend to every aspect of the analysand's experiences, inner workings, sufferings, and joys. The offering is so astonishing that, unwittingly, the patient imposes upon the analyst transferences from objects of the past in the effort to find antecedents for the analyst as a new listening and dialogical object. In fact, we can say that when the analysand begins to *believe* (Rizzuto, 2002) that the analyst has no other agenda than the *intention* to listen and to understand him/her as a person, we have an indicator that the analytic process is well in its way to achieve the level of dialogue indispensable for psychic transformation. I am talking about the type of object relation that I consider I must establish to sustain my analytic mode of listening: a profound investment in truly hearing the patient as a full adult object involved with me in analysis.

What is so peculiar about our invested listening? My answer is: everything. The setting and our behaviour within it promises and delivers safety, unswerving respect, careful attentiveness, absolute privacy, and the physical and psychical space for the analysand to bring to us his/her every thought, feeling, fantasy, desire, threat, and shameful or loving or hateful feeling. We open a field for seriously playing with every aspect of psychic and shared realities or, in Freud's (1914) words:

> We admit it [the compulsion to repeat] into the transference as a playground in which it is allowed to expand in almost complete freedom and in which it is expected to display to us everything in the way of pathogenic instincts that is hidden in the patient's mind. (p. 154)

Today 'everything' goes beyond 'pathogenic instincts' to encompass developmental events, subjective modes of experiencing, varieties of object relatedness, self-perceptions, intra-analytic events between the analytic pair, convictions, unconscious fantasies, as well as anything that has the patient entrapped. The possibility for each of them 'expanding in complete freedom' is what makes the analytic relation so astonishing. No ordinary human being can offer this freedom in a relationship without succumbing to necessary defenses as an affective shield against the painful inability to recognize oneself as a transferentially disagreeable interlocutor and against the affective discordance in the transferential persona imposed by the analysand upon the analyst. Neither can an ordinary person tolerate the fluctuating or contradictory moods and facets of him/herself that the analysand brings to successive hours or even a single hour. The analytic training, in particular the personal analysis, has prepared the analyst to enter into the analytic playground in which every aspect of the patient can and is invited to display its healthy and pathogenic components. The verbal, affective, enacted, and gestural manifestation of the patient become the very core of the analytic process. The analyst attends to them as expressions of the analysand's psychic reality, experiences, motivations, and preconscious and conscious intentions in the context of the relationship the patient is attempting to establish or avoid with her/him. The analyst goal is to find in any of them *the patient as the agent self* who is experiencing, speaking and relating, revealing and hiding, hoping and fearing during the hours they spend together. This agent self is the same adult person who has requested analysis and to whom the analyst, as a professional who is also an adult, has made a full therapeutic commitment.

In my way of working, it is the patient as an adult who becomes my essential interlocutor. I invite that adult to explore and to be attentive to what is happening in his/her mind, to capture the experience of the analytic moment, to discern feelings and reactions, to try to name them, to assist me to understand the total person who is addressing me. The adult I talk with is not only the visibly grown-up person on the couch but the psychic being who, I assume, is capable of functioning as an adult should, regardless of even blatant regressive pathology. What defines an adult person is the capacity for autonomy (Gullestad, 1992) in relation to issues of initiative and self-regulation as well as for responsible ownership of feelings, thoughts, actions, and the establishing of affective and interactionally meaningful relationships with others and with the realities of life. Obviously, people who request analysis have failed in some of these areas and cannot manage significant aspects of their actual life. Nor can they control their acting out or acting in during the analysis. They cannot accept their own feelings and intentions or own their fantasies and wishes. This phenomenon points to one of the core paradoxes of analytic work as I understand it. The patient has failed to master critical developmental tasks or to resolve intrapsychic and interpersonal conflicts that do not permit him/her to fully live a desired adult life. Yet, as analysts, we *assume from the start of treatment* that the patient is capable of taking up those adult responsibilities in working with us. It would be immoral to undertake the treatment of analytic patients if we did not *believe* that at a certain level, even unknown to them, they are capable of becoming our adult partner and collaborator in the analytic exploration. In other words, at the level of participation in the analytic dialogue, the analysand is offered the *symmetry of equal participation* that is necessary for the establishment of genuine communication between interlocutors. It may take the patient a long time to accept and achieve such symmetry even when it is offered to him/her from the start. The dialogical symmetry does not alter the fact that patient and analyst do not have symmetrical *functions* in their joint enterprise. It means that from the point of view of communication with one another, each partner is asked to *assume full psychic responsibility* for each word, gesture, or communication addressed to the other. In analysis the rules of relatedness to the total person of the analysand require that every expression can be explored and examined until it reveals its source, motivation, and desire, leaving nothing hidden, nothing as a private secret. Here, the asymmetry between the partners becomes obvious. The analysand is enjoined to give words to even the most private of thoughts, feelings, and fantasies. The analyst, in turn, attends to them and to similar manifestations in his/her own mind in order to find clues to make sense of the patient's communications at a particular dynamic and relational analytic moment so as to understand the patient experience and its unconscious sources *revealed in* those expressions. Then, the analyst has to ascertain the 'point of urgency' (Baranger, 1993) that needs immediate attention in the patient's communication to the analyst. Such points of urgency are progressive landmarks that unveil unconscious motivations emerging in the analytic dialogue. The analyst tries to understand the simultaneous dynamic, dialogical, and transferential affective components of that particular analytic moment and communicates to the patient what she/he is in the process of comprehending about the patient's experience. Frequently, the analyst's words bring to the analysand the relief of having accessed with another person aspects of him/herself that have been to this point either incomprehensible or shame producing. This is the type of intervention that best illustrates the analyst addressing the analysand as an adult that s/he has invested as a constant object, a person who can hear now what yesterday would have caused a symptomatic reaction.

Other conditions are necessary because patients are frequently regressed, convinced that we do not care about them, invested in remaining a victim, or find themselves highly suspicious of our competence or even good will. Once more, we must remember Corradi Fiumara's (1990) assertion that 'an individual can speak only if he is listened to' (pp. 1–2). Addressing the adult does not mean neglecting the regressed experience of the patient or the defensive manoeuvres in the analysand's efforts to avoid repetition of trauma and psychic pain. The stance of addressing the *constantly invested adult* does not preclude the use of all of our analytic techniques and efforts to address *simultaneously* the adult and the suffering child still alive in the patient's experience with us. That child must also be addressed with our tone of voice (Rizzuto, 2002), the content of what we say, and our affective efforts to be in touch with the patient's still felt infantile hurts. This is the great beauty of analytic work, to be able to have in a synchronic moment the diachrony of different instances of a lived life unified now in the dialogue between the analysand and ourselves. Such exquisite attentiveness cannot be achieved in circumstances other than analysis.

Progressively, after many moments of shared understanding, an analytic 'we' emerges between the participants (Gullestad, 1992) signalling that understanding the patient's reality is a shared enterprise. The 'we' of the therapeutic relationship, however, is not a copy of the caretaker's mirroring relationship. The analyst participation in the 'we' represents a a second-order confirmation, of the jointly articulated subjective reality of the patient which faciliates 'internalization of relational experiences promoting autonomous self-representation' (Gullestad, 1992 p. 129). Schafer (1983) describes the result of such work for the patient as 'experiencing the past in an articulated fashion for the first time' (p. 132). Gullestad moves a step further, proposing a modified theoretical model of human motivation by suggesting that

> being part of an emotional dialogue is in itself a motive. An extended vision of the individual emerges: Man is not only pleasure seeking. He has a need to communicate his feelings, to share them with others. (p. 125)

The analyst's object constancy

I have described analysis as two adults on equal dialogical footing committed to the task of making sense of the patient. The earlier question remains: What then could make the difference in our listening, that would permit the patient to feel heard, understood, and be able to continue the frequently painful transformative exploration of his/her own psychic life? My answer is twofold: firstly we treat the patient as an adult; secondly, we accept and even facilitate the regressive re-experiencing and working through with us of painful and traumatic events and inner processes.

The analyst's unswerving commitment to grant the patient the full status of a responsible adult in meaningful dialogue, regardless of the patient's regressed frame of mind, protests, devaluations, hatred, insults, even disregard for his/her words and good efforts progressively permits the patient to perceive and acknowledge that s/he is been given an *emotional object constancy and investment* unknown to him/her up to that point. The analyst has constituted him as an object/patient and commits every effort not only to make contact and establish a dialogue with the analysand but, most importantly, the analyst would not allow the patient's defensive manoeuvres to alter his/her commitment to hold the analysand as a constant valuable and responsible object that deserves the full attention and the investment of the analyst. I believe that the analyst's *emotional object constancy and investment* of the patient as an adult partner is the condition that makes analysis possible and that accounts for its efficacy.

The analysand's experiences of the analyst as a respectful and consistent object who *expects* the patient to be capable of making sense of his/her mind's processes, including unconscious processes, lead the analysand to the progressive discovery that regardless of his/her enactments, protestations, rebellions, accusations, refusal to join in the effort, the analyst remains *faithful* to the analysand as a valuable object that deserves analytic help and is capable of using it. In brief, the analysand discovers that, short of leaving the treatment, there is nothing to be done to alter the analyst investment in him/her as a valuable person that is deemed capable of mastering his/her psychic house.

In my opinion, this *emotional object constancy* creates the *conditions* for the exploration of all levels of psychic organization, from extremely regressed states to the sophisticated high level defences, frequently on the edge of consciousness of the neurotic. The concept of the analyst's *emotional object constancy* goes beyond the therapeutic alliance. The latter relies on the concious ego capacities and commitments between patient and analyst. The former refers to *an affective disposition* of the analyst who genuinely *believes* and *expects* that, with help, the analysand will be able to use his/her adult capacity for self-observation and enter a self-transformative process. The patient's conscious commitment to do analytic work is part of the treatment agreement. Once that agreement has been reached the analyst holds the patient in his/her own mind as capable of joining in and emotionally invests the analysand as a partner who *is expected* to do the analytic work.

The analyst's expectation is not a complete novelty for the patient. Jerome Bruner (1983) proposes that during the developmental stages, the parents offer the child what he described as the Language Acquisition Support System (LASS) to spur the youngster on to access the language appropriate for each developmental level. Parents invite their offspring to talk efficiently according to the child's age and continuously insist on new linguistic refinements which they frequently support with their 'speech lessons'. The parental pleasure at the child's mastery of speech conveys the message that the parents enjoy their youngster's progressive capacity for self-expression and language mastery. This attitude on the progenitors' part fosters separation from the object and facilitates the child's appropriation of the personal meaning of words. Frequently, the offspring internalizes the spurring parental words not only to comply with parental insistence on acting in accordance with the child's age but also as injunctions of the youngster's own guiding, loving and also restricting superego (Edgcumbe, 1981). The analyst's expectation that the analysand will move to new understandings as an adult partner also becomes internalized as aspects of the ego and superego. When affective insight and the feeling of having been understood emerge silently or overtly as part of the analytic process, patient and analyst share a frequently subdued but profound dialogical and personal pleasure, which can become part of the patient's guiding and loving superego.

I want to return now to the exploration of traumatic or very painful affective experiences that very frequently bring the analysand to regressive enactments, entrenched resistances, persistent defensive manoeuvres, and, at times, discouragement or even despair about the possibility of alleviation of pain. These are the analytic moments or prolonged periods of analytic work that require the most exquisite attention and affective communication on the analyst's part. The patient is emotionally taken up by the repetition in the context of the transference of previously repressed wishes, complaints, accusations or the reliving of dreadful moments of childhood terrors and sufferings. We do not want to shorten the displays of suffering or the accusations against our inability to understand it because we want to grasp even the subtlest of details that have contributed to the patient's persistent experience of the past pain in the present. We want to understand the complexity of the humiliation, the fear, the guilt, the desire or hope that act as the emotional pivot in the architecture of unrelieved pain or symptoms. I have published the case of Mr B (Rizzuto, 1991) whose intense fear of being criticized and shamed interfered with his ability to hear the analyst's words. He described his experience:

> I feel hurt that I said something . . . I made an effort . . . I have a sense of shame . . . of humiliation. A bad child: I can't transgress boundaries; I am ashamed of myself. I am frightened of superiors, older people, family members . . . I can't compete with you. I have to submit. I am overpowered and embarrassed. I feel defeated in relation to you. I have a sulking feeling of a bad, hurt boy. (p. 306)

I described in presenting the case how:

> These most painful analytic moments were followed by many hours in which Mr B had vengeful fantasies of overpowering the woman analyst, moving into her house, and bossing her around. He wanted her to feel the pain and humiliation of having to submit to his imperious orders. At the high point of his vengeful imaginary acts he would demand that she throw herself on the floor and he would make her his sexual toy: he would penetrate her anally, like 'a bitch', humiliating her as much as he felt humiliated. The revengeful fantasies reveal the obverse of meaningful communication: he matched affect prompted by the perceived rejection of him with his perception of the analyst's feelings of being humiliated by him; the complementary response followed talion law, a devaluation for a devaluation (p. 307).

The intensely felt fantasized enactments did not make much room for dialoguing with the adult man he was. During those moments, the furious and humiliated child, enraged at his complete impotence to make himself noticed in the way he wanted, needed all my respectful empathic listening to jointly understand that his childhood suffering and impotence had been real. I had to be there with him in his rage and acknowledge with him that his wishes for revenge offer some victory while gently guiding him, the child and the adult, to the recognition that his triumph was a Pyrrhic victory. He still felt like a dirty child incapable of recognizing himself as a true man. He was addicted to masturbating while fantasizing about having sex with the perfect woman. His reasoning had the following logic: 'Only the perfect woman could make him feel like a man. That her making love to him would confirm that he was a man' (p. 307). His core problem consisted in his active Oedipal wish to have his mother recognize him as a man when he was a child. He had been unable to accept that she had been a child for her, her child. At the time when termination was nearing in the fifth year of analysis he described his experience during the treatment and in life:

> 'For a long time I was embarrassed communicating with you . . . I did not want to come and be a little boy in your eyes . . . There is a real problem in being freer. I am so scared of being seen as

> a little boy that I have to come across as superman, the unapproachable person . . . My need as a child to create this impenetrable attitude . . . The defensive superman feeling: I want to have the perfect woman whose perfection reflects on me. It confirms that I am what I want to be. I call that image of myself a defence against the image of the defenceless little boy . . . In growing up I had intercourse with my fantasy and put a wall around me. The little boy must feel very threatened to need to put on the costume'. . . . Mr B could now give up the key element of the early childhood fantasy, the disavowal that he was a child. The acceptance of having been a child allowed him for the first time to feel like a man with the analyst and with his girl-friend. (p. 309)

How did we achieve such transformation from the suffering little boy who denied being one to the adult analysand who could accept having been a child and even still feeling like one in his regressed moments? It was no easy task because his fragile narcissistic equilibrium required extreme care not to add the slightest hint in words or tone of voice, in my manner of relating to him or in phrasing comments that I did not respect him fully even at his most regressed infantile revengeful moments when he was intent on making me feel thoroughly humiliated.

My technique consisted in attending *simultaneously* to the obviously enraged and impotent child and to the present-day man who could not feel like an adult. First, I helped him to describe in great detail his infantile feelings and devoted my attention to making sure I was understanding him as the ashamed child he had been. I also attended to every detail of his profound narcissistic rage as well as to the compensatory pleasure in his revengeful fantasies. My tone of voice frequently addressed that suffering child who had lived until now in the secret recesses of his mind, inviting him to share his misery with me. Then, whenever he seem to me to feel that I was with him in his pain, I talked with adult words to the adult patient who was capable of observing himself and of listening to my observations about him. I gently invited him to ponder about the sources of his fear of being humiliated by me. After a prolonged time of my alternating between deep empathy with the child and my inviting him to attend to his inner processes, *he* began to question whether his fear of humiliation and his need to put me down could not be a defensive manoeuvre to avoid doubts about himself in my presence. We noticed a change in him. For the first time in his life he became able to observe himself in a manner that had not been possible before. He had experienced during many analytic hours that neither doing the right or the wrong thing had modified my investment in helping him, my adult patient. He noticed that my asking him to attend to himself did not imply that I saw him as he saw himself: an impotent little boy who did not know how to be a man. The fear of being humiliated as a pathetic boy had given way to the *conviction* that I not only respected him, even if he felt like an irrelevant child, but also that throughout our conversations I had always addressed him as the man he actually was, competent and capable of joining me in doing the analytic work. At this point, he asked me explicitly to 'focus' on him because he was no longer afraid that I would see only the pathetic child he considered himself to be. He wanted more objectivity about himself because he could now feel that I could see in him more than he could see: the child and the man as a single unity. Then, he asked me to help him look at himself without having to despise himself. Such a request signalled the obvious diminution of his dread of being criticized and the fear of being overcome by shame. We had arrived together at the point of his developmental fixation when he could not tolerate being the child he was and we had help him overcome it. He could now empathize with the child he had been because he had began to feel like a real man with me.

Presenting the case of Mr B in a neat narrative is an over-simplification. The work demanded of me an extraordinary perceptual subtlety and a constant effort to keep the balance between empathizing with the child while keeping in touch with the adult. When he arrived for analysis, his shame about feeling only like a pathetic child did not permit him to muster the necessary respect to listen to himself in a dispassionate manner. He could only belittle himself, feel ashamed about his boyish condition or wish to inflict on others the constant humiliation he felt. My persistent stance of respectfully listening to the despised child while simultaneously conveying to him that he was in fact an adult who could join forces with me, convinced him that he could listen and examine himself in a respectful manner. The change indicated the internalization of my empathic stance towards the man and the child he was. Soon, the man who was my patient became able to empathize with the child he had been. He was now well on the way to achieving *the symmetry of equal dialogical participation* with me as my *adult* analytic partner who wanted to know himself and his inner reality. The continuation of our joint efforts in exploring his infantile predicaments brought us to reconstruct his persisting unconscious childhood fantasy and to its transformation into attainable adult desires. The analysis came to a satisfactory termination. He felt like a man, was able to marry his girlfriend, and became capable of using self-analysis to modulate the moments when the ashamed boy of the past wanted to claim its right to feel hurt and humiliated. Mr B had internalized as *self constancy* for the adult he was my investment in him as my adult analytic patient. We parted as two adults who had completed the task we had set out to do.

Not all analyses have such a happy end. Nonetheless, I remain convinced that our investment in the adult patient as the object we count on to do the work is an essential *condition* to be able to analyse.

In concluding, I want to insist upon the significance of the words I have italicized in the text: affective disposition, hope, belief, conviction, wish, expectation, and faithfulness. These are profound relational words that describe how the progression of a human relationship (Rizzuto, 2002), analytic or any other, depends upon what we want others to be or do and what we believe they are or want to be in relation to us. What we do in analysis includes a large measure of believing in certain types of psychic events that are not demonstrable, even when they are real. Such is the case in analysis when the patient reaches the critical *conviction* that we *want* to help him/her and becomes freer than before to join in the psychoanalytic exploration.

CHAPTER NINE

The past unconscious and the present unconscious

Anne-Marie Sandler

It is a great pleasure for me to have been invited to add a few thoughts to this wonderful book written to honour Jacqueline Amati Mehler and to acknowledge her many important psychoanalytic contributions.

Most of the chapters contained in this book describe new insights or reflections, which help us to widen our understanding of the workings of the mind and offer us better ways of listening and interpreting analytic material. It is in this vein that I would like to describe the concepts of the past unconscious and the present unconscious, concepts that my late husband and I have used as a helpful technical frame of reference in our work with patients.

In Freud's topographical model, a classical distinction is made between unconscious, preconscious, and conscious. We have often pointed out that to speak of the patient's unconscious when referring to all the processes that occur outside conscious awareness is misleading. It is true that both the preconscious and the unconscious systems of the topographical model share the quality of being descriptively speaking unconscious, yet we are all aware of the distinction which exists between the system Ucs and the broader descriptive notion of the term unconscious, which encompasses both the system Ucs (the dynamic Ucs) and the Pcs. By speaking loosely of 'the unconscious' we create a situation in which the preconscious is lumped together with the dynamic unconscious without regard to the fact that they are governed by very different rules and radically different functions and operating characteristics. This has been a source of great confusion in the literature, particularly in regard to the definition of 'unconscious phantasy'. Referring to unconscious phantasy without qualification does not indicate whether we are considering a current phantasy in the preconscious or a phantasy of the young child, which has been repressed into the system unconscious.

By introducing the concept of the past and present unconscious, we hoped to redress this situation. The *past unconscious* is a clinically based hypothetical construct, regarded as crystallizing in the first few years of life. The *present unconscious* can be thought of as having a very different type of functional organization from the past unconscious and is in some ways similar to the system preconscious of Freud's topographical model or closely resembles the unconscious ego of the structural model.

The past unconscious is more complex than Freud's dynamic unconscious, which was conceived of as the reservoir of repressed memories that can be reinvested by sexual or aggressive drives which, as instinctual wishes, press forward for gratification. The past unconscious contains the whole gamut of immediate, peremptory wishes, impulses, and responses of the individual that have been formed early in his life. The content of the past unconscious is dominated by primitive forms of thinking and by the use of defence mechanisms characteristic of the early years of life.

As psychoanalysts, we all know that early experiences are of crucial importance, but in our view these early experiences can never be recalled. They have been organized according to what cognitive neuroscientists have called procedural or implicit memory systems. All we can ever retrieve from our first years of life are memories of procedures in which experiences are encoded as rules of functioning. The past unconscious is, therefore, conceptualized as essentially a memory of procedures, which represent a totally different type of organization from the later declarative or autobiographical memory system. The primitive rules of functioning of the past unconscious will shape the form of the unconscious phantasies, thoughts, wishes, and memories as these arise in the present unconscious, and we refer to them as basic dynamic templates. These could be considered as structuring organizations that form the basis for the immediate here-and-now unconscious strivings and responses of the older individual.

The dynamic templates stemming from the past unconscious give form to all the intrapsychic content that arises in the depth of the present unconscious, particularly unconscious wishes and wishful phantasies. They act spontaneously and blindly, without thought to current adaptation, and it is the task of the rest of the mental apparatus to deal with it.

In the course of his or her development, every child will have had multiple interactions with others and made important identifications with significant objects, and these interactions and identifications will have become internalized. The child's phantasy life will be profoundly affected by such structured internal object relationships, including those that have been viewed as interactions with the superego. Identification and introjections and relationships with such introjects and identificates constitute an important organizing vector of the past unconscious.

In the past unconscious, we can imagine sets of procedures reflecting, among other things, the modes of mental functioning of a specific child, having been moulded by its specific endowment and developmental history. It evolves in the young child who has progressed along biologically and socially determined lines of maturation, along 'normal' or 'deviant' developmental lines, whose unconscious wishes and phantasies were significantly modified in the process, both in terms of the type of mental processes that underpin these wishes and phantasies, and the content of their beliefs and wishes. The developmental changes impacting the past unconscious include steps in terms of separation-individuation, changes in narcissistic resources, anxiety and sublimations and characteristic solutions to conflicts.

The present unconscious is 'dynamic' in the classical sense in that whilst its contents may become conscious, they are not necessary freely accessible to consciousness. The present unconscious can be regarded as the area of the mind containing the current preoccupations and the unconscious wishful phantasies, which represent the present-day counterparts of, developments from, and derivative of, those infantile reactions, which we attribute to and locate in the past unconscious. The present unconscious is a mental experiential world, essentially made up of the ways in which experiences and object relations are organized in the present. It is attuned to reality, but working outside consciousness and is orientated not to the past, but to the present. It regards the impulses from the past unconscious as intrusive and upsetting and has, as a major function, the updating of them in order to make them 'fit' the present and avoid embarrassment and preserve safety and self-esteem.

As wishful impulses and phantasies arise in the present unconscious, they have to be dealt with by the person of the present, by the adult part of the person. One could say that whereas the past unconscious acts and reacts according to the past, the present unconscious is concerned with maintaining equilibrium in the present. The present unconscious is much more accessible to us, although not entirely so, and is the central domain of the analytic investigation and the direct source of transference manifestation.

In our model, unconscious phantasies do not arise in the depth of the past unconscious, but in the depth of the present unconscious. They will tend to arouse conflict and disturb the inner equilibrium of the individual and are mostly modified or repressed outside consciousness. The defence mechanisms used by the individual to regulate the content of the present unconscious serve to disguise these unconscious phantasies by means of manipulations of the self and the object representations involved in the phantasy. Part of the self-representation may be split off and displaced to the object representation and vice versa. The rules governing the interaction with others are of particular importance as such rules will become the blueprint of the unconscious relationships represented in the 'now' of the present unconscious.

It is important to clarify that we refer to 'unconscious phantasies' as a designation for internal processes, as they exist in the present unconscious. The unconscious phantasies of the present unconscious have a constant here-and-now adapting function and they differ markedly from the past unconscious, which is infantile, peremptory, dynamic, and potentially disruptive to the present unconscious system. The past unconscious acts as a source of thematic distortion, amplifying the importance of particular ways of being, provoking specific unconscious expectations, feelings, and beliefs. Thus, central recurring themes will occur in the present unconscious, determined by specific powerful demands from the past unconscious.

Thus to summarize, it would be correct to state that a major part of the work of the present unconscious is to maintain inner equilibrium, to maintain feelings of safety and the integrity of the self by reorganizing the unconscious representations of the threatening phantasies through the use of a variety of defensive measures, essentially measures by which the unconscious content of the present unconscious is transformed. This unconscious content, however motivated, arises in the individual as if he or she were a particular young child. This unconscious content is not conceived of as arising in the past unconscious, which is viewed as acting as dynamic templates. The dynamic templates are sets of procedures or schemata reflecting the modes of mental functioning of the specific young child within each adult. The impulse, wish or memory that arises in the depths of the present unconscious is not, in this model, one that has passed in disguised form through a repression barrier between the unconscious and the preconscious. The censorship takes place within and throughout the present unconscious, with a final defensive transformation occurring before admission to conscious awareness. An unconscious wish arising in the depth of the present unconscious can be regarded as modelled on the template of the inner child's wishes, but the objects involved are objects of the present. It is important to remember that there is no direct access to the past unconscious. It consists of mental configurations that can never be 'recollected'.

In conclusion, I shall briefly describe the importance for our clinical work of the model of the past and the present unconscious. I shall attempt to highlight just one influence it has had on my work. I believe that the clear understanding of how the dynamic templates of the past unconscious, even though greatly transformed by the present unconscious, exert subtle pressures on the analyst is of immense clinical importance. These pressures are created through the unconscious attempts of the patients to actualize in the transference their wishful phantasies and their complex internal object relationships and expectations. These psychic structures create unconscious patterns of behaviour and need to be identified in the here-and-now of the sessions, mostly through the feelings aroused in the countertransference. I am aware that this focus on current unconscious material has created controversy. Many analysts asked how is it possible to understand patients without first acquiring a full knowledge of their past experiences. The model of the past and present unconscious aims at showing the need for the analyst to focus on the current unconscious communications between the patient and the analyst. If, thanks to the analyst's interpretations, the patient can accept the censored, warded off, wishful aspect of himself or herself, then we have the opportunity to anchor this new understanding by helping the patient to become aware of his current habitual patterns of functioning. We can then usefully attempt to reconstruct a link between these habitual patterns in the present and the patient's past experiences. However, on the basis of our model, we have become aware that we are only able to reconstruct the early past as best we can, as we are unable to really remember it.

I hope that, in this very condensed way, I have been able to illustrate why I believe in the importance of interpreting the here-and-now aspects of the material of my patients and why I think that work in the transference and countertransference is essential.

CHAPTER TEN

The mystery of the unsaid name: commonalities between God and Rumpelstiltskin

Theodore Shapiro

The subtitle of this essay may seem provocative insofar as I have juxtaposed God to an elfin benefactor in a Grimm fairy tale. Nonetheless, each text concerns cautions about naming. We are admonished not to utter the name of God in vain in the sacred text which contains the Ten Commandments. Furthermore, God is most frequently named indirectly as 'the Lord' or in a similar paranomic device, lest we be accused of sinning. Such prohibitions to the naming of God also exist in non-Judeo-Christian religions and cultures as well and with even harsher retaliatory consequences. Curiously, in Judaic practice, celebrants of the Lord have gone further in obeying the prohibition against saying God's name insofar as supplicants do not even utter 'the Lord' (Heb. Adonai) but rather 'the Name' (Heb. Hashem) when practising prayer or in discourse about benedictions. Thus, they are now twice removed from the proper name of God.

In addition, it is well known that among certain African, Amazonian, and other tribal peoples the use of proper names or taking photos by a stranger is prohibited for fear that the stranger will actually take control of the person by possessing the representational image that is produced or uttered. Thus, the signifier or name of mortals as well as gods is also infused with power.

The tale of Rumpelstiltskin includes some similarities to the prohibition described in naming God and the power of the representation. This fairy tale, gathered among others by the brothers Grimm during the early nineteenth century, presents a central elfin figure as the nightly visitor and benefactor to a maiden, married off to a king, who was told by her greedy father that she could spin straw into gold. Rumpelstiltskin, hearing her plaint, assists her in her chore for small rewards in the form of trinkets, such as a bracelet or ring, until he strikes a final bargain that her first-born child is to be given to him as a reward for his super-alchemical feats (turning a non-metal fibre into a precious metal). The forfeit for the bargain can only be broken if the young Queen guesses the nightly visitor's name. Thus, the designation, or naming, has the potential to break the secret bargain that up to now has empowered the Queen, but its final iteration will force her to give up her first born. In both instances, the sacred and profane, naming takes on magical power with consequences to the speaker.

There are many instances in our sacred texts and literature where similar references are made to the power of naming and its importance. It is certainly not by chance that one of the first tasks of newly created man in Genesis was to name the beasts of the field and the flora as well. The New Testament Gospel of John initiates with the phrase,' In the beginning was the word and the word was with God.' According to Jones (1914) the Annunciation, too, is an impregnation via audition. Odysseus' encounter with the Cyclops ends with the protagonist's response to his blinded victim that his tormenter was 'No Name'. These uniquely Western texts are matched across cultures by similar stories that employ empowerment by words as creative acts and gestural equivalents.

The magic words 'Abracadabra' (Aramaic for 'It will be done as I say') is but one example of an incantation that is filled with unexpected power for action, moving far beyond mere saying.

These historical and cultural examples have been incorporated into the modern study of language which reaches beyond the labelling power of words. Many modern linguists have declared the ascendancy of pragmatics over semantics and syntax as a means of deriving the core feature of signifying, and now they study how we 'do things with words'. Austin (1962), Searle (1969), and Lakoff (2003) have explicated the power of designating as *performatives* and *speech acts* in which the utterances have active consequential effects on the surround. Within such a system, naming God or Rumpelstiltskin represents more than a casual designation.

How can we understand these narrative gestures unless we address the significance of naming itself, both culturally and from the vantage of psychoanalysis? Or better, how can we use our psychoanalytic perspective to illuminate these disparate cultural phenomena? There is a long tradition from Freud onwards to extend our interpretations from the couch to culture. There are pitfalls in this venture but many scholars have utilized the psychoanalytic method to illuminate and enrich understanding of texts by using ample convergent data to support their conclusions. This proviso in place, I will proceed.

Within psychoanalysis, we examine the power of the word, designated both in classical Freudian linguistics and in more recent Lacanian designations such as 'Le Nom du Père' which stands for more than the name of the father. It designates a whole constellation of signifiers pertaining to power and the triadic Oedipal constellation. Freud's (1919) explication of the 'uncanny' brings home the idea that unconscious repressed derivatives are called up by a word that links experiences with repressed constellations. The sense of awe is linked to the 'uncanny' because it depends upon similar depth factors that are associated to the audible word. Indeed, the German word for uncanny is 'unheimlich' which is related both to the familiar, home, and secret, eliciting dual meanings. I, (Shapiro, 1976) and then others, have referred to the very act of interpretation as a naming event that illuminates the patient's thoughts and actions by representing what they do and what they say in a linguistic system that can be considered in consciousness. More recently, Fonagy and others (1998) suggest we pay attention to the 'mentalization' of unconscious constellations as a significant factor in our work as psychoanalysts.

A most general proposition in linguistic terms is that every utterance in words is an interpretation in so far as the choice of words binds the concept represented to a limited range of denotations and connotations within a code, i.e. it has a definition that excludes other dimensions of meaning. Psychoanalysts in practice listen carefully to usage as a clue to selective meanings. Similarly, psychoanalytic scholars attend carefully to texts for clues to better interpretations.

This brief review of the commonalities among linguistics and psychoanalysis and textual analysis suggests that we can approach the 'unnamed' from the vantage of the consequential power of 'uttering a name'. If we explore the power of giving something a name, we will then be able to contrast it with what we avoid when we prohibit naming. Two suggestive literary texts come to mind that exemplify this point. One is from Lewis Carroll's *Through the Looking Glass* in which Alice meets Humpty Dumpty, and the other derives from a play by Tom Stoppard , *The Invention of Love.*

When Alice encounters Humpty Dumpty he says:

> '. . . but tell me your name and your business.'
> My name is Alice, but . . .'
> 'It's a stupid name enough!' Humpty Dumpty interrupted impatiently. 'What does it mean?'
> 'Must a name mean something?' Alice asked doubtfully.
> 'Of course it must.' Humpty Dumpty said with a short laugh: 'My name means the shape I am – and a good handsome shape it is, too. With a name like Alice you might be any shape, almost.' (Carroll, 1960, pp. 263)

In the Stoppard play we encounter A.E. Hausman, the poet, in Hades meeting a friend who describes a group he belongs to where they have been defining the then gay community insofar as it could exist in England during the time of the restrictive Indecency Laws:

> Chamberlain: . . . We belong to a sort of secret society, The Order of Chaeronea, like the sacred bond of Thebes. Actually it's more like a discussion group. We discuss what we should call ourselves. 'Homosexuals' has been suggested.
> AEH: Homosexuals?
> Chamberlain: We aren't anything till there is a word for it.

These fragments provide us with examples of the significance of words in binding, not only the cognitive boundaries of thought, but also the affective features of the words we employ in language. Speech is the main vehicle of linguistic expression and the spoken word carries not only referential power, but as noted earlier, performative power. The link between references to God and Rumpelstiltskin will, I suggest, provide a means to grasp the depth meaning of the unnamed and the affects that accompany the prohibitions in naming. I will approach the matter of the unnamed from the converse side by studying naming and its role in culture. I will also make some further suggestions regarding the difference between negating and the 'unnamed'. Then I will examine the Grimm fairy tale as it may illuminate the prohibition of uttering the name of God. Let us begin with the linguistic texts that are relevant and proceed to the psychoanalytic contribution to our topic.

Linguistics and naming

The early twentieth century literature addressing naming and its fuller themes in the science of Semiotics was influenced by Ogden and Richards (1923) who showed clearly that names or words do not simply reference singular things and objects but refer to concepts or class categories. Taking a somewhat Platonic stance, they showed that words, except perhaps proper nouns, refer to ideas and concepts. Each word delimits the referential frame and segregates categories. Earlier in the century, Saussure (1911) wrote about signifier and signified to address the mental form of designating as a linguistic task. It took the later innovative work of Austin (1962) to initiate the more recent interest in the performative aspects of naming, i.e. their functional and pragmatic role in intentionality which Searle (1969) elaborated as speech acts. Words could never again be simple labels, but would from then on be seen as initiators or stimuli of intended action. Semantics expanded from the study of defining and designation to encompass rhetorical intent. The text could no longer be analysed and understood without knowing the context of its expression and perhaps the intent of the 'sayer'.

Wittgenstein's (1953) first foray into this realm also involved the idea that words took on significance only in sentences and therefore were contextually determined. While this early idea was later modified, others used the concept to advance the pragmatic effect of narratives. Lakoff's (1986) work in this area best explains the categorizing function of the mind. He sees this function as the central tool by which we master the idea of the world within naming categories honed in specific cultures. Names call up rather delimited and specified concepts that then are the stuff of the mind's 'filing system' within any culture.

Following an exhaustive review of the relevant literature on designating and categorizing (including some of the authors noted above), Lakoff suggests a number of features that must be included to afford a complete description of the categorizing function that establishes word boundaries. These include: family resemblance among a class of words, centrality, and gradients as we enlist more connotative extensions in use, metonymic reasoning, where the word itself stands in for a concept contiguous to the word, (e.g. Crown for King, White House for President). He also reminds us of generativity and polysemy, allowing for a dynamic extension of connotative significance of words to new meanings and usages.

He argues that the structure of thought is characterized by a limited number of cognitive models. Some categories are scalar with degrees of membership in a category while others are classical with rigid boundaries; some are metonymic, some are centrally organized emerging as spokes deriving from prototypes. He then notes that categories are not simply arbitrary as semanticists of the past suggested, but may be empirically derived from experience which includes bodily states and socially defined extensions of meaning, in accord with the models listed above. These latter notions should be particularly trenchant for psychoanalysts and will be addressed in the following sections.

He continues that concepts are not transcendental, i.e. that reason is not just the mechanical manipulation of abstract symbols. Nor do concepts merely provide internal representations of external reality. The mind is not simply a mirror of nature, but is limited by the needs of any language culture. These assertions are tested functionally by the following examples. Various cultures designate colours in accord with their needs even though the objectively measured wavelengths of colours can be detected independently of the designations. The perspectivism implied by these choices do not deprecate or trivialize the indexing systems of each culture. They merely suggest that designations are intimately limited by the specified requirements of each linguistic group and are linked to core experiences.

Among the simplest examples I can cite is the Levi-Strauss description of an Amazonian linguistic system where flora are simply divided between edible and not edible compared to our elaborate multinamed empirical Linnaean taxonomy and functional biological systems.

While linguistic systems are shared by needs of a culture, they can also be shaped within cultures to influence power distribution and the interest of sub-groups. In a recent book, Lakoff shows the powerful impact of words on politics. Slogans and word clusters (2003) influence our 'frames of reference' in construing the way we see things and as a result have powerful pragmatic effects. Thus, the defining features of a word prescribe limits to meaning but they also convey affective power in use. The name of God perforce must have pragmatic power as it is uttered or else it can become an empty icon chanted in ritual phrases.

These considerations direct us to the unnamed: If the 'named' is trapped by various dimensions or features within a category, it cannot be boundless in its signifying references and function. There is an injunction not to utter the name of the deity, because there is no name we can employ that does not have specified features that constrain it. A name limits our conception of God.

Nonetheless, some religions have seen fit to permit embodiments of God in various forms to make the deity palpable in human terms and accessible; as more than awe inspiring; as more than an ineffable boundless enigma that monotheism, in its purest form, requires. Parenthetically, the Old Testament does designate the name of God (Heb. Yahwe, Elohim) only to suggest later that when we see the tetragram signifying his name, we say instead, 'The Lord'. We also have the multiple incarnations in the Hindu religion, and we have the incarnation of Jesus in Christianity and the referential metaphor for God as father and 'all powerful'. These variations do not exclude the more mysterious and the 'not to be named' third element of the trinity, the 'holy spirit', or the god who appears as a burning bush in the Moses text simply asserting in a humanly audible voice 'I am that I am'. We preserve the unnamed in these variations as the special quality that determines the deity. In this vein, Lakoff introduces the common occurrence in culture of the expansion of prototypic names or basic categorization to extended or family words. We may look at the various designations of an incarnation as an aspect of the deity. They are symbolic extensions of the prototype of the most abstract representation of God.

Continuing the argument as it bears relevance to designating aspects of God, contiguous features are represented in classical Christianity as Saints, or in the Old Testament, as prophetic voices. Indeed, it is here where the spokes from the prototypic idea of God reach into polysemantic concrete representations. This need for concrete representations derives from religious groups' need to turn to a deity for comfort and justification of suffering. The notion of one ineffible God may at times be too abstract and difficult to grasp as a disembodied object of prayer. The demand for signs of presence and visible power require new representational qualities. We long for a name or an image to be magically uttered or seen. The Christian credo (Credo in Unum Diem) and The Hebrew 'Shema' (Hear oh Israel, the Lord is one) remain awe inspiring but remote abstract concepts without flesh. Such remote power is the counterpoint of the concrete representations preferred by various believers.

Although the 'one God' credo is abstract and remote there are a number of attributes which have been used to characterize the God head – all knowing, just, omnipotent, loving, and, most central, possessing the power to create. Creativity as an essential feature of God's power has been central to theological and social dimensions of belief. God is a force that creates. One Old Testament narrative showing the primacy of God as creator is exemplified in the Book of Job. The afflictions suffered by Job lead to a curious confrontation in which God reveals his essence by asserting his creative power. The voice in the whirlwind that represents God appearing to Job is humbling: God intimidatingly asks 'where were you when I created the universe?' thereby suggesting that Job's querying his personal pain is trivial in the face of the magnitude of the deity's works. The boundlessness must be referential not only in his ubiquity but in his unending creative works. A name cannot encompass such power.

In modern times, the religious anti-evolutionary movement has countered the Darwinian chance natural selection hypothesis with the idea of a Creative Intelligent Designer to account for our evolving to a state where we can even consider this matter intellectually. Thus, the believers add 'intention and intelligence' to the deity's work plan in evoking creation and grand design. The idea of intention in creativity provides yet another metaphor that anthropomorphizes God in the form of a dialogic partner in a speech act. The notion of an abstract force guiding history without intent or special consideration for man is too unnerving and intolerable for those who wish to maintain awe of the unique order in the non-artifactual world. Parenthetically, we have not even addressed the referential analogy pointed to by feminists in the practice of referring to God as a HE. Even the pantheists cannot bear the idea of an unembodied 'it'.

The linguistic analysis of the various dimensional and emotional constraints on the features of our defining God takes us this far. I hope to enhance understanding by adding a psychoanalytical point of view that explores the unconscious factors that enrich meanings of our subject. I will attempt to link the unnamed Rumpelstiltskin to the conundrum of the unconscious significance of God as our unnamed Creator.

Psychoanalysis and the unnamed

'The Unnamed' may be seen to have unconscious roots and significance that can be discovered by a psychoanalytically oriented probe. First, I will review Freud's and later psychoanalysts' forays into linguistic issues.

Freud (1900) was fascinated by problems of representation. Dreams, symptoms, and parapraxes all required transformational rules for their emergence into consciousness. These rules, similar to the tropes in narrative analysis were invoked, within a symbolic system that he believed were built into the mental apparatus. Freud's topographic theory was most closely allied to the Sauserian linguistic model accounting for the French Psychoanalytic School's continuing devotion to this earliest model. Lacan's (1956) devotion to Saussure and his specific employment of linguistic tropes also are found in the topographic model. Freud's use of thing and word presentation model permitted a split between the system ucs and the system pcs. He required that thing presentations be attached to word presentations in order to pass from ucs through pcs to system cs.

Freud's linguistics initially concerned interpretation in words as a means of rendering the unconscious conscious. The Oedipus complex, primal scene, etc. are but a few of the deeper unconscious constellations that lie at the basis of derivative social structures that are rendered in language. These complexes are transformed into designative units that are used to structure human relationships and narratives. I (Shapiro, 1979) have written that the structure of drives and wishes is syntactically arranged in a form akin to sentences with a subject, verb, and object, thus allowing for naming as a narrative statement.

Each verbal or symptomatic expression requires mental mechanisms or as linguists say, transformational rules, to establish their relationship to base or core meanings. Thus, there is much overlap between the idea of 'dream work' and literary linguistic 'tropes' such as metaphor and condensation. Indeed, Lacan's work draws heavily on this aspect of Freud's thought as it also directly references Saussure.

In rendering unconscious constellations linguistically, we *name* the yet unknown deeper constellations. We also tame the affects that are bound to formerly unconscious ideas permitting us to wrestle them to awareness. Metaphoric interpretations also show us that understanding entails rich physicalist references that reach to affects as well as to bodily features of definition (see Grossman & Steward, 1976). Lakoff too, from a non-psychoanalytic vantage, makes prominent reference to the bodily origins of many metaphoric structures, paralleling Freud's idea that ego was once body ego. Freud's bold statement merely addresses the idea that our infantile pre-verbal experience of the world does not transcend the subjective body centred experience, because the declarative form of experience is not available. Later linguistically based concepts are grafted onto these earlier templates and are recast as words (declarative memories) characterized by limited features for definitional clarity.

My own work at the interface of linguistics and psychoanalysis has been directed toward the importance of naming as interpretation. Rendering in words that which has been unconscious is a moment of recognition for a patient. The newly informed patient can then deal with a conscious verbal formula that references action dispositions toward others that can be applied to life experiences, understood, and modified since it is now a mental event. (I have already noted Fonagy's mentalization as but another variant form of the same process.)

Freud also made other forays into linguistic issues in his papers, *The Antithetical Meaning of Primal Words* (Freud, 1910) and *On Negation* (Freud, 1925) to name but two. *The Antithetical Meaning of Primal Words* is especially cogent for this discussion because Freud analogizes the discovery by cultural anthropologists that our earliest words may represent two antithetical meanings. Thus, one word initially pointed to both divergent meanings. Freud exploited the discovery to explain the idea that any word or sign may be used defensively to represent its opposite. In our current discussion of God's powers, we have revived the old Manichaean heresy that suggests a co-existence of forces of evil as equal to and opposite to God's power. The postulated dual power was disruptive to God's singularity and the monotheistic credo during the period of scholasticism. It raised the issue of existence implied in negation.

Negation differs from idea of the unnamed and will be addressed here as an addendum. Freud (1925) and the linguists agree that negation is a type of semantic designation that includes designation of the entity which is then denied by special markers such as not. We must first assert 'X' for it to be negated. This is not only so in symbolic logic, but in the psychoanalytic recognition that negation is a form of lifting repression, and recognizing an entity only to then verbally reject it in consciousness. Thus, negation requires expression of a word with all the constraints that apply plus a formal sign that denies. It is, therefore, different from the unnamed.

In religious terms, the Devil is recognized as 'the force that negates' according to Goethe (1953). While the devil asserts God's power by his opposition, he also contests it and tempts and exercises a counterforce to the assumed all encompassing good of the deity. This 'entity as counterforce' is not the same as the 'unnamed' God. The Lord's name (unnamed) remains the intellectual abstract representation of the Godhead as in the Credo. Believers keep it abstract and unnamed in order to maintain awe and abstract remoteness. We will return to the paper on antithetical meaning as it applies to Rumpelstiltskin and to God as I argue the unconscious meaning of the unnamed.

Rumpelstiltskin and God

I will make extensive reference to a scholarly article regarding Grimm's story as a starting point for my argument. Harry Rand's (2003) paper 'Who was Rumpelstiltskin?' provides a significant gloss on the fairy tale and a route to our expanding understanding about why the name is to be evaded and its meaning shrouded in mystery. In elaborating Rand's arguments, I will also offer some modifications and addenda that I believe will render the fairy tale more understandable and permit a more comprehensive understanding of the unnamed. In so doing, I will also extend the argument about what the 'unnamed' god represents. What would knowing or saying his name do to our faith and our awe.

Rand comments on the many variations of the folk story which is available in a number of languages and then settles into a discussion of what clues the name Rumpelstiltskin means from its etymology. His approach is designed to expand understanding of the deeper meaning of the tale. He also finds significance in the circumstance of the creation of this orally transmitted tale. The tales were created in Medieval 'Spinnstuben' or spinning rooms that were occupied by women who gathered to spin together. They amused themselves by telling creative tales, likely with negative and mocking references to men. The Spinnstuben may be compared to men's leisure time company in bars and pubs. The tales are significant in their intent to both entertain and narrate the plight of women during the Middle Ages. Thus, we can expect some interpretive passages and themes in the tales that serve the social and political aims of this 'spinster' (also derivative of the spinnstube) group.

Approaching the tale in this manner allows us to conjecture about the negative roles of men in the tales. In *Rumpelstiltskin*, a father, who uses his daughter as a means of raising his stature by marrying her to royalty and lying about her magical skills, and the King, wanting the maiden to satisfy his greed and his procreative powers for a son, are each prominently featured. Rand suggests that the only benign male in the tale, and its tacit hero, is Rumpelstiltskin. The little man lends his powers to facilitate the novice Queen's desperate plight and requirement to satisfy the King's greed by spinning straw into gold.. Rand's etymological analysis of the name Rumpelstiltskin and it's relevance to the story line is revealing.

Rand describes six essentials features about the night visitor:

1. He is male.
2. He is short but not described as one of the traditionally designated trolls or other 'wee-folk'.
3. He accomplishes vital work that seems magical.
4. His magical powers notwithstanding, he still wants a living child.

5. No one has ever heard his name – 'it is outside her vocabulary'.
6. When the Queen utters his name he shouts 'The Devil Told You!' and either disappears or self destructs in a number of ways by splitting himself in two or into many fragments according to which text is read.

Rand then breaks the name into stems and segments. This approach, incidentally, uses a particularly Germanic feature of constructing words from various stems which are agglutinated into a single compound word. Words such as 'mundtuch' or napkin are constructed from mouth and cloth or tischtuch (tablecloth). In this instance, we learn that the root, *Rumpel*, designates shrivelled or rumpled; and that the root, *stilts*, is related to the English word stilt or stiff; and the name ending *kin* may be a condensation of skin or -kin as in tiny, as in the French suffix -ette or -kin as in munchkin or manikin. Rand then indicates that, from this analysis, the little man is a 'flaccid penis'. He continues that such a little man, despite his powers, is rather benign and not aggressively harmful and the only male in the story who is sympathetic to the young Queen.

At this juncture I suggest that his conclusion is puzzling, because this is a powerful, indeed magical, little fellow, and the stem for stiff is just as prominent as the stem for rumpled. I contest the conclusion that the penis is flaccid by applying a similar analytic method. Indeed, 'the little man-penis' has features that would make the reader think of him as erect and potent. This change will become important to our understanding about why he has to be 'unnamed', and why his name has to be discovered and then uttered to alter the bargain with the Queen.

Etymological analysis of the name reveals the dual aspect of the little man's binary state, erect and rumpled. Freud's analysis of primal words offers a psychoanalytic means to understand the unconscious meaning of the dual opposing word stems. Thus Rumpelstiltskin, by virtue of his name, is represented as both erect (stilts) and flaccid (Rumpel) and, thus, personifies the nature of the penis itself, which exists in nature sequentially in both forms. The categorical features of each word root indicate the limits of meaning within a purely linguistic construct, as described by Lakoff. There is further reason to suggest phallic power from this narrative as well as the name itself. The power to create gold from straw is indeed a transformational miracle, suggesting magical power that is matched only by the miracle of conception and the transformation of the sperm and egg to a human form. The story redundantly expresses Rumpelstiltskin's wish to have the Queen's child as the price for the miracle performed. This wish is shared by the King or any husband. Thus, the new bride is expected to bear a child not only for Rumpelstiltskin but for and by the King. It is not of passing consequence that, at the time of creating this tale, children, like wives, belonged to the male leader of the household as chattel.

There is also unexploited symbolism in the tearful bride's waiting for her husband's entry or 'sexual intrusion'. She must do the impossible, make gold from straw (a baby from intercourse), without understanding the role of the penis in the task. The tale suggests that the novice bride relies on childish images of romance and sexuality without knowledge of coition. The apprehension concerning the King's anticipated entry is relieved when the elfin creature bursts into the room, unasked for, but welcomed, particularly when his miracle is performed. Her apprehension about the magnitude of the task of spinning straw into gold is alleviated by the amiable elf. Psychoanalysts are familiar with the body-penis equation in which the part stands for the whole, as in metonymy. The little man, as penis, also serves as a complement to the small gifts from the Queen at each evening's end. They are each circular feminine enclosures, a ring and a bracelet, which are not hard to decipher in this context as female genitalia. Thus, both the very entry of the little man into the queen's space, and the nature of her gifts, are graphic symbols of the King's nightly sexual intrusions. In the end, we have to accept the erstwhile maiden's grasp that the creative little man has produced the pure gold, a baby, to be born at a future date.

Intercourse and procreation are not linked by temporal contiguity, but by new knowledge of the relationship of conception to birth. It is a surprise for the nubile girl to learn that the baby has not grown 'ex nihilo' in a mother's womb, but that it is in part a product of the work of the little man who enters nightly and magically and figuratively spins straw into gold. The tale is about discovering the creative power of the male, and the role of the phallus in procreation. It tells why the male has a claim on the baby born nine months later. This is simultaneously an age old tale of primal learning and personal coming of age.

Once told in this manner, we have a suggestion why the little man is unnamed. His name is not known or voiced because of the phallus' awesome creative powers. The maiden's repression and lack of knowledge move hand in hand as self-deception and also to support the awe of magical creation. What should be a miracle of the gods is in fact a material product of the work of the human corporeal penis and figuratively of the imaginative phallus. A more homely interpretation might be read as follows: the innocent maiden, victimized by her greedy father, enters the marriage bed not knowing about the means of procreation and its link to intercourse. The Phallic/manikin bursting into her room is discovered to be the creative force of life itself – once the name of this intruder is discovered, some mastery occurs by new knowledge. The name helps the young woman to assimilate and adapt to marriage, intercourse, and procreation by its signifying function linking an idea to an experience in life. Naming again comforts by the acquisition of new knowledge that both reveals and contains the boundaries of the unknown. Like a proper interpretation, it elevates the repressed into words to be contemplated in thought.

Let us recapitulate. The tale of Rumpelstiltskin is a metaphoric restatement of the act of mental assimilation by the pre-nuptial girl signifying that the intrusion of the male penis is not just an exploitation of her virginal body, but the means of creating a child. The Oedipal girl's sense of despair and exploitation by the father in giving her to another man is gradually overcome by the bride's anticipation of the gift of a child. The additional theme in the story of the girl outwitting the little man represents a bit of feminine politics where the passive is turned into the active. It is a reference to issues that were salient during the middle ages. The Queen triumphs over the 'King and his little man' by prospectively winning her child. Ownership in the middle ages, of course, was a masculine privilege, and this triumph could be seen as the potential preemptive power of motherhood, even in the face of the 'Droit de Senor'(See Jones, 1925).

The Spinnstube women were very likely delighted by the young Queen outwitting the small man, as well as the inclusion in the story of his self destruction when his name was uttered. His cry that the Devil was the source of the discovery puts us in mind of the counterpoint between the natural forces at work in the story. The imagery of the nightly entry of the small man into the 'Queen's room' in association with the circular gifts is unmistakably a representation of intromission. It also reminds us that the worry about an evening visitor with the intent of intercourse might also be related to other regressive anxieties of young children regarding a variety of night intruders – robbers, kidnappers, sandmen, etc.

In light of the interpretation above, we can see that the unnamed creative body part was not named, because then the awesome nature of procreation would be delimited to a mere physical act. Nominalization curtails the imagined fancied power of the male member. Say it and it is! Abracadabra! Shazam! The magic of words as performatives and speech acts becomes apparent. We do indeed do things with words. We can also magically pretend things do not exist if we do not say their names.

Now I will pull together the various strands of my argument. I have juxtaposed the prohibitions against uttering the name of God and the challenge and forfeiture game that centres on discovery of the name of the elfin night visitor to the Queen of a fairy tale kingdom. One situation involves a prohibition against uttering a name while the other affords power to reverse a bargain by she who discovers and says a name. These are clearly somewhat different, but both affirm the power involved in naming and saying. Each narrative is an example of attempts to delimit the meaning of the object by representing it in a word that constrains it in a cognitive frame. Each also provides the listener with a sense of the power of utterance when considered from the vantage of a performative in which 'saying' is a form of 'doing'. The more magical and awesome aspect of the experience has been explained by the Freudian analysis of the sense of the uncanny that belongs to the repressed from which the 'unsaid' draws its affective power.

How do these two stories fit then? In the Rumpelstiltskin tale, we find it is an allegory of the procreative, or simply creative, power of the penis. If I were to employ a more abstract Lacanian interpretation, we might say the phallus is the imaginary representation of the power relationships among humans. There are many similar culturally bound symbols to point to. The Greco-Roman 'Herms' which adorned the front courtyards of our Western ancestors are concrete reminders of domestic phallic power and guardianship. These stone steles were intimately tied to the protective power of the phallus as well as creative representations of fertility. They are but another historical representation of imagery parallel to the tale of Rumpelstiltskin.

In the case of the unnamed god, I have argued that this is a similar reference to an abiding and unfettered creative force. The syllogism presented could be solved as follows: the meaning of god is the phallus or in body language, the penis. The regression from abstract to bodily derived words that represent corporeal flesh and blood is not new to psychoanalysts or to linguists. I have elaborated the body-phallus equation and the many more abstract representational references that represent regressive human forms. The linguists, too, show that body language, metaphor, and metonymy abound in our daily word play. Freud's quip that sometimes a cigar is only a cigar is, of course, the psychoanalyst denying his own theoretic position.

Contrariwise, 'God the creator' is represented in abstract terms that are remote from representation of the body, especially in monotheism. Such tropes permit us to place our fate outside human hands in an abstract awesome force. Many monotheistic believers gathering at times of need retain the awe reserved for the mystical by not saying God's name. However, if the responder to our prayers is not to be seen as a sham, making him more distant secures awe. The Wizard of Oz, of course, comes to mind insofar as he is discounted to be 'just a man' and the pyrotechnics around him are humbug. Nonetheless, many religions also alternate between the awesome abstract and the concrete as exemplified in various practices that bring God to flesh and human representation while others do not even say his name.

This duality of need is visible even in cultures supporting Christianity, where the 'word has become flesh'. The theology maintains the mystery of the trinity with a holy spirit in reserve for awe. The plea for 'Imitatio Christi' is a flesh and blood model in the form of a human, but the spirit remains in the background. Similarly, the Hindu incarnations and the prophetic anointments of the Old Testament use a force that is unnamed. In human terms, we return to my syllogism: the name of God is equated to the creative power of the penis. It is a symbol of the procreative force within and across generations.

This force is a powerful image that is not immediately obvious empirically. The procreative power of the phallus has to be discovered insofar as there are nine months between intromission and conception to birth. This linkage had to be discovered not only by the Queen in the tale, but also by primal peoples. The discovery may have displaced some of the awe reserved for the deity as progenitor, establishing a power vacuum that our ancestor males took advantage of to become the kings and possessors of power over women. Socially and politically, the power grab down-played the role of the female as a procreative force, even though many generations of diverse cultures honed fertility images and practiced rites solely devoted to the generative power of women.

From the purported awesome impregnation by polytheistic gods, newer cultures elevated men to thrones and a new hegemony by showing they were doing God's work.

There remain many representations of female goddesses and more recently female saints, followed by beatification of the Virgin Mary. Indeed, since males could not reproduce without females, the creative force is in fact a dual responsibility. This fact is symbolically stated in the tale of Rumpelstiltskin. Every Rumpelstiltskin must have his bracelet or necklace to exercise his creativity. The key to the relation of Grimm's tale to God rests in the unknown name. Once the name is discovered, its utterance frees the maiden from her bargain, and the little man's awesome gift is no longer necessary in the face of the greater miracle of birth.

I am sure that the male dominated culture at the time of the 'Spinnstuben' created feminine unrest and envy. We of the twenty-first century hopelessly repeat these same religious (Can women join the Clergy?) and social (Should women in the workplace earn as much as men?) conflicts by the continuing argument between the sexes. This does not make the argument regarding the symbolic significance of the 'unsaid' less cogent. There is a need to bring our human condition under the sway of higher forces such as deities who fill our need for the ritual experience of uncanny awe and belief.

The 'unnamed' protects us from the banality and confined humanity of the named. Any name entails limits and constraints because it has restrictive categorical meaning – but the abstraction is not the thing. Nonetheless, linguistic analysis shows that each abstraction can be analysed into baser corporeal references. Our use of a psychoanalytic method of analysis, in turn, helps us to understand the roots of awe that are also features of our symbols. The discovery of the creative power of the genitalia is relived in each adolescent in the recognition that sexuality is related to procreation just as our primal ancestors uncovered the same fact of life that helped elevate men to thrones. The awe accompanying the worship of God is based on repressing the deity's powerful attributes. Moreover, we do not casually utter the name of God, because to say his name is a speech act that represents an enactment of that awesome power.

References

Austin, J.L. (1962). *How to do Things with Words*. New York: Oxford University Press.

Carroll, L. (1960). *The Annotated Alice: Alice's Adventures in Wonderland and through the Looking Glass*. USA, Clarkson N. Potter.

Fonagy, P., & Target, M. (1998). Mentalization and the changing aims of child psychoanalysis. *Psychoanalytic Dialogues, 8*: 87–114.

Freud, S. (1900). The interpretation of dreams. *Standard Edition 4:5* London: Hogarth Press, 1953.

Freud, S. (1910). The antithetical meaning of primal words. *Standard Edition* 2. Hogarth Press, 1957.

Freud, S. (1919). The uncanny. *Standard Edition, 17*. London: Hogarth.

Freud, S. (1925). On negation. *Standard Edition, 19*. Hogarth Press, 1961.

Goethe, J.N. (1953). *Faust in the Permanent Goethe*. New York: The Dial Press.

Grimm, J. (1944). *The Complete Grimm's Fairy Tales*. New York: Pantheon Books.

Grossman W.I. & Stewart, W.A. (1976). Penis envy: from childhood wish to developmental metaphor. *Journal of the American Psychoanalytic Association 24*: 193–210.

Jones, E. (1914). The Madonna's conception through the ear in essays. In: *Applied Psychoanalysis Volume II* (pp.266–357).

Lacan, J. (1956). *The Language of the Self: The Function of Language in Psychoanalysis*. Translated by A. Wilden. Baltimore: The Johns Hopkins Press, 1956.

Lakoff, G. (1987). *Women, Fire and Dangerous Things*. Chicago: University of Chicago Press.

Lakoff, G. (2003). *Don't Think of One Elephant?* White River Junction: Chelsea Green Publishing.

Levi-Strauss, C. (1966). *The Savage Mind*. Chicago: University of Chicago Press.

Ogden, C.K. & Richards, I.A. (1923). *The Meaning of Meaning*. New York: Harcourt Brace & World 1946.

Rand, H. (2000). Who was Rumpelstiltskin? *International Journal of Psychoanalysis, 81*: 943–962.

Saussure, F. de (1911). *Course in General Linguistics*. New York: Philosophic Library, 1959.

Searle, J.R. (1969). *Speech Acts: An Essay in the Philosophy of Language*. New York: Cambridge University Press.

Shapiro, T. (1970). Interpretation and Naming. *Journal of American Psychoanalysis, 18*: 399–421.

Stoppard, T. (1997). *The Invention of Love*. Grove Press.

Winnicott, D.W. (1953). Transitional objects and transitional phenomena: a study of the first not-me possession. *International Journal of Psychoanalysis, 34*: 89–97.

Wittgenstein, L. (1953). *Philosophical Investigations*. New York: Macmillan.

CHAPTER ELEVEN

Texts and pre-texts in psychoanalytic clinical practice: languages and idioms

Adriana Sorrentini

In the first of his *Introductory Lectures* (1916), Freud shows that although medical training accustoms us to seeing and touching, coming into immediate contact with the patient and, through direct perception, becoming persuaded of certain facts, in psychoanalytic treatment we depend almost solely on the exchange of words between analysand and analyst.

Not *mere words* of course, but words that hold their ancient enchanting power, that can relieve pain and cure, or condemn to despair and death. Words that convey knowledge, words that inflame multitudes, that carry feelings *and are the universal means by which men influence each other*, all of which creates the supreme importance of words in our discipline.

We know that it is not the same to think as to speak our mind, and thus, during the psychoanalytic session, analyst and analysand pronounce words that attempt to convey thoughts, feelings, and sentiments. If thought can become conscious, it is because the word came from the outside as a conscious perception, so that – except the sentiments – everything that would become conscious must be transposed into an external perception. On the basis of acoustic mnemic residues, which are the word-representation, without forgetting the optical mnemic residues – which are ontogenic thinking and phylogenetically older – thought processes are formed thanks to the hypercathexis of thinking; they become real and effectively (wirklich) external, and this fact makes them true. The unconscious representation cannot be discerned as a thing; that is, it remains unknown – Unerkennen – while the preconscious representation is connected to word-representations, this being the condition of becoming conscious. However, not all the preconscious is joined to the word-representation; there may also be a direct hallucination of the optic residues with full evidence and vividness, a feeling that is self-produced by the psychic apparatus; therefore, we can say that the words of a discourse, through which the thought becomes conscious, are also hallucinations.

The word is mediation, and when it is pronounced, it is hallucinated as a feeling, and the internal thought processes become perceptions, validating that *all knowledge comes from external perception*, in the direction proposed by Haeckel when he affirms that 'there is nothing in the intellect that does not come from the senses', for example the word residues that come essentially from acoustic perceptions.

The two members of the analytic dyad tend to be surprised and amazed by a word or a slip of the tongue that, once spoken, is heard by both with new meanings, thereby becoming an interpretation (Deutung).

For Freud, what is psychic is unknown in and of itself, is unconscious, so that the analytic task is to help something to become conscious through the word of the interpretation or the construction, which focuses consciousness on the repressed representations, or presents the split-off parts of the ego, what is buried, orienting it toward an unconscious that differs from the one described in Chapter 7 of *The Interpretations of Dreams* (1900), that of the drive, which is a different constitutive level of the psyche.

Actually, we sometimes make a construction that addresses actual, non-representational, non-repressed unconscious material that was never conscious but is part of the buried, the somatic, and the actual. The usual construction, which refers to a forgotten fragment of the patient's history, is a historical reconstruction of infantile[1] material. We shall come back to these concepts below.

In *The Ego and the Id* (1923), we learn that all perceptions – Wahrnehmung – that come from the outside through the senses and the feelings – Empfindung – and the sentiments – Gefühl – coming from the inside, are conscious. In the Project (1887–1902 [1895], p. 308), consciousness is already described as providing *qualities* of sensations, perceived as *'sensations which are different* (anders sind) *in a great multiplicity of ways* (Mannigfaltigkeit) *and whose difference* (Anders) *is distinguished according to its relations with the external world.'* This quality and diversity (E. Kant) allow us to discern a thing because it is different from something else, from 'that qualitative-quantitative other' that is intense and forced, but different from the pure quantity described in the Project.

The representation – Vorstellung – refers to a memory, an autonomous function of the psychic apparatus, while the feeling is the presentation of something to the conscious. In order to become a representation, a preconscious residue must be cathected, meaning actualized and activated. The impressions of infancy demand reproductions, and their repetition is wish fulfilment; this occurs automatically as a repetition compulsion, different from memory – Erinnerung.

We recall that in Kant the object (Objekt) is constructed by a synthesis of feelings into an object-representation that we refer to a 'thing-in-the-world' – Ding – a material thing. Therefore, 'presentation' applies to feelings or to products of fantasy, the affect and somatic manifestations, while 're-presentation' is synthesis and assumes something given by feeling and bound by understanding, which does not reflect an object but is the object, as are the object-representation (Objekt-Vorstellung), the thing-representation (Sach-Vorstellung, always unconscious), and the word-representation (Wort-Vorstellung).

The connection between the representation and work is the condition of becoming conscious, the basis and aim of psychoanalytic work, which attempts to find lost connections. Finding this connection allows us to formulate an interpretation, making conscious something of the analysand's repressed, which brings us to understand the importance of knowing his or her language well, with all the nuances, idioms, and idiomatic expressions that allow us to grasp the double meaning in the discourse.

A brief digression in relation to this subject: when I was reading *The Babel of the Unconscious* (Amati Mehler, Argentieri & Canestri, 2002), I became absorbed in considerations concerning the importance of languages in the formation of the psyche. In my case, my maternal language is Italian, and, since my mother was a French teacher, a bit of the latter language; when I was nine years old and we moved to Argentina, I had no knowledge of the Spanish language, undoubtedly a traumatic experience, since I was obliged to learn it quickly in order to communicate with the environment outside the family. Luckily, I could soon speak and write correctly in Spanish, and then English was added at school. Later, when I was studying at the university, I began to study German. I would not say that I have a command of these languages at all, but that the many mnemic residues and word-representations in me have an effective and operational preconscious presence.

I had never noticed how often a word came to my mind in different languages and, many years later, as a physician and psychoanalyst, I tended to make associations in a different language, either single words or sayings, poems or bits of songs, without realizing how much they helped me, as they still do, to understand something more about what is latent in the heard discourse and what is happening in the real of the session.

On one occasion, a female patient tended to repeat a complaint-ridden narration of everything she had to do to support her household, educate her children, and find time to study and advance in her training, alone and unnoticed, without help, all expressed with a quantity of anguish that seemed to go far beyond the manifest content of her narration and producing, in the countertransference, an uncomfortable, guilt-producing feeling. At one point, my evenly suspended attention felt a jolt when it heard: '. . . and I can't go on like this forever . . . like a violet butterfly! . . .' The absurdity of the expression made me jump. I recalled her Italian origin, like my own, and awkwardly heard myself asking her if she remembered how you say 'violet butterfly' in Italian . . . silence . . . then, anguished, and in a thin, shaky voice, she replied: 'farfalla violata . . . no . . . viola!', the last word uttered with pain and rage.

We were able to reconstruct a forgotten scene in which, when she was about five years old, she had suffered sexual abuse by the father of a little girl she used to play with. She then remembered that, not knowing what was happening, she had felt disturbed by the way this man, taking advantage of a situation while playing with the little girls, had her crawl between his legs so that she was pressed against his genitals. She fell silent, feeling guilty for thinking that the daddy might have been doing something bad . . . she must have been in the wrong, the bad girl able to experience strange and disturbing feelings. She managed to stay away from this man, but had kept – forgotten – a painful secret, for over thirty years.

Certainly, the evenly suspended attention, in the abstinence of the setting, grasped the emotional intensity with which the word 'violet' was said and led to associations by homophony and meaning, composing the signifying chain 'violet – viola – violate – violation', surprising the analyst by the emergence of a scene with sexual content in which she is involved in the countertransference, which was doubtless the source of her countertransference guilt feelings.

It is not my intention to present this case and the transference and countertransference vicissitudes we worked on, but to share the idea of the complexity of the multiple routes to access the unconscious, on the basis of the word and its polysemy, the affect provoked by the resisted representation, body language and its many expressions.

The existence of traumatic mnemic residues that created an inner experience of pain (Schmerz Erlebniss) because of a high level of excitation, felt as unpleasure by consciousness, and the need of discharge, had also left its trace in her body, where what was impossible to say found a way out by changing into somatic language: in it, the guilt-producing excitation was perceived as pain – physical and mental – expressed in the hypochondriac language of her constant complaints and demands.

This inner experience of pain creates an extreme facilitation to feel pain in any experience that might offer points of analogy, as in the case of the tragic incestuous experience that came up in the field of the transference in the session, in the actual scene that unfolded there.

The mechanism of repression, in the unconscious ego, chooses its substitute formation by analogical laws and by contiguity with the repressed representation with which the similarity does not access consciousness. This similarity or analogy is with one of the qualities of the representation. When the patient was a little girl, her mother used to call her affectionately 'little butterfly' ('Farfallina'), so that the expression 'violet butterfly' carried all the pain and guilt connected with betraying her mother through what she had experienced and kept secret with her friend's father, a displacement of her own father in unconscious fantasy, a seduction fantasy rich in sexual implications, evoked by the excitation of desire and frustrated by the abstinence implicit in the session.

The tragic incestuous content is presented clearly in the regressive situation created in the transference field that envelops the analyst-analysand binomial, where the analyst hears the patient's discourse as free association: words that carry the language of the unconscious, if we are willing to hear and accept that we know what it is saying, if we admit that we understand the language in which desire expresses itself. Without this condition on the analyst's part, there will be no analysis.

The ambience of the session is created by its setting

The psychoanalytic session results from a particular encounter between two persons in a singular, ineffable ambience. It differs absolutely from other possible encounters, even considering them in terms of assistance, affection, confidences, confessions or any other type. It is regulated by the circulation of words, affects, and experiences in a transference field where the word transports both the analysand's occurrences and the psychoanalytic interventions.

We stress the originality of the temporal-spatial parameters in which the session takes place.

The manifest space is concrete and profane: a room used as a consulting room that, in virtue of the setting established, acquires the characteristics of a virtual, 'sacred' or fane space, a magic circle or centre[2] where the tragic-incestuous scene of the unconscious is invoked and can unfold, an internal, a-temporal world, with all its uncanny splendour.

Mircea Eliade (1972) maintains that all hierophany (manifestation of the sacred) transfigures the place that was its theatre, a profane or common space, into a sacred one appropriate for the repetition of the manifestation that singularized it and differentiating it from the rest of its surroundings. An area is secured for the repetition of that manifestation, on condition of entering there to come into contact with that force, communicating with the netherworld – for us, the unconscious – something that requires careful preparation through personal analysis and rigorous abstinence in the session, considering the danger involved.

The resistance to the psychoanalytic setting, which leads to the session, resides precisely in the ambivalence created by this *sacer* space that attracts and repels, is useful and dangerous, which becomes taboo by making contact with death and immortality.

We know of repeated attempts to trivialize the setting, with justifications of modernization and adaptation, rationalizations similar to the *logic of soup and arguments of meatballs* that Freud mentions in connection with transference love or, on the contrary, the use of a dogmatic practice, empty of meaning and theoretical grounding, which also invalidates and ridicules it.

The other parameter is time: the fifty minutes agreed upon in the contract and repeated several times each week correspond to profane time or clock time, which in the session acquires a very different characteristic, since we consider time in terms of periodicity and eternity. Periodicity – in magic and in religion – refers to the indefinite use of a mythical time converted into the present, since all rituals[3] have the quality of 'now', like the psychoanalytic session, which unfolds in the a-temporal present of the unconscious and where everything is actual and original, even though verb tenses may be used to establish past and future, in function of the resistance that arises in response to the inner experience that is occurring or, *a posteriori*, to construct the history on the basis of something original that occurred 'now'.

The believer feels he or she is a contemporary of the trans-historic events that, repeated in theophanous time – manifestation of the Unconscious Ideal – are present. The present indicative is the verb tense of the session, in virtue of the synchronicity of the unconscious. For our patient, all the material that we analyse is synchronic, actual, and present. This is an experiential quality, indispensable for the therapeutic efficacy of psychoanalysis, since it would otherwise carry no conviction, but would be reduced at most to an interesting theoretical explanation of the person's sufferings.

The setting situates the psychoanalytic dyad in the non-place and non-time where the session unfolds. Plato (*Tim.*, 37) considers that 'Time is the mobile image of eternity'. The session occurs in the eternity of the unconscious and takes place in the temporality of the fifty minutes agreed upon in the contract.

The history is constructed little by little, introducing time and the idea of repetition, on the basis of the encounter, where the synchronicity of the unconscious material presents both phylogeny and the infantile, while the drive shows its peremptory character, demanding discharge 'now', and the object is present in the person of the analyst.

The forgotten or repressed is acted in the transference in such a way that we and our patient acquire the conviction that *we must not treat his condition as a historical episode, but as an actual power*, when we observe that *the patient experiences as something real-objective and actual* (Freud, 1914): the commotion generated in the unfolding of the transference scene, to which the analyst puts words in order to handle the impulse that demands action as a memory.

The word circulates between patient and analyst, but it is the latter who gives meaning to the different languages that express human suffering. We also know that the word expresses much more than what it says, and this extra in it is what must be heard by the analytic ear. The spoken word is accompanied by other unsaid meanings, its polysemy determining it as a pre-destined mistake.

The psychoanalyst's interventions: transference-countertransference

Once they are ensconced in the session, that ineffable ambience encompassed by the setting and impregnated with abstinence, the analytic dialogue begins.

This occurs between an analysand, lying on the couch and deprived of a view of the analyst, who speaks of his thoughts and tries to say everything that occurs to him, be they memories or thoughts, affects or emotions; and an analyst who responds with a certain type of listening, who abstains from any interest or curiosity about the manifest narration and gives herself up entirely to her *unconscious memories* (Freud, 1912), so that, turning her own unconscious as a receptive organ toward the patient's emitting unconscious, she hears sounds that shape acoustic traces connected to meanings that evoke a word-representation (Wortvorstellung) in her pre-conscious, and in consciousness, a word – Wort – that she attributes to her analysand.

Freud goes on to say that, based on the incitement of these *sound waves, the physician´s unconscious is capable of re-establishing, from the residues of the unconscious communicated to him, the same unconscious that has determined the patient's occurrences.* It is clear that this cannot possibly happen if there are too many resistance 'blind spots' (Stekel, 1911) in the analyst's mind. There may be an understanding and empathic dialogue so to speak, but not a psychoanalytic one, no analysis but only narrations, confidences or opinions exchanged in the manifest. To concentrate our efforts on the aim of *performing an operation in the best possible accord with the rules of the art* also means being conscious that abstinence is a condition *sine qua non* of analysis, since it excites desire and the incestuous drive impulses that it forbids.

The rule of abstinence definitely falls on the analyst, who renounces the satisfaction of all desire or temptation, preserving his sobriety, continence, and moderation in response to the seduction and direct or displaced sexual demand that emerges at some moment in the transference; he avoids talking about himself, offering himself as an example or intruding on the analysand's private life, placing a limit on narcissism that also reminds us that, although it is our job to do the analysis, it is the analysand's prerogative to make a new synthesis.

Ethical reasons are added to the technical rationale for the prescription of abstinence, not a question of moral imposition but of the correct application of the theoretical principles that sustain psychoanalytic clinical practice. Our ethics are rooted in good praxis.

We know that we work with the most explosive forces: the repressed-buried drive impulses, and that we need to accept, sustain, and analyse the power that we have to bear, based on the transference of images of primary objects, both threatening and guilt-producing; we are conscious of the danger of acting out the idealization and power they confer on us.

The analytic cure demands that it be done in a state of a degree of privation capable of putting desire in the fore, since the inevitable frustration makes *need and longing* subsist as the motor of analytic work. The situation of privation excites desire that gradually approaches its fulfilment in the manner of a dream, by cathecting the image of the analyst as a preconscious representation, recent and insignificant, the cathexes belonging to the repressed object of the Oedipus complex.

It happens that this process goes on, since libidinal regression reaches back to the tragic residues of the Oedipal tragedy,[4] which are capable of generating hallucinatory wish fulfilment that is just as inner as the feeling of reality in a dream; the inner experience[5] – Erlebniss – which takes place in the real of the session, is accompanied by affective and neuro-vegetative reactions that manifest the actual and somatic, expressing the transference in the person of the analyst, now converted into the original object and not merely its representation. This configuration of the session, thought of as a dream in which the psychoneurosis unfolds, is subject to interpretation – Deutung – the intervention by which the psychoanalyst presents the analysand with the unconscious meaning of his or her acts: an idea, a failed action, the various representations of the return of the repressed, the substitution of what has been forgotten. It attends to the break in associative consistency in the discourse, where free association functions in correspondence with evenly suspended attention. The words tell of images and scenes that go through the analysand's mind through representations and ideas that can, if pursued, liberate affect until they resemble an anxiety dream. There is some discomfort, and what is now innerly experienced tends to be narrated metaphorically by describing scenes that happen in other places with different people and in verb tenses that generally refer to a more or less remote past, depending on the resistance they generate.

As an example, allow me to recall a well-known anecdote experienced and told by Freud himself in Letter 70 (1887–1902) to Fliess (October 3, 1897), telling of his guilt feelings related to the Oedipus complex he discovered in his auto-analysis; what is striking is that in the retelling, he does so symptomatically, putting it farther away in time, since, according to Jones, the event that he had placed at age two occurred when he was four, and also using expressions in Latin, a dead language, to refer to the resisted, saying: '*. . . later (between the ages of two and two-and-a-half) my libido was stirred up towards matrem, namely on the occasion of a journey with her from Leipzig to Vienna, during which we must have spent the night together and I must have had an opportunity of seeing her nudam . . .*'[6] The impact of seeing his mother naked before his eyes can only be expressed in a dubitative tone, in Latin and at an earlier moment than the real event. Words spoken in a different language lack the incestuous charge of the mother tongue, Latin carries the roots of the original, repressed in the contemporary German and, paradoxically, highlights what it means to conceal.

Continuing with the session, the excitation of desire and its inevitable frustration can produce a malfunction of the censure, permitting some achievement of the unconscious: what began as a dream and with the liberation of affect took on the characteristics of an anxiety dream, is now hallucinated as wish fulfillment and becomes a nightmare

Thus, the representation spoken by free association – psychoneurosis – is interrupted, displaced when the actual presentation breaks in and the metaphor is lost, followed by silence, anxiety, and somatic manifestations – pain or lethargy – that offer dialectics that differ greatly from any known language. From the psychic facet of the word, repressed by resistance, the somatic expression of the affect, whose paradigm is anxiety, follows. The analyst experiences the interruption of his or her evenly suspended attention because of the intrusion of an uncanny presentation that invades the transference field, displaying the tragic scene.

Here, our resource is the construction of the act, the description of the scene with words that analysts find on the basis of their inner experience, ideas, and the perception of their own somatic reactions (anxiety, excitation, pain, lethargy, etc.). This construction is what we use as a technical resource when the actual, the non represented presents itself, a material fated to be buried – Untergang. For this, analysts need to be willing to let themselves be used in the scene they happen to experience innerly in the countertransference, and to accept participation by taking the place of the transferred object, whatever it is, only to put a word where there never was one and to offer a representation, always provisional, that can allow this material to enter the associative circuit.

Therefore, some processes and contents inaccessible to consciousness need to be brought together and translated into conscious expression, meaning interpreted. But others need to be constructed on the basis of signs contained in the affective conglomerate presented. We recall that the Latin verb *construere*, composed of *cum*: 'with' and *struere*: 'to accumulate or pile up', is at the root of the English *construct*, which means to erect, build, and make something again. In grammar, it refers to putting words into order or putting them together according to the rules of grammatical construction, transforming that disordered accumulation or pile into a phrase, discourse or conclusions with meaning. Quantity must be subordinated to quality, which allows us to differentiate and put things into order.

In order to construct out of the conglomerate of large quantities, the analyst experiences innerly and analyses, differentiating and separating, de-constructing the effects of recognition of the tragic elements, and finally offers – skillfully – a construction of the act. It is something original and actual that occurs in the real of the session and provokes a conjecture, an ordering of the residues or relics that are gathered into the active exteriorizations of the transference on to his or her person. This is a different kind of transference, with an intense actual-experiential – drive – quality, that makes the analyst into an original object, cathected with drive, quite different from the usual representation that can be cathected libidinally, as occurs in psychoneurosis.

In *An Outline of Psychoanalysis* (1939), Freud highlights a certain coincidence between the id, which represents the inherited past – the constitutional that comes with birth – and the superego, with the influences of the *past assumed by others*, which substitutes race, family, ancestors, progenitors, and subsequent substitutive persons, while the ego *is governed principally by what one has experienced, which means whatever is accidental and actual*, which exerts effects and causes alterations in its structuring, and must be altered again therapeutically through analysis.

Freud alerts us to the importance of the word and free association, while Lacan formulates the hypothesis of the unconscious structured as a language. Last but not least, in the old schools of grammar, 'construction' means translating from Greek or Latin into a modern language. This implies translating a prehistoric[7] text in an archaic, dead language into a shared and contemporary tongue, giving words to the 'dead'[8] (Cesio, 2005).

The construction attempts to assemble, complete, and put order into these signs – Anzeichen – these piled-up residues, trying to build and re-make something, getting something living from the prehistoric piece, of which the essential has been preserved, though ***'buried underground***[9] *and inaccessible to the individual.'*

We are not referring to repressed material but to something corresponding to impressions and inner experiences that were not bound but buried underground: they have no representation and, therefore, no signification in the ego; not having been constituted into experience, they lack the psychic elaboration corresponding to the prehistory, which means that they have become neither memories nor memory, so that this material remains subject to the repetition compulsion, a manifestation of the death drive.

In this archaic mode, analysand and analyst find their boundaries blurred and mixed, in the tragic incestuous inner experience unfolding. It is the analyst that, through auto-analysis, must rescue him or herself from the scene and describe it, providing words whose lineal quality permits us to conceive of 'this that is occurring now' and is original, as a supposed repetition, a concept that introduces time and space, thereby constructing history.

The asymmetry makes the analyst the party responsible for signifying, putting into order, and naming the unnamed that will exist thanks to the word that creates it. As we said, constructing the act and describing the shared, inner experiential scene allows us to express in words the invading affect that demands discharge in action – Agieren – as tragic repetition. Transforming tragedy into drama means passing from prehistory to history and thus having memory, representation, recall, and word.

Consideration of this aspect of the technical resource of construction broadens the frontiers of psychoanalytic work and gives continuity to the Freudian investigation, since it conceives of a method, among the analyst's interventions, that makes it possible to include contents that never went through consciousness, the circuit of the psychic handling of their elaboration. It provides the actual drive contents, foreign to the ego, with the missing metaphor, which thus acquire a representational and symbolic level, an original experience and the capacity to come into what is historical and psychoneurotic, through reconstruction.

The stimulus to study and investigate is constant in our complex discipline, when we bear in mind the Freudian challenge: *It is only a question of analytic technique whether we are or are not able to entirely bring to light what is hidden.* I fully agree with my dear friend, Jacqueline Amati Mehler when she says, in a paper I had the pleasure of translating into Spanish, that as psychoanalysts, not only are we able to access deeper analytic work today, but also that better knowledge of the archaic object and its vicissitudes in psychic organisation has broadened the horizons of psychoanalytic theory and technique, so that we can now treat pathologies that were once considered unanalysable by our specific method of investigation and treatment (Amati Mehler, 2001).

Notes

1. 'Infantile' and 'unconscious' refer to the quality of the material, and have no bearing on place or time.
2. The magic circle is drawn by the shaman to establish the barrier between two heterogeneous spaces: an inside, where the magic happens, in opposition to the outside of profane reality. As for the 'centre of the world' or 'omphalos', it refers to the one Pausanias describes in Delphos, situated at the centre of the Earth. Varrón describes the omphalos as a tomb, that of the sacred serpent of Delphos, the Pythoness. It was considered the intersection between the world of the dead, the world of the living, and the world of the gods. A tomb can be an 'omphalos': a 'mortis et vitae locus'.
3. 'Ritual' refers to a set of pre-established rules that are repeated the same way each time.
4. The tragedy is a sealed unit that includes: parricide, incest, and phallic castration, followed by the Oedipus complex: tender love for the mother, ambivalence for the father, and the threat of castration. Freud describes this sequence in Chapter 3 of *The Ego and the Id* (1923), but it is F. Cesio who describes and terms it as the 'Oedipal tragedy'.
5. Vivencia [inner experience] is the term proposed by Ortega y Gasset to translate the German word Erlebniss, and indicates that something is merely experienced but not qualified as a real event. It differs from 'experience', which is precisely acquired with an object of external reality.
6. The bold type is mine.
7. Prehistory encompasses a period extending from the existence of humankind in the world and the beginning of our history. In psychoanalysis, it is material that is presented in the session in an actual, a-temporal way. The subject's history begins with the Oedipus complex, which can be salvaged from infantile amnesia and reconstructed from its residues.
8. The 'dead' is a construction made on the basis of buried contents, discovered in actual manifestations, such as lethargy, and is constituted by vicissitudes of phallic castration, the buried, tragic, primary Oedipus complex.
9. The 'buried underground' is the buried, which emerges from its tomb as hypochondria, actual neurosis or somatic illness.

References

Amati Mehler, J. (2001). El objeto en psicoanálisis. *Rev. de Psicoanal. LVIII, 4.*

Amati Mehler, J., Argentieri, S., & Canestri, J. (1993). The babel of the unconscious. polylingualism in psychoanalysis. *International Journal of Psychoanalysis, 71(4).*

Amati Mehler, J., Argentieri, S., & Canestri, J. (2002). *La Babel del Inconsciente: Lengua madre y lenguas extranjeras en la dimensión psicoanalítica.* Buenos Aires: Lumen.

Baranger, W., & Baranger, M. (1969). *Problemas del Campo Psicoanalítico.* Buenos Aires: Kargieman.

Cesio, F. (1987). Tragedia edípica. Sepultamiento. Acto. Transferencia y Repetición. *Rev. de Psicoanal.*, Vol. *XLIV*, N°1.

Cesio, F. (1994). Psicoanálisis de la 'vivencia' en la sesión, abstinencia y neurosis actual. Una introducción al análisis de las manifestaciones somáticas. *Rev. Latinoam. de Psicoanal., I, 1.*

Cesio, F. et al. (1992). *Freud y La Palabra.* Buenos Aires: Kargieman.

Cesio, F., & Sorrentini, A. (1998). El poder del analista. *Rev. de Psicoanal.*

Corominas, J. (1973). *Diccionario Etimológico de la Lengua Castellana.* Spain: Gredos.

Eliade, Mircea (1972). *Tratado de Historia de las Religiones.* Mexico City: Era.

Etcheverry, J.L. (1978). Sobre la versión castellana. *A.E.*, I.

Freud, S. (1887–1902). Extracts from the Fliess papers: draft n. letter 70 (1897). *Standard Edition, 1,* 1950.

Freud, S. (1887–1902). The problem of quality: in project for a scientific psychology. *Standard Edition, 1,* 1950.

Freud, S. (1887–1902). The experience of pain. *Standard Edition, 1,* 1950.

Freud, S. (1900). The interpretation of dreams. Chapter VII. *Standard Edition, 5.*

Freud, S. (1901). The psychopathology of everyday life. *Standard Edition, 6.*

Freud, S. (1916–1917). Introductory lectures on psycho-analysis. *Standard Edition, 15.*

Freud, S. (1923). The ego and the id. *Standard Edition, 19.*

Freud, S. (1937). Constructions in analysis. *S.E.* Vol. *XXIII. Standard Edition, 23.*

Freud, S. (1939). Historical truth. In: Moses and monotheism: three essays. *Standard Edition, 23.*

Freud, S. (1940). An outline of psycho-analysis. *Standard Edition, 23.*

Real Academia Española (1984). *Diccionario de la Lengua Española.* Madrid: EC.

Sorrentini, A. (1998). El Padecer actual, Vol.7. *Hipocondría,* Vol. *9. Las intervenciones psicoanalíticas,* Vol. *10.*
Sorrentini, A. (2000). Dolor y sufrimiento. *La Peste de Tebas.* Vol. *16.*
Sorrentini, A. (2003). Sentimiento de culpa. *La Peste de Tebas.* Vol. *26.*
Sorrentini, A. (2004). Encuadre psicoanalítico. *La Peste de Tebas.* Vol. *31.*
Sorrentini, A. (2005). Necesidad y deseo. *La Peste de Tebas.* Vol. 32, BA, Arg.
Sorrentini, A. (2005). Conciencia-Realidad-Fantasía. *La Peste de Tebas.* Vol. *34.*

CHAPTER TWELVE

Symbolism in love and sex

Ethel Spector Person

> . . . It was not the French symbolists who invented the trend from the explicit statement to the implicit hint, from the obvious to the allusive and oblique; it is as old as art itself. All mythologies started with symbols, veiled in allegory; the parables of Christ pose riddles which the audience must solve. The intention is not to obscure the message, but to make it more luminous by compelling the recipient to work it out by himself – to recreate it. (Koestler, 1964, p. 337)

Freud brilliantly delineated the nature of symbolism in dreams, symptoms, art and creative writing, fantasies, myths and folklore, religion and superstition. This paper focuses on the ways in which symbolism is incorporated into our knowledge and experience of love and sex, and the role of the culture in shaping symbols of love and sex.

Symbolization and symbols

Questions still persist about the origins of the symbolic process, the stage of development in which symbols become organized, the extent to which they require altered states of consciousness, such as the sleeping state, for their implementation, and the degree to which symbolic expression is related to underlying conflicts. Beebe and

Lachmann (2002) note that Piaget proposed that symbolic thought first emerged in infants no later than nine to twelve months of age. Greenspan and Shanker suggest that symbolization, 'the way symbols and internal representations emerge from earlier behavior remains an unsolved mystery in modern psychology' (Greenspan & Shanker, 2005, p. 354). They, too, point out that the earliest roots of symbols and internal representations are often an outgrowth of early infant behaviour, and that children need to meet two goals in order to achieve the capacity for creating meaningful interpersonal representations and symbols: (1) affect or emotion is integral to the formation of symbols, (2) 'affectively meaningful symbols of self and others become the basis for internal representations. Images without affect can lead to memories without meaning . . . A representation or symbol emerges [only] when perception *is separated from its action'* (*ibid.*).

A symbol, the product of symbolization, represents a particular thought or feeling expressed through the act of invoking an image of a concrete or natural thing to stand in for it. For example, the lion is a symbol of courage while the lamb is a symbol of meekness. Parables, fables, allegories, emblems, and dreams all encompass one or another symbol. In the Eucharist, the bread and wine serve as symbols of the body and blood of Christ.

Signs and symbols need to be distinguished from one another. In contrast to symbols, signs reside in consciousness; they convey the meaning of a specific concept by one or another arbitrary or conventional connection. Loewald's depiction of signs is excellent: 'Signs bring to mind something that they point to, indicate, or recall. For instance, fever is a sign of illness; wet pavement is a sign of rain' (1988, p. 46). There is a self-evident connection between a sign and what it represents.

Unlike a sign, a symbol is a conscious, manifest representation that encapsulates an unconscious or latent thought content. A symbol is invoked (out of awareness) to represent something else. Symbols represent a form of compromise between unconscious motivation and conscious mental processing. Some form of similarity links the symbol to what it stands for. Symbols are generally concrete in distinction to the more complex ideas that they represent; they are condensed expressions of those ideas. As Meissner points out, 'The image of a house can represent the body, money can symbolize feces, a pillar can refer to a phallus, or a bowl of flowers or a window can represent the female genitals' (Meissner, 2005, p. 31). A symbol serves as a vehicle to express what has been repressed. It allows unconscious content to surface in a cleverly disguised way, either to keep the nature of the latent meaning out of consciousness or to render it as consciously acceptable. Symbols play a major role in dreaming and dreamlike processes. Symbolism can be individual or can be communal as is often expressed in the visual arts and in religious icons. Thus 'the cross is a symbol of sacrifice and salvation, the menorah is a symbol of the faith of Israel in a god of light and life . . .' (*ibid.*).

Observers have noted a cross-cultural similarity in some symbols, which suggests that different cultures share similar themes originating in similar early life experiences, particularly in those relating to the body. For example, Ferenczi made a connection between faeces and money: Faeces, mud-pies, sand, pebbles, marbles, buttons, jewels, coins. He acknowledged that the value adults attach to such objects conditions their unconscious equations. Abraham observed that, 'The child first takes pleasure in substance that is soft and yielding, then in hard and granular material, and finally in small solid objects with a clean and shiny surface. In the Unconscious, these objects all remain equivalent to excrement' (quoted in Healy, Bronner, & Bowers, 1930, p. 323).

While symbols can be observed in everyday speech, enactments, and conscious fantasy, they are particularly prominent in the interpretation of dreams. Freud discovered the importance of symbolism in dreams, pointing out that dream images had a definite meaning even though they were disguised. He observed that when his patients associated to dream fragments, they frequently reported images that were more closely connected with suppressed material than with everyday life events. He interpreted the manifest content as representing unconscious wishes or thoughts, that had been disguised through a process of symbolization.

Freud's examination of dream content showed that the ideas or objects represented in dreams were often highly charged with unacceptable feelings and burdened with conflict. It was because of the forbidden meanings of symbols, derived as they were from instinctual levels of motivation, that their meaning remained unconscious. Other kinds of symbol formation are regarded as the same or similar to what is described in dream symbolism.

Any one symbol conveys multiple meanings. The figure of an eye may be symbolic of sight and knowledge, or on a more prosaic note, a painting of an eye may be hung on the door of an ophthalmologist. In Greece, I became enamoured of the 'evil eye' which was said to ward off danger, and I have for years, off and on, worn an 'eye' on a chain. Consciously, I assumed that I just liked the look of it, which I did, but there were undoubtably layers of magical meaning behind my off-and-on wearing of the eye. In discussing dream symbols, Winnicott described how 'a given symbol can, by displacement or substitution, come to represent more than one thing – balloons can symbolize breasts, but because of their lightness and playful quality, they may also represent states of manic elation' (1935).

What is sometimes omitted in discussions of symbolism is its communicative component, the fact that symbolization may be utilized in the form of speech to connect with someone else or to test that person's limits by speaking suggestively or symbolically on behalf of a particular goal. Bromberg has elaborated on the interpersonal aspects of symbolization in language. As he describes it, 'Human development is seen as mediated not by the increasing ability to manage and integrate instincts and unconscious wishes, but by a progressive capacity to symbolize and communicate to another person through the use of language, "who you are" rather than simply what you need or want. The therapeutic action of psychoanalysis is predicated, therefore, on the capacity of the analytic situation to require the patient, as a continuing task, to symbolize progressively in an interpersonal context, previously unformulated aspects of self as they emerge' (1998, p. 57). He concludes that 'in this light, Freud's basic rule of free association – the patient's stated commitment to try and fully reveal himself and the meaning of his words and behavior – is not simply the doorway to the "real" material, but, in the context of participant observation, is part of the continuing "task" built into the analytic structure . . . It keeps the analytic process from becoming solipsistic by making it inherently interpersonal through its demand quality . . .' (*ibid.*, pp. 57–58). In extending Bromberg's insight into the interpersonal nature of symbol and symbolization, we must take note not only of individual (and sometimes idiosyncratic) symbolization but also of symbols that are borrowed from pre-existing cultural symbols, whether ethnic, religious, or patriotic. My discussion focuses on the ways in which symbols play important roles in love and in sex and on the role culture plays in symbolization.

Symbolism in love

H.G. Wells wrote an analysis of the longing for love that has long been a priority in the emotional lives of those who live in Western culture. He tried to solve the riddle of why we came to love whom we did, proposing that we have in our minds a pre-existing conception of what love is. As Wells put it, 'I think that in every human mind, possibly from an extremely early age, there exists a continually growing and continually more subtle complex of expectation and hope; an aggregation of loving and exciting thoughts; conception of encounter and reaction picked up from observation, descriptions, drama; reveries of sensuous delights and ecstasies; reveries of understanding and reciprocities; which I will call the Lover-Shadow ... I think it is almost as essential as our self consciousness. It is *other* consciousness ...'

He goes on to say that, 'When we make love, we are trying to make another human being concentrate for us an impersonation or at least a *symbol* of the Lover-Shadow in our minds ...'(Wells, 1984, p. 53, my italics). Here he is emphasizing the fact that we have a pre-existing image of the type of lover we might desire, and that we fall in love with someone who corresponds to that pre-existing ideal. Wells' position is that we choose our lovers in tandem with an internal psychic processes, in short, with imagination. First we create an image of the complex qualities that seem to us to constitute the ideal love. We each have different priorities, generally unconscious, for those qualities essential to our image of the Lover-Shadow (Wells, 1984, pp. 53–55). Once we have created that image, we can imaginatively transform someone we meet into the embodiment of that product of our minds. Wells describes the person we choose as the *symbol* of our pre-existing ideal.

Consequently, a lover may fall in love at first sight if and when someone appears who corresponds to his or her already well-developed image of the Lover-Shadow. The lover experiences this person as an almost perfect 'fit' with the pre-existing or preconscious idealized image of an imagined love object – in effect the very image that Wells denoted as the 'Lover-Shadow'. The wished-for merger can be expressed through love, intimacy, and sexuality.

Stendhal, a great enthusiast of love, symbolized the act of falling in love through a specific metaphor: 'A branch or bough is stripped of its leaves in winter and thrown into an abandoned salt mine. Months later, the branch is pulled out and is covered with brilliant crystals. It is, so to speak, crystallized. Even the tiniest twigs are spangled over with sparkling, shimming diamonds, and the bare bough is no longer recognized' (Stendhal, 1947, p. XV). Here the crystallization of the bough is metaphoric or symbolic for the development of love. Despite the fact that love is the result of such a process, and so recognized by Stendhal, love is nonetheless experienced as a radical transformation.

It was in thinking about love that Stendhal observed how symbols of status may sometimes change our perceptions. Writing in the nineteenth century, Stendhal described the sensibility that informed the hierarchical society of that milieu: 'The Duchesse de Chaulnes used to say that a duchess is never more than thirty years old to a snob; and people who frequented the court of that upright man, King Louis of Holland still recall with amusement a pretty woman at the Hague who could never bring herself to think a man anything but charming if he was a Duke or Prince.' Put simply, the symbolic importance of an individual sometimes takes priority over the reality of his or her appearance or quality.

At the other extreme, observers are sometimes surprised by the apparently ridiculous choice of the decrepit or unappealing love object of one or another of their friends. Carson McCullers made this observation somewhat dramatically when she wrote of love that 'the most outlandish people can be the stimulus for love. A man be a doddering great-grandfather and still love only a strange girl he saw on the streets of Cheehaw one afternoon two decades past. The preacher may love a fallen women. The beloved may be treacherous, greasy-headed, and given to evil habits. Yes, and the lover may see this as clearly as anyone else (but that does not affect the evolution of his lover one whit. A most mediocre person can be the object of a love which is wild, extravagant, and beautiful as the poison lilies of the swamp. A good man may be the stimulus for a love both violent or debased, or a jabbering mad man may bring about in the soul of someone a tender and simple idyll' (McCullers, 1971, pp. 26–29). Her subtext is that the choice of the beloved is formed without conscious evaluation or judgement. The beloved strikes a chord in the lover; one or another of the beloved's attributes is symbolic for some attribute of which the lover is in search. How else might we understand love at first sight?

These vignettes, taken together, indicate that the lover's choice of the beloved has something to do with a predetermined attraction for specific characteristics. The object of choice has a certain kind of face or voice or carriage, a symbolic resonance, that draws the lover in. Lovers may be surprised to discover that their friends view their erotic choices as reminiscent of their mother, father, or former lover. But the reality is that our choice of a lover frequently conveys a symbolic reiteration of an earlier relationship. That the object of love may symbolize someone from earlier life is observable in many of our clinical cases, in which choice is sometimes based on the prototype of an idealized parent or, quite the opposite, on someone who is depreciated and who represents the otherness longed for.

Symbols figure heavily in the trajectory of love as it is expressed in the conventions of marriage. The bride's white wedding gown is a symbol of sexual purity. The engagement ring and then the wedding ring become the symbols of being partnered with, belonging to, or merging with the beloved. For many decades, the wedding ring served as a symbol of a man's 'ownership' of his woman, insofar as it was the wife who invariably wore a wedding ring while the husband seldom did. The ring also serves as a symbolic warning to other men that the woman wearing the wedding ring is off-limits. But in recent decades, many men wear wedding rings. This is one of the changes that grew out of the advent of the women's movement in which some women insisted on parity in 'symbols' of 'belonging' or 'ownership'.

Important symbols are intrinsic to the traditional marriage ceremony. The father of the bride gives her away, thus affirming his hegemony over his daughter. Though his parents may accompany the groom down the aisle, no-one gives him away; he is already a free man. The bride and groom together cut the first slice of the wedding cake, an act said to symbolize lifelong harmony; some suggest that the bride and groom's feeding one another a bite of the wedding cake symbolizes intercourse. Sharing the cake with the wedding guests affirms the unification of two families. One might say that the prenuptials and nuptials connected to marriage are steeped in symbols that are meant to represent and cement the permanency of the union.

However, it is important to note that romantic love is far from universal. The experience of love varies widely according to epoch, culture, class and caste, and even gender. Put simply, romantic love does not have the same priority or valence in all cultures. While romantic love draws on a fundamental human propensity, in particular, the longing for transcendence as the means for ameliorating the basic isolation of the human condition, different cultures promote different kinds of symbolic longing and different avenues to transcendence (among them religion and war).

Symbolism in sex

Some authors have suggested that sexual symbols comprise the vast majority of all symbols (Healy, Bronner, & Bowers, 1930, p. 207). Men and women usually employ different sexual symbols. Unlike the propositions of classical psychoanalysis that tie the symbols of masculinity and the symbols of femininity almost exclusively to anatomy, history demonstrates that sexual symbolism is dependent not only on one's body, but also on the divergent ways in which female and male sexuality are regarded in different epochs and cultures. That is, sexual symbolism implicates not only sexual organs and sexual acts, but also the way in which sex and gender are conceptualized in a specific historical epoch. Because contemporary changes in the way sex and gender are viewed have impacted women more than men, changes in the way women have revamped the symbolization of their sex and sexuality are more dramatic than what has been observed among men.

Symbolization in male sexuality

The longstanding, cultural stereotype (or ideal) of male sexuality has been of a kind of phallic omnipotence and supremacy, a phallus invested with the power of mastery. This ideal depicts a large, powerful, untiring phallus attached to a very cool male, long on self-control, with experience, and competence sufficient to make women (or men) crazy with desire. As Zielbergeld described it, 'It's two feet long, hard as steel, and can go all night' (1978, p. 23). This language conveys the way in which the penis is symbolically invested as the heart and soul of masculinity. René Girard observed the consequences of such phallic pride. As he wittily observed, 'Sexuality is one of those primary forces whose sovereignty over man is assured by man's firm belief in his sovereignty over it' (Girard, 1977, p. 34).

Some have claimed that the rocket was designed in the classic phallic shape, appropriately so, since it is an object of great power and thrust as well as symbolic of the 'male' urge to conquer. Thus, it has been argued that just as man the hunter set out to penetrate his domain so, too, the astronaut acts to penetrate space.

Kate Millet, in her book *Sexual Politics* (1970), pointed out that descriptions of male sexuality and the penis were not restricted to explaining sexual function but symbolically represented ideas of ascendancy and power (1970, p. 46). Such formulations symbolize a view of male sexuality as power-seeking and domineering with the penis as a potential weapon.

What is the function of the many novels that symbolize male sexuality as all-powerful? The emphasis on the power of the phallus and control over female (or male) partners should be understood, at least in part, as a compensatory response to anxieties engendered in the male developmental experience. Some of these anxieties can be understood as an amalgam of castration anxiety, fear and envy of both sexes, and the fear (or experience) of loss of the love object or the loss of love.

However, such fears can be temporarily abated through macho fantasies. There is a genre of popular fiction in which the common theme depicts the hero as extremely macho, adventurous, and virile. Men's preoccupation with such books and movies is comparable to women's fascination with love stories. The female novels are so popular that the word 'harlequin,' after the publishing house of the same name, has become a descriptive term. An equivalent term for the male novel is what I have called 'Herotica'.

A passage from Eric van Slustbader's *The Miko*, captures the way male sexuality is portrayed in this body of writing. The plot hinges on the idea that Akito, a woman trained in the arcane mystic and martial arts, is sworn to avenge a loved one by killing the hero

Nicholas. Although portrayed as a master assassin in perfect control of all her feelings, when she meets Nicholas, she feels compelled to have a sexual encounter with him:

> For the first time in her life Akito was open to the universe. Nothing in all her long arduous training had caused this ignition inside of her.
>
> She was so dizzy that she was doubly grateful for his strong arms about her. All breath had left her as he had uttered her name, how she ached for him! Her thighs were like water, unable to support her. She felt a kind of ecstasy at his touch she thought only possible in orgasm . . . Swept away, still a dark part of her mind yammered to be heard. What strange force had invaded her mind? What turned her plans of vengeance inside out? What made her feel this way about a hated enemy? [p. 277].

Her response is either part of the author's fantasy life or a depiction of what he thinks the average male is attracted to. Here, a man's power is validated symbolically through the idea that the most powerful of women is overcome by his charisma and overwhelming erotic power.

Another prominent feature of the erotic life of heterosexual men is preoccupation with lesbian themes. In part, the fantasy of two women making love suggests an abundance of women whose primary interest and sole function are sexual, ensuring that the man will never be humiliated by the absence of a sexual object. What is symbolically at play for the men is the self-reiteration of personal power through the power they exert over women who bend to their charms and to their power. One observes the symbolization of the penis as conferring power in the growing practice of penile inserts to enlarge the appearance of the penis. (This is analogous to women's augmentation of their breasts).

Sexual symbolism is often expressed in dreams and in fantasies. S.T., a successful professional, came into treatment because of recurring depressions. He was extremely proud of his beautiful, well preserved wife and obviously pleased by her voracious sexual appetite, although he was morbidly jealous of a lover she had prior to their marriage. He had initiated threesome sex, mostly with one other woman, but occasionally with another man. He enjoyed talking about how much his wife liked these sexual encounters. He was proud of her rapture but also pleased because she was so clearly at his disposal. He also maintained a number of ancillary sexual partners, although he in no way regarded this as being unfaithful.

During his depressions, usually triggered by business reversals, he became impotent. This was invariably followed by an obsessive preoccupation with his wife's former relationships, pathological jealousy, and the suspicion that she was currently unfaithful. He would then reject her and accuse her of being a dog in heat. During one depressive bout, he had a series of paired dreams with slight variations. In one dream, his wife was all-powerful and drove a chariot while he clung to her feet, and she fertilized the land with great streams of water. In a second dream, he controlled two giant stallions and dragged his wife along behind him. These oscillations in his perceptions occurred very rapidly and revealed how he perceived his wife and himself as locked in a bitter struggle for power, yet yoked together.

In these two dreams, the symbolism speaks for itself. One dream encapsulated his fears, the other his desires. Symbolism may appear in either direct or indirect ways. Some men have sexual fantasies or requirements that the women they sleep with have shaved pudenda. This appears to reflect one variant of a man's wish for the woman to be completely exposed, to conceal nothing whatsoever; the symbolic wish for power is gratified through the feeling that the man is able to possess a woman fully, visually as well as sexually. She is 'on-call' to his desires. The repetitive recourse to naked, erotic women in advertising appears to speak to some men's unconscious need to be surrounded by sexually available and willing females. It is, of course, the symbolic need for 'on-call' women that provides a good deal of the market for prostitution. Needless to say, many of these demands and fantasies are stoked by a man's need for symbolic endorsement of his phallic power.

What are the origins of man's symbolic desire for control and domination of women? The male's fear of the female, of his inability to please her (and his anger at her) stem from different developmental levels: fear of the pre-Oedipal mother who abandons, of the anal mother who intrudes/indulges, of the phallic-narcissistic mother who falsely seduces/denigrates masculinity, or the Oedipal mother who cannot be fulfilled, rejects, and falsely seduces. It is these potential fears that a male sometimes attempts to overcome with fantasies of sexual power and enactments of control.

The male's ambivalence about his control over his genital equipment and sexual prowess can be traced to physical aspects of the adolescent induction into genitality. While the experience of spontaneous erection and ejaculation is a release phenomenon, its subjective meaning may be ambivalent: although a man takes pride in the pleasure and power of his phallus, he often fears that his penis is not really under his control. The idea that the penis has its own separate identity is reflected in the tendency of young men to personify their penis by giving it a pet name. The young man's tragedy has been described as having a gun and ammunition but no control: by the time control is achieved the ammunition has been taken away. As a result, male sexuality frequently becomes imbued with issues of control and dominance, yet the adolescent's sense of lack of control over the penis is never completely resolved. Consequently, the penis remains a locus for symbolic elaboration, male pride, and some version of macho sexuality.

The fear of female unavailability and rejection leads to compensatory fantasies featuring a cornucopia of sexually available women. What is haunting in such fantasies is the magically exaggerated picture of male sexual prowess and a wishful desire for a different sexual world. As a consequence, men may be internally driven to conquer women, to posses them, and to do so repeatedly.

Symbolization in female sexuality

While there appears to be some consistency in Freud's application of sexual symbols as they apply to men and our contemporary understanding of male sexuality, there is a disconnect in most contemporary thinking about female psychology as interpreted by Freud, and, consequently, there is some disparity between symbolization of female sexuality in Freud's era contrasted to our own. Freud believed that the trajectory of female development leading to femininity exhausted the possibilities for women (*New Introductory Lectures*, p.173). But women's sexual powers are now celebrated.

Freud recognized many symbols as sexually derived. He interpreted containers, including boxes, cases, chests, and ovens as representations of the womb. He placed emphasis on the symbolic references to the female genitals in referring to women as an 'old box' or the 'weaker vessel' (SE XV, p. 161). He referred to a man's complaint if he 'found the door open', by which I believe he meant that the woman was no longer a virgin. In Freud's examples, some women appear to have internalized the metaphors men used for them, for example, 'I laid the table for him, but he turned it round.' A derivative expression (fantasy) suggested that 'Lame children . . . come about through the man's "turning the table round",' a concrete symbolization of the particular sexual act in which the woman is entered from behind (*ibid.*, p. 162).

Just as many male sexual symbols that have to do with power are associated with the phallus and the phallic shape, so too have symbols of female power been connected to breasts, beauty, and, ultimately, to an active kind of participation in sex. It has been remarked that the high-heeled shoe has two different symbolic valences. On the one hand, the strictures it puts on walking accentuates the symbol of circumscribed power (comparable to the binding of women's feet in China) but, at the same time, the very high stiletto heel suggests domination.

Many symbols of female sexuality have to do with fertility. In earlier centuries, reproduction, human fertility, and continuation of the species were some of the greatest preoccupations of human kind. As a consequence, each society prayed to fertility gods and goddesses. In addition, specific images were imbued with sexual symbolism. Women and young girls often wore fertility dolls around their waists in order to enhance their likelihood of becoming pregnant. In our own culture, women's preferred sex symbols seem to have as much to do with sexual appeal and personal power over men as with fertility. Some men appear to regard big breasts as symbolic of sexual intensity, as a result of which some women resort to breast implants.

Symbols of fertility are different in different cultures. Such fertility symbols include fertility dolls, which were sometimes worn by women and young girls in Angola to enhance their fertility. These were often made of corn cobs, forked sticks, and beeswax, with the corn cob itself sometimes being a symbol of fertility. Many of these symbols are not anatomically representative but refer to the earth's bounty. Fertility has often been represented by pineapples, thought to be symbols of life and fertility, and also by flowers, such as lilies and tulips, which were believed to symbolize love. The pine cone, which in ancient times served as an emblem of Venus, goddess of love, was believed to be a symbol of life and fertility. So, too, was the cornucopia, the horn of plenty, spilling over with fruit deemed a symbol of fertility. Interestingly enough, the cornucopia because of its shape, which is that of a hollow horn, has been used to represent both male and female (Bruce-Mitford, 2004, p. 70).

The symbolization of female sexuality is far from static. Traditional symbols undergo change in association with a change in sexual mores as they relate both to women's sexuality and autonomy. While female sexual symbols once referred primarily to conception and birth, such symbols now focus just as heavily on sexuality and on sexual allure. These changes are apparent not only in patients' dreams and associations, but also in themes manifest in contemporary film and fiction.

However, it was only with the effectiveness of birth control that there was, or could be, a major shift in how women regarded and symbolized their own sexuality. Effective birth control meant that women could enjoy sexuality without the fear of becoming pregnant. In the 1970s, the writer Snitow pointed out that, 'The idea that women can have sex in the world too is still exotic, but writers can now explore this possibility in their work, all of which has been touched in some way by the resurgence of feminine consciousness' (Snitow, 1980, p. 161). She emphasizes how the women's movement enlarged women's dreams and demonstrated that women writers were no longer writing about sexuality 'as an isolated entity, but as a complex occasion in which certain words, thoughts, memories, and predictable tensions between men and women play as large a part as the body or any ideal of love' (*ibid.*, p. 173).

While I have been discussing essentially generic symbols, symbols may sometimes be so idiosyncratic that they are not amenable to generalization. Hanna Segal gives an example of a very ingenious symbolic mode of representation: 'As part of a long dream a patient dreamed of *a column of soldiers marching eight abreast*. Rather perplexed by that part of the dream, [Segal] asked her what she thought. She answered immediately: "Ate a breast, of course. What else could it mean?"' (Segal, 1991, p. 9).

Bassin writes about the way in which the body ego acts as 'origin and container for symbolization'. While she is primarily addressing symbolization in women, the body ego clearly plays the same role in both sexes. Bassin draws on Winnicott, 1988, who described the body ego as 'the imaginative elaboration of the body'(Bassin, 1996, p. 177). She suggests that such an imaginative elaboration 'allows sufficient play for indeterminate contributions from both the body and psyche that are elaborated in affect-latent object relations (e.g., identification from significant Others arising from separation-individuation, primal scene, and Oedipal drama) to the body' (*ibid.*). The consequence, as she points out, is that the body ego has both a symbolic and metaphoric relation to the body.

Bassin points to Jones's 1938 formulation of symbolization, 'as requiring repression between symbol and fantasy in which symbolization has a defensive cast'. But she notes, in contrast, that, 'In Loewald's (1988) model, symbolization is part of ego development, without the traditional emphasis on defense. Here the creation of a symbol emphasizes a hidden linkage and restores the breach between primary and secondary process. These memorial symbolizations are to be differentiated from the fetish (another memorial decastration in that they do not disguise what is symbolized' (*ibid.*, p. 181). Though it was not his emphasis, Loewald's formulation can be read as going beyond sexuality *per se*; he describes a kind of symbolization that allows women to own their individuality; here symbolization transcends sexuality to establish autonomy.

Conclusion

While there is some continuity between romantic and sexual symbolism as portrayed in earlier eras and in our contemporary culture, there are also important differences. Our contemporary observations demonstrate how romantic and sexual symbols change with the cultural *Zeitgeist*. This does not distract from the importance of symbolization or the origins or meaning of symbols, but it does emphasize how the culture, and not just biology or early life events, plays a major role in creating symbols and dictating symbolic function. There have, perhaps, been fewer changes in the symbolization of male sexuality than in the symbolization of female sexuality. This may be so insofar our concepts of male sexuality have not undergone the same degree of re-theorization as has our understanding of female sexuality. Female sexuality could not be fully re-thought or re-symbolized until the discovery of reliable birth control. Analogously, women have also achieved more control in their romantic relationships, in large part because they are now able to support themselves and are no longer so dependent on marriage. The point I am emphasizing is that culture acts to re-codify symbols such that they differ to a greater or lesser degree in different cultures and different epochs. Put another way, it is the unconscious as it intersects with the culture that impacts symbolization and decrees the interpretations that will likely be made of contemporaneous symbols.

References

Bassin, D. (1996). Reconciliation of masculinity and femininity in the postoedipal model. *JAPA 44*, suppl.: 157–190.

Beebe, B., & Lachmann, F. (2002). *Infant Research and Adult Treatment: Co-Constructing Interactions*. Hillsdale, NJ: The Analytic Press, Inc.

Bromberg, P.M. (1998). *Standing in the Spaces: Essays on Clinical Process Trauma and Dissociation*. Hillsdale, NJ: The Analytic Press, 2001.

Bruce-Mitford, M. (2004). *Signs and Symbols*. London: Dorling Kindersley in Association with Barnes and Nobel.

Freud, S. (1937). Analysis terminable and interminable. *Standard Edition, 23*.

Freud, S. Symbolism in dreams. In: *Standard Edition, 25* (pp. 149–161).

Girard, R. (1977). *Violence and the Sacred*. Baltimore & London: Johns Hopkins University Press. (Originally published in Paris, 1972.)

Greenspan & Shanker (2005). Developmental Research. In: Person, Cooper & Gabbard (Eds.) *The APPI Textbook of Psychoanalysis* (pp. 335–360). Washington, DC: American Psychiatric Publishing, Inc.

Healy, Bronner, & Bowers (1930). In: *The Structure and Meaning of Psychoanalysis* (pp. 335–360.). New York: Alfred A. Knopf.

Koestler, A. (1964). *The Act of Creation*. New York: The Penguin Group, 1989.

Loewald, H. (1988). *Sublimation: Inquiries into Theoretical Psychoanalysis*. New Haven: Yale University Press.

McCullers, C. (1971). *The Ballad of the Sad Café*. New York: Bantam Books.

Meissner, W.W. (2005). The dynamic unconscious: psychic determinism, intrapsychic conflict, unconscious fantasy, dreams, and symptom formation. In: Person, Cooper & Gabbard (Eds.), *The APPI Textbook of Psychoanalysis* (pp. 21–37). Washington, DC: American Psychiatric Publishing, Inc.

Segal, H. (1991). *Dream, Fantasy and Art*. London: Routledge.

Snitow, A. Barr (1980). The frontline: notes on sex and novels by women 1969–1979. In: C.R. Stimpson & E. Spector Person (Eds.), *Women: Sex and Sexuality* (pp. 158–179). Chicago: University of Chicago Press.

Stendhal (1947). *On Love*. Translated by HVB under the direction of C.K. Scott-Moncrief. New York: Liveright.

Wells, G.P. (Ed.) (1984). *H.G. Wells in Love: Postscript to an Experiment in Autobiography*. Boston: Little Brown.

Winnicott, D.W. (1935). The manic defence. In: *Through Paediatrics to Psycho-Analysis: Collected Papers* (pp. 29–144). New York: Brunner/Mazel, 1992.

CHAPTER THIRTEEN

Does the Pierce's semiotic model based on index, icon, symbol have anything to do with psychoanalysis?[1]

Riccardo Steiner

1) 'You are better than my librium, because you give me equilibrium', a patient told me in a sort of manic state, who had just been admitted to a psychiatric hospital in North London where I worked during my training as a psychoanalyst, many years ago. The following day, when I met him again, he did not recognize me and looked very frightened and confused. I tried to remind him what he had told me the day before, but he became very agitated and started shouting at me: 'I am not a horse . . . I am not a horse . . . you want to poison me . . . you want to give me the librium for a horse . . .'[2]

2) Working together with a very perceptive and intelligent social worker and occupational therapist, still in the same hospital in North London, we managed to move a British patient out from a very serious catatonic and mute state that had lasted for several months. He started working in the garden with us and at one point began speaking again. But he claimed to be in Argentina and pronounced a few Spanish words. During the period of his catatonic state, sitting on his chair without speaking, he had heard the social worker addressing me in Spanish, a language I could understand and speak much better than English. The patient therefore was convinced I was a South American, although no

mention of my background had been made in my conversations with the social worker. We dealt only with professional matters.

3) One morning, a private patient of mine came into my consulting room looking terribly suspicious and agitated, and did not want to lie on the couch. The patient was standing in the middle of my room, looking at me. I could see only half the patient's face. I noticed that there was something under the pullover that the patient was holding with both hands. After a few seconds of silence, during which I looked at the patient with the most benign and at the same time interrogative expression on my face that I could find, the patient started whispering a few words: 'I must protect . . . I must protect . . . I must protect the baby . . .' When I told the patient that at that particular moment he felt I was threatening the baby-patient himself, the patient took out from under the pullover a little doll and a pair of scissors and told me not to say anything more, because my words would physically hurt the 'baby', meaning the doll. The patient was prepared to use the scissors to cut my words and my throat.[3]

4) During the preliminary interview with a patient of mine, who had had previous therapy and was acquainted with the British psychoanalytical way of looking at a patient's personal history, the patient told me spontaneously that the mother and other relatives had reported to the patient that a few weeks after the patient was born, the mother developed a mastitis. The mother had to go to hospital and, according to the patient, the mother made the patient feel responsible for all this.

After a few sessions, the patient had a dream in which a cow that had become very restless and noisy could not feed the newborn calf, which also looked very disturbed. Asked by me to associate about the dream, the patient told me 'It must have to do with my mother,' and plunged into a heavy silence. In order not to put my interpretations into what the patient had said, this being just a sort of newborn analysis, I asked whether the patient could remember what the patient had told me during the first interview about the mother's illness in her breast and whether there were some links between the dream of that episode and what was going on in the analysis. The patient stood up and left the room in a sort of state of panic. But after a few moments, the patient came back and told me that I had mentioned the breast and it had been too frightening just to hear the word.

5) A patient with a long, chronic history of eczema, which had been present since the patient was born, and who later on developed serious asthma that lasted through childhood, adolescence, and beyond, for months and months could only whisper or cry, which made communication even more complicated. My attention and ability to concentrate were pushed to their limits because, in spite of me telling the patient that I could not hear what was being whispered, the patient did not raise her voice. However, during one session, probably feeling a bit better, the patient was able to tell me that the reason for coming to sessions with me was to see my room and the couch and 'feel' the security of the physical contact with the couch and to tune in with my breathing, rather than to speak or try to understand. I was, therefore, mainly functioning for her as one of the breathing masks she used for her asthma attacks, or a sort of rather indifferentiated but very perceptible holding other.

6) During a particularly anxious moment in his analysis, a patient who had been left by his partner constantly returned to a specific place where they used to meet and walk together. Furthermore, during weekends, the patient compulsively walked up and down the road where my consulting room is. All these ritualistic moves helped him control his anxieties, because the places and the roads reminded him of what he had lost and was in need of. However, he was quite aware of the rather illusory nature of what he was doing or trying to recreate in himself.

7) This patient had an extremely complicated and difficult relationship with his parents and his mother in particular. After her death, the patient had to look after her belongings. Among other things, there was a series of boxes containing historical personal family correspondence that would have been very silly to destroy. The delusional hatred of this patient for his family and mother was still so strong that it would have been impossible to keep all those documents at home. The patient more than once mentioned that the fact that those documents could be put in the attic of the home where the patient was living was too disturbing because it was still as if, through their visual and physical presence, the mother of the patient could have been felt as

present too. A solution was nevertheless found, because a library agreed to store and look after the documents. The patient was aware of the 'as if' quality of his feelings, but could not cope with them, at least at that moment.

8) This patient had a long-standing problem with her father. They did not meet for a long period. During the analysis, the patient started feeling better and thought it would be possible to contact her father again. At one point, they decided to meet. Prior to their meeting, the patient had to phone him and during the Friday session she got more and more excited and manic about the phonecall and the meeting and started speaking louder and louder, repeating 'my father, my father' several times in different contexts. I was struck by her tone of voice and the emotional 'weight' that the vocal 'a' in the word 'father' started carrying when my patient was pronouncing it. But I also noticed that at one point I was almost automatically repeating 'my father, my father' myself, and I felt I had to open my mouth wider and wider. I could visually represent me doing that in pronouncing the name 'father'. I did not say that to the patient, although I stressed how excited she must have felt, waiting to speak to, and then meet, her father and leaving me behind, perhaps like her mother in that context.

On the Monday, she came back and told me: 'Oh . . . I had a weekend full of my father . . . I phoned him . . . and we will meet . . . and I had a dream . . . In the dream I was eating a big leg of lamb.' I think the dream speaks for itself. Incidentally, the word 'lamb' even contained a syllable of the Christian name of my patient's father!

How would one consider or, to use a term that I do not like very much because it is too rigid but is at the same time quite useful, 'classify' the short clinical vignettes I have just described? Of course, it depends on one's own theoretical and clinical upbringing. But, I think, particularly today, when so much has been written on the subject, rightly or wrongly, there would be a general consensus in considering the first three vignettes as examples of 'concrete thinking and feeling', to use the language of classical psychiatry – which is of course also part of psychoanalysis – or, to use the language of the psychoanalytical tradition to which I belong, as typical examples of 'symbolic equations' (Segal, 1950, 1957) in which projective and introjective identification of a pathological kind linked to anxieties of primitive persecution and fragmentation or highly split and idealized primitive libidinal impulses play a major distorting role. Indeed, looking at the first vignette, after having got totally manic about me, the patient, via projection and fear of introjection, confused me with a mad poisoning therapist who had confused him with a horse. In the second vignette, the patient, giving up momentarily his rigid catatonic defensive state, had tried to cope with the persecutory and fragmenting anxieties by '*becoming*' whom he thought I was, living in my supposed country of origin and speaking my maternal language. The third vignette seems to show again an enormously persecutory anxiety in the patient, who projected his murderous feelings into me, attributing them to me.

If those examples are so typical, why did I think it was worthwhile mentioning them, one might well ask. Well, there are a few reasons why I did so, which I will try to explain and which I think could help me try to develop not so much a set of new ideas as an attempt to focus on, and from my point of view, to better work, clinically-speaking, with patients of this kind, if one takes into consideration the characteristics and nature of the other five vignettes, comparing them with the first three that I have already mentioned. Indeed, it seems to me that the other vignettes do represent what I would call *provisionally* a sort of *fluctuation* in the way patients communicate their anxieties and problems, which also had countertransferential effects in me, as far as symbolization was concerned. At times, the way of communicating seemed to be very similar to, if not identical to, the symbolic equation, as in the fourth vignette of a patient who was a borderline case in which psychotic features were very strong and at times briefly prevailed. The other examples, in my opinion – and, of course, had I more space to describe the clinical cases, it would have been easier to demonstrate it – seem to belong to a 'spectrum' in which borderline *psychotic* features were less intense, also because of a major awareness of what the patients were communicating. And particularly as far as the last of my eight vignettes is concerned, the communication of the patient seemed to be very similar to what today we mean by 'symbolization' in a 'neurotic' way in our discipline, thinking particularly of what followed after the Friday session in the dream, in which, symbolically, she was orally 'incorporating' the father or his penis.

Although I am quite prepared to be criticized for getting on my usual idiosyncratic hobby horse, I think it would be first of all quite useful and even interesting to briefly remind the reader of how M. Klein and H. Segal later on came to describe equations, symbolic equations, and symbols, without forgetting the historical context in which they were making their observations. Even in our field, discoveries do not happen miraculously and the tendency to have to focus on 'the here and now' today in every field of psychoanalysis, makes us, to my mind, forget the complexity of the issues and the slow, at times painstaking, repetitive process of change based on the borrowing, consciously or less consciously, of concepts and definitions by single scholars in different contexts, which leads, via accumulation and change of meaning due to new ways of observing and making sense of clinical data, to new discoveries.

Sometimes, re-reading or simply reminding ourselves of old texts, putting them in a broader historical context, can help us to better understand the danger of the professionalization of our discipline, which compels us to apply mechanically and rigidly concepts that, when they were first introduced, implicitly or explicitly contained potential new questions, and provide the answers to the problems they tried to solve or clarify. Maybe all of this can be of some help in trying to go further.

The term 'symbolic equation', was used by Melanie Klein in her famous 1930 paper *The Importance of Symbol Formation in the Development of the Ego* (Klein, 1930, pp. 220–225) to describe the difficulties her little patient Dick had to symbolise because he was rigidly blocked both emotionally and intellectually, nearly unable to speak and to play, with a fixed interest only in a few things, particularly trains and doors. Klein, in reality, had already used the term, which she borrowed from the famous 1916 paper of E. Jones, *The Theory of Symbolism* (Jones, 1916, pp. 139–140)[4], making at the same time use of Ferenczi's 1913 paper *Stages of the Development of the Sense of Reality* (p. 79) in her earlier work, particularly in a 1923 paper entitled *Early Analysis* (Klein, 1923, pp. 83–104), in which Klein attempted to rethink Jones' final conclusions concerning symbolism in psychoanalysis.

Klein, at that time, was still working on the continent using clinical material from her first cases in Budapest, where she went from Vienna and had been deeply influenced by Ferenczi but had already decided to go to Berlin to work with K. Abraham, before arriving in 1926 in London, helped by the Stracheys and E. Jones. Even her biographical vicissitudes seemed to reflect a constant need to move, to shift, to find new objects, which curiously enough seemed reflected in her very dynamic views about symbolic equations, symbolism, and sublimation of those years.

I cannot, of course, go into detail here concerning Jones' paper, perhaps the most typical example of Jones' orthodoxy to Freud. The founder of British psychoanalysis had tried to have the final word in a long, extremely lively, and creative debate about symbols in psychoanalysis compared with other ways of understanding symbolism that had characterized the first twenty years or so of the existence of our discipline. Indeed, Freud had started using the term 'symbol/symbolic', particularly in his *Studies on Hysteria* (1895)[5], not to mention what he had already come across in his pre-analytical research on aphasia (Steiner, 1981, 1982) and in the *Project for a Scientific Psychology* (Freud, 1895; Steiner 1975), to describe and make sense of the unconscious meaning of the symptoms of his patients and then made of sexual symbolism in particular, one of the corner-stones of the way the patients, but also normal people, express their wishes and conflicts in the dream. Just think of Freud's *The Interpretation of Dreams* (1900) followed by the fundamental revision of the same book in 1914 and further revisions later on, in addition to what one can find in his clinical cases, particularly that of Little Hans (1909), the Wolf Man (1914) and the Schreber case (1911), and in his theoretical essays, *Three Essays on the Theory of Sexuality* (1905) or in his metapsychological paper, *The Unconscious* (1915), as well as *Totem and Tabu* (1913), just to mention at random some of the main papers in which Freud had further elaborated his theory of symbolism. The 1914 edition of *The Interpretation of Dreams* is of such interest because together with the famous lecture 'Symbolism in dreams' of the *Introductory Lectures on Psychoanalysis* (1916–1917, pp. 149–169) and almost simultaneously with what Freud stated about the unconscious primary phantasies, particularly in the case of the Wolf Man (Freud, 1941; Steiner, 2003) and their universality, it contains the final thoughts of Freud concerning the universality of certain sexual symbols present in the dream and unconscious life in general. I have to assume the reader understands all this and how it can be related to what Freud meant at that time by sexual drive, self-preservative drive, aggressive drive, and related phantasies, by defence, repression, unconscious, etc. Just remember that we are still in the years of the so-called 'topographical model of the psychic apparatus' in which the repression of libidinal sexual infantile phantasies and activities and the core role played by the Oedipus complex were thought to be the main causes of the disturbances symbolized in the symptoms and in the dreams. And if one excepts the Schreber case, Freud did not speak openly about psychotic cases. Although, and this has to be stressed in this particular context, besides Freud's observations (1913), some of his colleagues or followers like Bleuler, who later on would publish the most important descriptive research on schizophrenia, inspired by Freud's thinking, had already, in 1910, as Freud himself reports, noticed that schizophrenics, as Bleuler called patients affected by dementia praecox, could understand very easily Freud's sexual symbolism (Freud, 1911 edition of the *Interpretation of Dreams*, 1900, p. 351).[6]

Why do I stress so much all this, which was completely forgotten later on? Because already at that date, if not before, Freud and some of his pupils were aware that adult patients affected *by dementia praecox were able to practically bypass the symbolism and immediately perceive what the symbolizer was hinting at, reminding of, but also hiding.* One should not forget that Freud's sexual symbols in the dreams and in the symptomatic behaviour of his patients were considered to be hiding their original sexual content due to the work of repression of the dream itself, etc. That is also the reason why in those first two decades of psychoanalysis there had been an explosion of interest in applied psychoanalysis, because literature, anthropology, folklore, mythology, history of religion, etc., seems to confirm the wealth of the 'symbolic material' Freud discovers.

Today, the observations of Freud, Bleuler, and others, considering, incidentally, also the enormous importance that Bleuler gave to the power of unconscious effects in distorting the proper way of thinking and behaviour, could be considered as referring to symbolic equations, descriptively speaking.

Curiously enough, but also symptomatically enough, the beginning of the First World War seemed to have slowed down, if not stopped, this enormous interest and enthusiasm in studying sexual symbolism and interpreting the whole cultural world through Freud's discoveries. I cannot deal here in detail with Freud's conflicts and doubts about Stekel, who was probably the most gifted but also eccentric interpreter of symbols of Freud's pupils. Neither can I deal with Freud's criticism of Silberer and, of course, particularly of Jung[7] who in those years had started criticizing Freud more and more for his pansexualism, which affected mainly symbolization and Freud's views about it. I dealt with all this better in my 1975 book. But I had to recall all this because the paper of Jones, who so deeply influenced M. Klein, H. Segal, and the British schools of psychoanalysis in general, as I will briefly mention later on, cannot be understood if one forgets the context in which it was written. Jones, with his typical attitude of the warden of Freud's orthodoxy when he had to deal with his male rivals, the other pupils around Freud, was trying to critically answer and dismantle what he called the 'post-psychoanalytical school' represented by Jung, Silberer, and also, to a certain degree, Stekel (Jones, 1916). Jones tried to rigidly differentiate Freudian psychoanalytic symbolism from other ways of understanding symbolism in other fields of culture. The true, unique symbolism of psychoanalysis was mainly, for Jones, a sort of *defensive process*, a form of compromise between what is symbolized and the repression which forces the original content of the symbol to hide. 'Only what is repressed can be symbolized' claims Jones and, of course, what is repressed are the infantile wishes and sexual phantasies and only what can be repressed can be symbolized. Furthermore, Jones tried to sharply differentiate the true psychoanalytical symbol from sublimation, although he saw a necessary link between those two processes and stressed that the progressive symbolization of the child was important in order to understand the widening of his ego interests and the approach to reality of the child and later his approach to science, art, and other creative activities. He stressed particularly the importance of interest and pleasure in pushing the child to symbolize. Therefore, making use of his evolutionistic, cultural background, Jones saw a sort of movement forwards, inherent in symbolization, provided it could be overtaken by sublimation (Steiner, 1975).

In spite of his rigid categorizations, I think that one of the most important aspects of Jones' paper is that he tries to deal with the ontogenesis of symbols using, obviously, Freud, who stressed more than once the relationship between the infantile way of thinking and symbolism and also, in general, the primitive pre-individual way of thinking (to which symbols seem to refer). But, Jones also used the work of Ferenczi, who had dedicated more than one work in 1913 to the problem of the ontogenesis of symbols beside what one could find in Abraham's *Symbol and Dream* (1909). Jones uses, therefore, but also, in some way, substitutes Ferenczi's notion of identification: identification that the child makes between his body and his organs and the inanimate world in which the small child constantly projects himself and his organs, according to Ferenczi (1913). Jones substitutes all this with the expression 'equation, symbolic equation'. The child equates his organs with external objects but also he equates his parents' organs with his own and with external inanimate objects. Then he gradually starts symbolizing, investing the world with new sexual meanings. But then he has to repress and, in the end, he can start sublimating: symbolism, the true psychoanalytic symbolism, although important, is left behind as a regressive way of thinking and feeling. Yet we have here a first clear description of a process which will attract the attention of M. Klein as early as 1923.

But what one notes in Klein's 1923 paper *Early Analysis* (Klein, 1923, pp. 77–105) – without which we could not understand her landmark paper of 1930 that I mentioned a few pages earlier, and on which I will make some comments in a moment – is the fact that Klein seems to think more positively than Jones about the passage from symbolic equations to symbolization and sublimation. In her 1923 paper, in which, following Freud's changed views concerning the role played by the death drive in human development, which had led Freud to the formulation in 1920 of the so-called 'structural model' of the psychic apparatus, based on the life and death drives, Klein attaches great importance to aggressive inhibited impulses and drives, focusing mainly on the classical Oedipus complex, and acknowledges that sublimation is very important. Yet, due also probably to the fact that she was working mainly using her revolutionary method of play technique with her small patients, she accentuates the dynamic role present in both symbolic equations and in symbolization from the most primitive symbols to the most elaborate ones. It is not that she denies the pathological characteristics of the entire process when the child is inhibited, but she seems fascinated by the child's emotional and mental movements, by the child's instinct to know, or epistemophilic instinct as she calls it, starting from the first symbolic equation, to symbolization and sublimation. In both her 1923 and 1930 papers, she also reminds the reader of Ferenczi's notion of identification, 'the forerunner of symbolization' (1923, pp. 75–76; 1930, p. 220), which she links to the formation of symbolic equations first of all, to the point that towards the end of her 1923 paper she openly claims that: 'The impulsion constantly to effect by means of fixations, a libidinal cathexis of fresh ego activities and interests genetically (i.e. by means of sexual symbolism) connected with one another and to create new activities and interests is *the driving force in cultural evolution of mankind.*[8] This explains why we find symbols at work in increasingly complicated inventions and activities, just as the child advances from his original primitive symbols, games and activities, to others, leaving the former ones behind' (Klein, 1923, p. 104).

And that explains why, in her 1930 paper, at one point resuming her work done during the Twenties and quoting again as her sources Jones and Ferenczi, she claimed: 'Some years ago, I wrote a paper based on those concepts (she was referring to Ferenczi's notion of identification and Jones' symbolic equations), in which I drew the conclusion that symbolism *is the foundation of all sublimations and talents, since it is by way of symbolic equation that things, activities and interests become the subject of libidinal phantasies*'[9], (Klein, 1930, p. 220).

In her usual condensed, and at the same time not very precise, way of expressing herself, Klein mentions here both symbols and symbolic equations, using the same terminology 'symbolic equation' for normal and pathological development – something the reader must bear in mind, as I will stress again later on – and one has, therefore, to be careful how one reads these sentences. But it is obvious that she was thinking of the strict, nearly overlapping link between symbolic equations and symbols, particularly in the earliest phases of development of the child. Considering all that, and remembering also that in 1923 she referred to a very interesting and forgotten paper by Groddek on the compulsion to use symbols[10] (Klein, 1923 p. 104), one could perhaps say she was giving new life, through her work – which I have to say seems at times to remind one of the importance attributed by Jung to symbolization – to what Freud had observed in *The Interpretation of Dreams*. There, Freud (1900), partially inspired by Scherner, a rather mad, eccentric but genial late Romantic writer and follower of Schelling (Steiner, 1981), whose theories on the dream's symbolization had deeply influenced him, had underlined that it was the unconscious activity of the 'imagination' which one had to consider, if one wanted to understand the symbolism of the dream created by this phantasy (1900, pp. 83–84).

This unconscious imagination or capacity to create symbols – what Freud called in German '*unbewußte Phantasie . . . die symbolisierende Tätigkeit der Phantasie* ('the symbolizing activity of the imagination', Freud, 1900, G.W., vol.II/III, p. 88, as well as pp. 230–231, p. 340, etc.) – was present and very active even in very small children, according to Klein and those who followed her pioneering views in those years. That was due, as Klein claimed in another paper of the 1920s, *Psychological Principles of Early Analysis* (Klein, 1926), to the fact that communication between consciousness and the Unconscious was much easier and more fluid in small children. Furthermore, echoing the most daring phylogenetic hypotheses of Freud and his followers, Groddek in particular, Klein stated (1926, p. 134): 'In their play, children represent symbolically phantasies, wishes, experiences. Here they are employing the same language, the same archaic phylogenetically acquired mode of expression as we are familiar with from the dreams.'[11]

And if it were not too risky to make such a comparison, because of E. Cassirer's criticism of psychoanalysis (1945), one could even be tempted to remind the reader that in the third volume of his *Philosophie der Symbolischen Formen* (1927), written more or less in the same period, but completely unknown to Klein, Cassirer had stressed the enormous importance of the symbolic function in our minds.[12]

Too often – I say that incidentally here – Klein's notion of unconscious phantasy, which has so many links with the notion of 'imagination' (Steiner, 2000), has been confused with the actual primary unconscious phantasies to which, together with unconscious symbolism, Klein started attributing enormous importance in her work of those years and even later on (Steiner, 2003). But this notion seems to overlap with the capacity to create symbolic equations and symbols.

Furthermore, due also to her work using her play technique, Klein seemed to accept and to hint at an answer to what probably was, and still is, the most complex problem related to the unconscious capacity to create symbols, linked to the unconscious imagination. Klein followed some of Freud's statements, particularly those related to Sperber's theory (Freud, 1916–1917, p. 167) and those of some of his colleagues. Groddek, for instance, mentions the existence in the child of a philogenetically inherited language, as we have seen. But what sort of language was it? The Freudian evolutionistic Lamarckian views accepted by Klein, even as far as the primary unconscious phantasies were concerned (Steiner, 2003), seemed to imply that at the origin of humankind there had been the body and sexuality, which were responsible for all sorts of ways of communicating to which, at one moment, verbal language attached itself. Language became necessary for better communication. But the figurative non-verbal language, the same language that Klein observed in her very small patients, was the one which had prevailed at the beginning of humankind: long, short, open, closed, etc., all this was, originally, linked to the erotic body and was equated with sexuality, auto-erotic sexuality, but also that of the primary scene. . . Although in the case of her little patients, Klein could not deny that they had been *born inside a sort of historical language* spoken by their parents. But in their plays and symptoms they were like the representative of this archaic, prelinguistic language. Phylogenesis and ontogenesis were overlapping in Klein as in her masters. Pathology and normality in some ways too. As we will see, the same terminology will be used to describe normal and pathological phenomena.

Freud had oscillated in his hypotheses (Steiner, 1975) because sometimes, as in the case of Cecile M. and the *Studies on Hysteria* (1895) that I have already quoted, or in what I have just reminded the reader, he seemed to imply the existence of this universal, non-verbal, archaic, figurative language, which went beyond and before spoken language and at other times, he was more cautious (Steiner, 1975).[13]

Nevertheless, Klein took from Freud what she thought was more useful for her, but since those years, due to the importance that the symbols and primary unconscious phantasies linked to the body and sexuality had in her work, *and due to the fluidity between unconscious and conscious processes, she was increasingly implying that, for her, even sublimation could never be conceived without any reference to the original symbolic equations and first symbolizations related to the body and the primitive phantasies connected with it*. I cannot here deal with what all this implied. I would simply remind the reader that beside, beyond, and before psychoanalysis, the problem of the nature and origins of thought, and its relationship with verbal language, has a long history in Western culture: it can be traced back to Plato's Cratilus. But, without ending up in a sort of Reader's Digest way of dealing with those issues, one should at least remember that in the 1920s and 1930s, in a more restricted field of research – that of psychology – Piaget, Vigotsky and Wertheimer, among others, were tackling similar problems (Steiner, 1975).

What Freud called unconscious imagination, Groddek called a compulsion to symbolize coming from the Unconscious and M. Klein called a kind of symbolizing function, implied a capacity to find the identical or the like in the unlike one, following the rules of the primary process logic. But, with the development of the child, it implied the capacity to make sense of what had been symbolized using verbal language, transforming those figurative images into verbal ones and repressing them in order to sublimate. In those years, Klein already considered verbal language to be a powerful tool with which not only to symbolize, but also to sublimate (see Klein, 1923; 1926, pp. 71, 73, 84), something she will reiterate later on (see Klein 1927, p. 314; 1952, p. 98).

Now, if, after this long and discursive detour, we come back to Klein's 1930 paper, I hope it will become clear why I had to spend so many words in trying to clarify the origins of the expressions 'symbolic equation', 'symbol', and 'sublimation'.

What Klein describes in her 1930 paper (written when she had started working in London, rather isolated at first, but well accepted by 1926) is not a developmental phase of the child but a blockage, an inhibition of that development. Dick, the little four-year-old boy, had an emotional and mental maturity of a child of fifteen to eighteen months when Klein saw him. He could barely speak, could not play and had a sort of fixation on a few inanimate objects. After a 'feeble beginning, symbol formation in this child had come to a standstill,' (Klein, 1930, p. 224). There had been 'a cessation of phantasy life', symbolism had not developed and there was 'a lack of symbolic representations' (Klein, 1930, p. 225) in what he was doing, due also to the apparent lack of affects in the child. Klein pointed out that he was therefore stuck in a terrifying, omnipotent, paranoid world of rigid symbolic equations. Why? Now we arrive at M. Klein's most interesting, even if for many people questionable, explanation: this was due to Dick's sadism towards the mother's breast, the father's penis, and the bodies of the mother and father, which were equated by him, *due to the projection of his own sadism,* with terrible, persecuting, external and internal objects that paralysed his mind and emotions, like a terrible, omnipotent, internal and external primitive superego, which was a notion on which she was working in those years, retrodating its origins to the first introjections of the mother's breast by the baby. At the same time, Klein had been increasingly convinced of the importance of Freud's notion of the death drive (Segal, 1979; Steiner, 1975). Interacting with the life drive since the beginning of life, mobilized by the trauma of birth and by the frustrations coming from the earliest environment,[14] under stress, the death drive found expression in the omnipotent sadism of the baby linked to what, at that time, Klein used to call the paranoid phase, or later on 'position', of the development of the baby. This phase or position embraced the first months of his life. The sadism was activated in the baby by the presence of an internal, terrible, omnipotent, distorted and distorting phantasy life, concerning his own body and the body and organs of the mother and father since the beginning of the baby's life, contrary to what Freud and his Viennese and other followers thought at the time. Klein, therefore, was postulating and clarifying in those years her most revolutionary hypothesis: the existence of an object relationship, a rudimentary conscious communication between the baby and the mother, and also the father, since the beginning of his life – what she called, borrowing the term from Abraham, 'partial object relationship'. As far as Klein saw the development of the child in those years, normal development began under the pressure of his anxieties, but also of his libidinal impulses towards the mother and father to create symbolic equations, immediately followed by rudimentary symbols, in order to find relief and substitute satisfactions, but also a way of discharging his murderous, omnipotent aggression onto inanimate objects, which become equated with the original ones. And then the baby starts symbolizing the original objects of his desire and hate: mother, breast, body, father's penis, etc. Later on, the baby will start sublimating, losing his omnipotence and becoming more realistic. In Dick's case, the process had stopped, due to the violence of his sadism and his projected sadism, the consequent omnipotent, retaliatory, paranoid anxieties and the impossibility of mobilizing his loving libidinal impulses towards his parents. Therefore, although the child seemed so aloof, *the emotions, the affects were primitive, omnipotent and of enormous intensity in him. The anxiety about the destructiveness, not so much, or only, libido and interest, as in the case of Jones, becomes for Klein the functional engine of symbolic equation – symbolization – sublimation. That is the major shift Klein introduces in the theory of symbolization in 1930* – although she always attached great importance to the curiosity in the child. She called it the epistemophilic drive.

It is important to notice that in this paper Klein very clearly describes the mechanism of expulsion or violent projection which precedes repression. At one point, she also links Dick's sadism to the earliest phases of the Oedipus complex. According to Klein, who followed and developed at the same time Freud's and Abraham's views, Dick's sadism was an oral one to which urethral, muscular, and anal sadism associated themselves, confused with early Oedipal phantasies (Klein, 1930, p. 232).

Dick, therefore, could not play, could not speak, and could not feel emotion, because more or less consciously, he was frightened that what he had wished and projected concerning the mother's breast and body and father's penis could, *without any proper symbolization* directly persecute him in turn and destroy him with the same intensity of his own sadism. The inanimate object could, for instance, *be* (symbolic equation) a persecutive penis or a persecutive mother's womb.

Klein, playing with him, through the verbal interpretations of his sadism, managed to help him play, lessen the rigidity of his archaic superego, mobilize his loving impulse towards her and his parents and become interested in the exploration of the outside world with much less anxiety.

But what is also of extreme importance, in my opinion, thinking of what I have already noted, quoting Bleuler's and Freud's observations concerning psychotics' capacity to immediately understand symbols, is that Klein was finding *the same phenomena* in Dick, who could not play because the little train, for instance, was for him a dangerous penis. Now, is it not curious that Klein, with the help of a medical colleague, Dr Forsyth, an extremely intelligent member of the first generation of British analysts, diagnosed Dick as affected by 'dementia praecox' or 'schizophrenia'? It is in the paper (Klein, 1930, pp. 229, 232) that she discusses the general issue of schizophrenia in children, due not only to regression, but also to inhibition, insisting that schizophrenia and psychotic illness, causing enormous scandal in many areas of traditional psychiatry in those years, are much more frequent in children than had been thought until that time. But the origins of the illness had to be traced back to very, very early phases of development. And the way of communicating of schizophrenic children could, I believe, be described as 'pathological symbolic equations', due to the intensity of their anxieties and projections. The same term, therefore, could be used both to describe normal and pathological development. Indeed, as I have already mentioned, remember that both Freud and Klein, and others too, had emphasized that children know symbolism when they are very small and that when repression takes place they forget it. What mattered more, perhaps, was that the odd phenomena observable in adult schizophrenics and psychotics could be traced back, ontologenetically speaking, to the early phase of development. Incidentally, in this paper, Klein did not deny the importance and influence of the environment in the pathology of the little Dick. And it was during those years that she tried, following her ideas on the early object relationship, to very clearly describe the point of fixation in early infancy of schizophrenia, paranoia, and manic-depressive illnesses.

Scattered observations about adult psychosis, children, severe child disturbances, phylogentically-based hypotheses on the existence of primary unconscious phantasies and symbolisms, and archaic figurative language gradually began to be linked together. According to Klein, of course, not everything was clearly established, and to better understand Klein's conclusions concerning the issues in which I am interested, I should discuss in detail Freud's, and his Viennese colleagues', radical interpretation of the development of the child, which led Klein to postulate the existence of what she, since 1935, had been calling the 'depressive position' to differentiate it from the paranoid position. Suffice to say here that because it is strictly related to the problem of symbolization and sublimation, the depressive position, which according to Klein starts in the second quarter of the first year in the life of the baby, is characterized by a diminution of the way in which the baby experiences the world during the first months of life, in which extremely persecutory anxieties of separation, highly erotised destructive and libidinal impulses, partial object relationships based on primitive distorted phantasies dominated by violent projections and introjections of the external parents, splitting and denial or excessive idealization, are chaotically prevailing. It is during those months, as I have already mentioned, that in both normal and pathological development, 'symbolic equations' are created and prevail. But, and this is what makes the depressive position so important, *it is only when, and if, the baby reaches the depressive position that symbolization and sublimation can really begin.*[15] Indeed, the depressive position is characterized by the emergence of ambivalence towards the external and internal objects, by the presence of strong, loving, and reparative feelings, and by a greater tolerance of separation, which allows the impulses to blend, and extreme erotisation and sadism towards the frustrating, abandoning mother to lessen, which leads to a more realistic perception of the parents. Klein called this relation a 'total object relationship'. It is during those months that a more realistic experience of the Oedipal complex starts to take place and repression starts working, allowing a better, but not too rigid according to Klein, differentiation between the ego and the Id, as she called the Unconscious following Freud's latest view (Klein, 1935). It is during the depressive position that the first rudiments of verbal language start to emerge (Steiner, 1975, 2002). As we know, Klein considered verbal language to be an enormously powerful tool for improving symbolization and sublimation in the baby. The baby is able to tolerate real separation because it can start symbolizing and sublimate (Steiner, 1975). Ten years later, in a paper written for the Controversial Discussions between her and Anna Freud and her Viennese followers entitled *The Emotional Life and Ego Development of the Infant with Special Reference to the Depressive Position* (1944), in which, in a masterly way, Klein resumed her views concerning the importance of the depressive position in dealing with the issue of symbol formation, she stressed that the understanding of the depressive position helped her to realize the importance not only of separation, *but also of mourning for the lost security and omnipotent possession of the mother's breast and father's penis as partial objects in the process of symbol formation* (Klein, 1944, pp. 781–783). Because it was only through the process of mourning and its depressive feelings that the baby could really find at last a substitute for the lost objects in the outside world and create internal substitute objects too (Klein, 1944, pp. 781–782). This is, to me, perhaps the most important 'addenda', regarding the issue I am concerned with, that Klein brought to her previous views in those so seminal years.

Of course, the introduction of the depressive position allowed Klein to better clarify even the point of fixation of psychosis in childhood, because it is when the baby, due to all sorts of internal and external circumstances, *remains stuck in the paranoid position*, as she still called it during those years, that he is bound to become psychotic and not go beyond symbolic equations. Certainly, this is only an elementary summary of what Klein implied when she introduced the hypothesis of the existence of the depressive position in the baby, which is considered a real landmark in her work. This was clearly evident in all the interchanges during the Controversial Discussions with A. Freud (1941–1945) (King & Steiner, 1993). All this had to be considered, even by Klein and her followers, for instance S. Isaacs (1943), as simply 'probably reflecting' what went on in the life of the baby and child. Klein, confronted with the violent criticism of the Viennese and others, could not deny the hypothetical, inferred character of what she described. Although she never openly referred to Freud's notion of 'Nachträglichkeit', one has the impression that the deep access to very primitive, pre-verbal aspects of the unconscious that Klein claimed to have through her technique of dealing with very young children, using the basic tools of psychoanalysis, gave her a sort of deep enthusiastic conviction that she had opened up new vistas to psychoanalysis. She had been able to link adult psychotic disturbances to their infantile origins, making use of the most daring of Freud's views and developing them further. She understood that symbolic equation, symbolic formation, symbolization, and sublimation played a fundamental role in all those achievements.

But in mentioning the attempt to successfully treat adult psychotics using her hypotheses, I am already touching upon what still needs to be said about the last landmark in Klein's way of thinking and clinical practice.

In 1946, she published a paper called *Some Notes on Schizoid Mechanisms* in which she introduced, at least partially, the notion of 'projective identification', borrowing the definition and some conceptual implication too from E. Weiss (Steiner, 1999). Later on, in 1952 (pp. 1–24), she came to a better definition of what she had anticipated in 1946. Due to the fact that so much has been written on this subject (Sandler, 1987) – and one should also not forget introjective identification, strictly linked to projective identification – I have to assume the reader is familiar with the concepts.

Regarding the issue I am concerned with, it is, I think, fair to say that Klein makes sense in a better way of her previous work, came to a better understanding of the most primitive interrelationship between baby and mother, and also father, still based on her persuasion of the fundamental importance of the anxiety of separation at birth, of the existence of a rudimentary ego that is aware of this separation and on the role played by the death and life drives linked to unconscious primary phantasies and the way they start manifesting themselves through symbolic equations, followed by symbolization, etc., from the beginning of the life of the baby. The presence of Freud, Ferenczi, Jones, and Abraham – her illustrious predecessors – can be clearly felt in her insistence on the old notion of identification, the notion of projection of parts of the ego into the external object mother and then father, followed by introjection, and particularly her new description of omnipotent splitting as well as fragmentation of the ego and its omnipotent projection into the mother's breast, which can lead to the omnipotent, persecutory phantasy of the fragmentation of the mother's breast then reintrojected by the baby, plus her insistence on the need to penetrate and control omnipotently the mother's breast and body through projective and introjective identification of all this helped her and her pupils to better make sense of the process of fragmentation in schizophrenia. Indeed, it is in this paper that Klein chose to call from now on the paranoid position, the schizo-paranoid position, bearing in mind that schizo-paranoid anxieties, as she had claimed before for the paranoid ones, are part of normal development too. One has the impression that with the introduction of those descriptive concepts, Klein was achieving a clearer description of the baby as a psychological being, from the beginning insisting not only on his eroticism or destructiveness, but also on other needs, for example to project into the mother even parts of his ego in danger of being destroyed.

All this, and much more, started helping Klein and her pupils to better understand the highly complex pathological communication of psychotics, but also to better clarify the communication primitive of more normal patients.

And yet, in my opinion (Steiner, 1975), as I have already mentioned, and as I will try to show in a moment, projective and introjective identification will be transformed by her pupils, particularly Rosenfeld and Bion, from their original defensive or destructive meaning into the main explicative tools for understanding all sorts of communication during the first months of life of the baby and even later on.[16] Projective and introjective identification, as I suggested earlier, did not bring any substantial change to the descriptive sequence of symbolic equation, symbol formation, symbol, and sublimation.

Indeed, if one has a quick glance at the latest papers of Melanie Klein, those of the Fifties and Sixties of the past century, one notices that in one way or another, she comes back, when necessary, to: the notion of symbolic equation in *The Mutual Influence in Development of the Ego and the Id* (1952, p. 58); symbol formation in *The Origins of the Transference* (1952a, p. 51), *Some Theoretical Conclusions Regarding the Emotional Life of the Infant* (1952b, p. 83), *On Observing the Behaviour of Young Infants* (1952c, pp. 115, 137, 138) and *Some Reflections on the Oresteia* (1963, pp. 277, 299); symbolism in *On Observing the Behaviour of Young Infants* (1952c, p. 138) and *Some Reflections on the Oresteia* (1963, p. 298). The references to sublimation are so numerous in connection with symbolism that I cannot quote them all here. But what is also interesting is that Klein returns to, and mentions, her old papers on the subject, the ones of 1923 and 1930 that dealt with those issues. Particularly important is her 1963 paper *On Some Reflections on the Oresteia*, because at the end of it, Klein restated the links she had already made in the 1920s and 1930s between symbolism and talents and also genius, stressing that the creative person is able to transform the infantile symbols, emotions and phantasies connected with them into his or her adult creation (Klein, 1963, p. 298).

In my last statements, I mentioned several times Klein, her pupils, and the use they made of Klein's views in particular to treat adult psychotics in the years immediately after the Second World War. Do not forget that Freud and his most orthodox followers had been and remained very sceptical about the possibility of treating adult psychotics using psychoanalysis. In order to better understand the issue in question, which is strictly related to the work of those pupils of Klein, and here I am thinking of H. Rosenfeld, H. Segal, and W.R.

Bion, and one should not forget R. Money-Kyrle, one has to consider several factors which interacted and led to certain specific results. Things had radically changed in psychoanalysis since the Second World War, the arrival of the Freuds and the Viennese analysts in England, and others who migrated to America, due to Nazi persecution. The isolation from Europe and America for a while, the changed alliances and situation inside the British Psychoanalytical Society after the 'Controversial Discussions 1941–1945', which I have already referred to, had given to M. Klein a prominent place inside the British Society, in spite of the presence of A. Freud and the increasing importance of Winnicott. She could now rely on a group, if not a school, of devoted followers, and could see the immediate application of her new views in the work of her pupils.

H. Rosenfeld and H. Segal, and later on W.R. Bion (although his work would soon show a different quality) found Klein's discoveries and hypotheses so revolutionary that they began working with adult psychotics without having to find any further cultural stimulus outside London and a certain tradition of the British pioneers. They could continue to rely mainly, if not solely, as Klein did, on the great and bold tradition which blended clinical, theoretical, and applied psychoanalysis in all sorts of field and helped and stimulated first Freud and then Ferenczi, Abraham, and Jones, to write about symbolism and then the same M. Klein too.

Yet, as we shall see, due to the changing times and the pressures of the empirical British tradition, which, for instance, would lead Money-Kyrle and Bion to question the more phylogentically based hypotheses of Freud and his followers (Steiner, 2003),[17] something will change or be elaborated in a different way also as far as the problem of symbolization in psychoanalysis is concerned.

But, due to the reasons I have just mentioned, one has almost the impression that in those years the enthusiastic followers of Klein worked in something akin to an enclave. It is true, for example, that Rosenfeld (1954) made a reference to the work of Goldstein and Vigotsky concerning concrete thinking. Together with the reference of Segal to concrete thinking in her paper *Some Aspects of the Analysis of a Schizophrenic* of 1950 (p. 104 and passim), these expressions seemed the only hint of what had been claimed by other researchers, who did not use the same framework as Rosenfeld, Segal, and Bion.

Bleuler's research and the work of Storch, which incidentally had been translated and published in America at the beginning of the 1950s, were completely ignored.

In discussion with Rosenfeld some years ago, he told me that he had discussed the technique with the Swiss therapist M. Sechehaye, who had employed it when dealing with a famous case of schizophrenia [1951]), and that Sechehaye did not agree with her. The research of the French school working with psychosomatic patients that would lead Marty and others to a very interesting theory of difficulties in symbolizing (1963), were of course also ignored, not to mention Lacan's theory of *le Réel, l'Imaginaire et le Symbolique* and the role played by what Lacan meant by 'the law of the father'.[18]

North American research concerning symbolization and thinking from a psychoanalytic viewpoint, such as Kubie's famous paper of 1952, or Rapaport's *Organisation and Pathology of Thought* (1951), a real bible of the so-called ego psychology of those years, were felt too distant from Klein's approach to be considered. The same can be said of the interesting work of Arieti (1955). That may sound like a criticism, but at the same time, it shows the euristic power of the model suggested by M. Klein.

In reality, if one excepts Bion's original, but copious in its references to philosophy, literature, etc., and, particularly in his later years, too convoluted retranslations of the observations of Klein, Segal, and partially of Rosenfeld, of those years, the model on which the so-called post-Kleinian or contemporary-Kleinian generation has tackled the issues I am concerned with was firmly established in the 1950s. I just mentioned Bion's thinking and work, but in my opinion, despite what he later on contributed in redefining in his own terms what mental apparatus and capacity for thinking or inability to think means in psychoanalysis, the basic references to the model I am going to briefly describe will remain substantially unchanged, because he will always in one way or another refer to symbolic equation, symbol formation, and symbolization as conceived by M. Klein and re-elaborated by H. Segal during those years.[19]

I will briefly remind the reader of what H. Segal had observed. In 1950, she published a paper, *Some Aspects of the Analysis of a Schizophrenic*, in which she reported the difficulties a young adult patient had in symbolizing, referring incidentally to another patient she had observed but not treated who, asked by the doctor why he could not play the violin, answered in a typical way, if the reader remembers what I said about Bleuler and his patients: 'Fancy masturbating in public?' (Segal, 1950, p. 104).[20] Segal's small vignette has become a classic in the field and that is the reason why I reported it.

In reminding the reader that her patient could not differentiate between 'being like something' and 'being something', Segal referred to Klein's famous paper of 1930, but she stressed that her adult patient, contrary to what according to Klein had described in the case of Dick, had been able to form symbols but then could not use them because he equated them to the object itself (Segal, 1950, pp. 104–105). Now, as far as I understood Klein's statements in her 1930 paper, even in the case of Dick there had 'a feeble beginning of symbol formation' (Klein, 1930, p. 224), but perhaps one should also consider that Dick was a child whom, incidentally, Segal defined following the diagnosis of Kanner as autistic and not schizophrenic in a later paper (Segal, 1957, p. 52),[21] whereas Segal's patient was a young adult and one cannot discard the presence in this adult patient of more developed aspects of the ego, which could lead to the formation of more symbols, but this is a matter to which I will return in a while. What is curious is that in this 1950 paper, Segal never used the definition of projective identification, probably due also to the fact that Klein came to its proper definition only in 1952, as I said earlier. Interestingly enough, Segal also gives examples of the difficulties this patient experienced detaching himself from the literal meaning of something; a cigarette had to be a cigarette, because if Segal gave him a symbolic interpretation, it could transform itself, could be equated directly to a penis, losing its symbolic representational character (1950, p. 110).

In a postscriptum dated 1980, Segal claimed, thinking of the process of splitting and fragmentation of the ego of her patient, that she could not use at that time Bion's notion (1957) of 'pathological projective identification' (Segal, 1950, p. 119).

The person who mentioned very clearly projective identification in relation to the difficulties psychotic patients in general have in symbolizing was in reality Rosenfeld who, in 1952, making use of Segal's paper of 1950 and also making sense of what he had already discovered and observed since his first paper in 1947, claimed that the symbolic equations of the schizophrenic and manic depressive patients were due to the *intensity* with which they were using projective identification. In his typical, very down to earth, and pragmatic style, Rosenfeld spoke of the 'quantity of the self' projected into the analyst. It depends on the quantity of the self, due to the force of the projection, how much the patient gets confused to the point he cannot differentiate anymore between phantasy and reality, the content of the symbol and the symboliser. Everything becomes the same (Rosenfeld, 1952, p. 77). Even Rosenfeld claims that the capacity to form symbols was very present in his patients and was only temporarily lost due to the violence of the projective identification. In this paper he describes how perceptions and functions of the self, such as memory, could be recovered once he had interpreted to the patient how much he had projected himself into him. What does all that mean? I will mention in a moment the theoretical formulations of Bion, even concerning this issue. But beside asking the reader to remember what Rosenfeld said about the 'quantity' of the self projected violently into the analyst or the outside world, I think it is worthwhile quoting here what Bion, later on, syntetically and graphically claimed about those issues. In his *Brazilian Lectures* (1974, p. 92), Bion stated that he only analysed psychotics who could come to his consulting room and did not claim that they could be compared with those hospitalized and in his *Bion in New York and Sao Paulo* paper (1980, p. 70), he made the distinction between healthy and unhealthy psychotics, meaning that the healthy ones have vestiges of rational conscious behaviour and 'something can be done to develop them. The insane psychotic, on the other hand, finds his way into psychiatric hospitals where usually he deteriorates.' But see also Bion (1953).

It is true that Segal and Rosenfeld had access to hospitalized patients, yet one has to consider that even pathological symbolic equations as conceived by the whole Kleinian School seem also to imply the presence of a relatively accessible, sane part of the psyche of the psychotic patient.

The paper of Bion (1957, 1967) to which H. Segal refers as dealing with what she called 'pathological projective identification', as far as I know, does not contain this term. However, H. Segal is absolutely right in pointing out their importance in better understanding some of the specificity of the difficulties in symbolizing experienced by schizophrenic and psychotic patients in general.

To even summarize what Bion claimed in his 1957 (1967) paper on *Differentiation of the Psychotic from the Non-psychotic Personalities*, to which I would also add the previous *Notes on the Theory of Schizophrenia* (1953, 1967) and *Developments of Schizophrenic Thoughts* (1956, 1967), would be impossible, due to the complexity of the issues involved. Suffice to say that Rosenfeld's intuitive descriptions of the world of schizophrenia, particularly those contained in a seminal paper *Notes on the Psychology of Confusional States* (1950)(1967) and Segal's points of view in her 1950 paper and the references to Klein's 1930 paper, linked now by Bion very clearly to projective identification, are re-translated by him into a rather new model of the thinking apparatus, if compared with that of Freud (1912)(1924). Bion himself hints also at the existence of a pre-thinking apparatus using material from his own clinical observations of schizophrenic patients. What is quite clear from those papers is that Bion considers in detail the single vicissitudes of the functions of the mental apparatus, what Klein, Segal, and Rosenfeld termed 'ego' or 'self'. According to Bion, those functions are split, but also extremely attached, fragmented, and projected violently by the schizophrenic into the outside world and introjected again. Memory, attention, perceptions, and verbal thinking, therefore, are projected, split, *and fragmented*, according to Bion. What emerges from all this is the 'psychotic part of the personality' as Bion calls it (1957, 1967), which is probably best described when Bion speaks of the minute part of those functions of the mental apparatus violently projected and encapsulated in the external reality, creating 'bizarre objects', a surrealistic but very real and powerful way of describing the confusion between self and object, so characteristic of pathological symbolic equations.

The psychotic therefore attacks and fragments his own psychic apparatus, which is then projected outside,[22] and does not only attack the external or internal objects. This leads to a denial of the external and internal reality and of emotions. But what Bion manages to emphasize, using Segal's ideas, is not only the importance of verbal thinking, which in the formation of symbols he links to the depressive position and which is constantly attacked by the psychotic, but also the hypothesis that what the psychotic attacks is also the unconscious primitive pre-verbal 'iconographic linked to sight' function of thinking, developing ideas that were originally Freud's, particularly in his paper 'The Unconscious' (1915, 1923, 1924). This primitive way of thinking, contrary to what Freud thought, is at work from the beginning of life, if one accepts, as Bion did, Klein's idea of the existence of a rudimentary ego and therefore of a rudimentary principle of reality in the newborn baby. This pre-verbal iconographic way of thinking in normal development gradually links itself in the preconscious with what Freud called 'word representations' – verbal thought – of which it is a necessary precondition.[23]

Bion tried to clarify what he meant by all this, what he referred to in 1959 (1967, p. 106) as 'embryonic thought, which forms a link between sense impressions and consciousness', later on adding new details of how to approach and tackle the issues from different angles. But the core of his views are expressed in the papers I have quoted, in which Bion constantly refers to Klein's papers of 1930, 1935, and 1946, and the views of H. Segal, who had just published her seminal paper 'Notes on symbol formation' in 1957.

Before dealing with Segal's paper, I think it is extremely important to remember that in the papers I have just mentioned, Bion also introduced the idea of the existence of a 'non-psychotic part of the personality' in psychotics. This part can deal with repression and, if not destroyed by splitting, projection, and fragmentation, can have access to the depressive position and can therefore symbolize, as his colleagues too had intuitively noticed. It depends – and I would like to bring the attention of the reader to Bion's words – on *'how much'* the psychotic part can prevail on and obscure the non-psychotic one. Symbolic equations and, to use my suggestion, their more or less pathological qualities, in Bion's terms are linked to this 'how much' and in Rosenfeld's terms, 'to the quantity of the self involved in projective identification'. However, as far as schizophrenic patients are concerned, Segal is right in emphasizing the particular obnoxious quality, and not so much the quantity, that projective identification and also introjective identification have in Bion's description, because this quality is responsible for the blocking of the transformation of the symbolic equations in symbols and for the pathological quality of the symbolic equations themselves.

The existence of the 'non-psychotic' part of the personality, which for me is linked to the formation of what I call 'normal symbolic equations', where projective identification is more benign, can only be understood if one remembers Klein's hypothesis of the coexistence from the beginning of life of what Freud (1912) called the 'pleasure and reality principle'. If the embryonic reality principle in the schizoparanoid position is not attacked and destroyed by the violence and the particular quality of the projective identification, even for the psychotic there is a chance of improvement. Otherwise, one could reach what I (Steiner, 1975) called the 'grade 0 of symbolization' in extreme cases,[24] such as, perhaps, the totally deteriorated hospitalized patient.

Rosenfeld, in his seminal 1950 paper on confusional states, mentioned a terrible confusional 'implosion' in some cases of schizophrenic patients that makes them totally inaccessible to any interpretation. But there is no doubt that even this notion of Bion's seems to imply a more optimistic view about the possible treatment of some psychotics than the one expressed by Freud, who understood psychosis as a total withdrawal of the patient from reality.

I think also that because Segal refers to some ideas of Bion first expressed in his 1959 (1967) paper *Attack on Linking* – undoubtedly one of Bion's masterpieces – I need to spend a few words on it. Here, at one point, Bion introduces the idea of a 'normal degree of projective identification' without defining the limits within which normality lies (p. 98). Again, I would like to draw the reader's attention to Bion's way of expressing himself: this is also the paper in which Bion openly discusses the role of what he will call the 'container', the mother who can absorb, or is not able to absorb, the projections of the baby and to metabolize them, or fail to do so, creating in this last case a terrible, vicious circle that leaves the baby experiencing a 'nameless threat'.

These are extremely important observations, even as far as the issue of symbolization is concerned. But in the case of psychotics, Bion – following Klein's ideas on the role of constitutionality, in which envy, for instance, can play a nefarious role – stresses that total responsibility should not be assigned to the mother (p. 106).

As the reader can see even in the case of the existence of normal projective identification, Bion, like his colleagues, does not have a proper, precise 'instrument' with which to measure the limits of its normality, which, incidentally, to my mind, plays a fundamental role in what I call normal symbolic equations.

Now it is time to discuss H. Segal's paper of 1957, *Notes on Symbol Formation*. It is a mainly theoretical paper in which, starting with a discussion of Jones' contribution to symbolism (1916), Segal agrees with Klein who, as we know, had slightly objected to the rigid definition of psychoanalytic symbol, stressing the importance that symbolization had in sublimation as such.[25] Segal does not want to deny that sublimation has its own characteristics, but she thinks – and was not the only one in those years – that isolating psychoanalytic symbolism too much does not allow psychoanalysis to find a link with other ways of understanding symbolism. She thinks that Jones had underestimated the role of anxieties and affects even in sublimation. Furthermore, she stresses the Kleinian point of view of a sort of continuity in the life of the individual between early primitive phantasies and desire and the later development of the individual. This more mature development could not be understood unless the wider concept of symbolism is admitted (Segal, 1957, p. 51). It seems that she is saying that sublimation would be inconceivable if it did not contain all the previous phases of symbol equations, early symbols, more mature and sophisticated symbols . . . But what she very clearly succeeds in doing is to describe – this time mentioning projective identification – the differences between symbolic equation and the symbols of the depressive position. What she is saying is not completely new: what matters is how she formulates it. She claims that she now wants to use the term 'symbolic equation' to describe what happens in the schizoparanoid position, a term used by Klein in 1930 that she wants to use in a slightly different way. And she returns to the case of Dick. She now thinks, contrary to what M. Klein thought, that even Dick had probably created numerous symbolic equations, which, due to his anxiety and persecutions, he had to annihilate, withdrawing his interest from reality (Segal, 1956, p. 54). Personally, I do not see a great difference between the numerous symbolic equations of Segal and what Klein meant by symbolic equations in the case of Dick, except for the fact that Segal now claims that even Dick had created numerous symbolic equations, whereas – as I have already emphasized – Klein (1930) had spoken of 'a feeble beginning of symbol formation' (see). In both cases there is evidence of a mental function able to create symbolic equations, which for various reasons could not develop further. To me, Segal's insistence on the fact that symbolic equations, as in the case of Dick, are also made by projecting part of the bad self, which leads to the annihilation of them, and are created by the baby to avoid the experience of separation, and therefore the existence of the notion of time, is more interesting than her statements concerning her use of the term 'symbolic equations' as defined in order not to split too much, as she had done in her 1950 paper, between equation and symbol. All this, as Klein in her own way, and particularly Bion in those years, had stated, seems constantly to hint at the existence of a part of the personality that from the beginning of life is at least potentially able to symbolize: the non-psychotic one.

In her paper, borrowing some ideas from Morris, the American philosopher and semiotician, Segal tries to define symbolism as the relationship between the object symbolized, the symbol, and the person. She uses this description to better clarify the primitive distorted relationship between the ego (the person), the object symbolized, and the symbol, starting with the symbolic equations in the case of the adult psychotic. They indicate a disturbance between the ego and the object symbolized and the symbol. But that, in some ways, following her model, has to be implied also in the baby, although in the baby symbolic equations are also the normal way to start symbolizing. The difficulty in understanding is due to the fact that Segal uses the same term to describe adult pathology, child pathology, and normal development, as Klein did, as I have already mentioned. That is the reason why I suggested differentiating between 'normal' and pathological symbolic equations (see). The differentiating criteria for Segal in those years were the quantity and quality of projective identification – and introjective identification too, one should add – as I have already mentioned.

In child and adult psychosis, the distorted relations between the object symbolized, the symbol, and the person, lead to a pathological equation between the object symbolized and symbol, due to what Segal this time calls 'massive projective identification' of the self and of the internal objects into the external world, followed by distorted introjective identification (p. 56). She seems to echo here both Rosenfeld and Bion. All this, although very clear, does not seem to me particularly new. But where her paper becomes more interesting is where she deals with the formation of symbols in the depressive position in normal development. Here, her insistence (p. 54) on the gradual development of the ego and on the gradual change in the ego's relations to its objects, seems to me to touch on a very important point until now not very clearly expressed. Although in need maybe of further help coming from baby observation and Kleinian-orientated developmental psychology!

Segal insists that it is only for reasons of clarity that she makes a strong distinction between what she now calls early symbols, and by that she means symbolic equations,[26] and fully formed symbols during the depressive position and *even after* (my emphasis) (Segal, 1957, p. 54). Therefore, she seems to suggest at least potentially a developmental sequence which goes beyond the depressive position of the first year of the life of the baby. As I said, what is of particular importance is what she adds in describing the particular characteristics of the symbols created in the depressive position. After having recalled what Klein meant by it, Segal mentions the fact that 'now symbols are clearly created not only to displace anxiety or libidinal and destructive impulses from the original objects, but *to save* them' (my emphasis) and 'guilt experienced in relation to aggressiveness is far less than that due to an attack on the original object' (Segal, 1956, p. 55). Thus, the symbol is not equivalent to an original object and 'the increased sense of reality . . . make symbols be felt . . . as created by the ego and therefore never completely equated with the original object' (p. 55, *ibidem*).

I could go on quoting, but there are a few other points I would like to stress. Segal comes back several times to describe the regression from symbolization, used in a sublimated way that belongs to the depressive position, to the symbolic equations using clinical material from her patients. When projective identification is used, Segal finally concludes, 'as a defence against depressive anxieties, symbols already formed and used as symbols and sublimations may revert to symbolic equations' (1952, p.57). If there is a really important part of this paper, it is the new vistas Segal opens up using the interplay, the to-ing and fro-ing, between the schizoparanoid and depressive positions, to understand symbolization and its deterioration as well as its creative function, to the extent that she stresses how true symbolization linked to sublimation of the depressive position might allow sense to be made of, and a solution found to early unresolvable conflicts or phantasies of the schizoparanoid position. These are really important points as far as creativity in every field is concerned (Steiner, 1999; but see also Bion, 1962a).

What is interesting is also the postscript to this paper (Segal, 1957 [1979, 1986]). In commenting on it in 1979, Segal states that now she would not attribute such importance to projective identification *per se* as the cause of concretization and pathological symbol formations. And, again influenced by the thinking of Bion, who had begun expressing this view in his papers in the 1950s (1959), but elaborated on them much later,[27] Segal says: 'One has to take into account the particular relationship between the projected part and the object projected into: the container and the contained' (Segal, ibidem, p. 60).[28]

Now, to describe what Bion started writing about the container and the contained would lead me too far. It is obvious, however, that more attention, according to Segal, should be given to the way the external object is able or not able to contain the projections of the baby, and of course one should consider Bion's notion of maternal reverie (Bion, 1962b) or his further elaboration of the model of the psychic apparatus when he introduced the notion of 'alpha function, beta elements' (Bion, 1962a, 1962b, 1970). They all contributed to a better understanding of the reasons for using symbolic equations or the way one comes to symbolization.

Indeed, and this is a point that clarifies H. Segal's statements concerning the capacity of normal people to be in constant unconscious contact with their process of symbolization (Segal, 1957, p. 105), Bion's views concerning the alpha function, and alpha and beta elements, led him to further clarify, from his point of view, the model of the mental apparatus, particularly as regards repression (Bion, 1970). He saw it as a contact barrier which allows for a great fluidity between the conscious and unconscious, much more than the notion of repression in Freud. The contact barrier helps to better understand how symbols are created in normal development (Segal, 2001b).[29]

As I said, I cannot deal here with the application of Bion's thinking to autism (see Meltzer, 1978).

Segal's most recent paper on symbolism (Segal, 2001a) does not add very much to what she has already observed. However, in stressing again the importance of the depressive position inside the framework of Bion's 'container-contained' model for the process of symbol formation, to the point that she claims that only what has been properly mourned can be symbolized (Segal, 2001a, p. 147),[30] she states that in recent years she has become increasingly convinced that 'accepting the reality of the father and the Oedipal couple is essential in this process' (Segal, 2001a, p. 154) and she refers to Britton's contribution (1989). Without taking anything away from Britton's interesting views concerning the Oedipus complex, one has to say that not only Segal but other Kleinians too seem to have forgotten what Klein had already stated in 1944 concerning the depressive position, symbol formation and the recognition by the baby of the parents as separate individuals, and the beginning of the more normal Oedipal complex. The Kleinians insisted too much, for years, on the early relationship between the baby and the mother, even as far as symbolization was concerned, forgetting the role played by the father (Steiner, 1975).[31]

Before coming to my last observations, I would like to mention the work of two British analysts who wrote some interesting contributions to the issue of symbolization more or less in the same years in which Segal published her seminal papers. They are not Kleinians in the strict sense, but it is obvious that in spite of the strong disagreements between the Kleinians and the so-called British Independents, particularly in the 1950s, a sort of *commun penumbra,* if not common ground, of concepts on those issues seems to have remained or existed.

I said 'seems to have remained', because M. Milner's views on the process of symbolization were actually published in a *Festschrift* for M. Klein. Milner had been supervised by Klein and discussed some of the issues of her paper with her. I am thinking of Milner's paper *The Role of Illusion in Symbol Formation* (1952). I have in mind not so much Milner's views concerning the necessity of a moment of illusion in the formation of symbols, as the necessity of maintaining the illusory identity between the self and the object to which one can return later, which Milner regards as being of paramount importance in order to understand creativity, something that she elaborated on herself, but also found in Winnicott's views concerning development.[32]

What is interesting is that Milner, during broadly the same years as H. Segal and others too, including Kubie (1953) in America – although from a completely different viewpoint – were claiming the same, was questioning the rigid defensive notion of Jones' definition of psychoanalytic symbolism as a pure defence process, claiming incidentally that this rigid conception of symbolization did not allow psychoanalysis to properly communicate with 'workers in related disciplines, such as epistemology, aesthetics and philosophy of sciences. It was interfering with what might be a valuable collaboration in the work of clarifying some of the obscure issues about the origins of thought' (Milner, 1952, p. 105).

The other colleague of H. Segal whom I have in mind is C. Rycroft, and in particular his paper *Symbolism and its Relationship to the Primary and Secondary Process* (1956). It is a very dense and at times difficult paper to understand. Nevertheless – and I am selecting here only a few aspects of it – it was Rycroft who, in using the work of Klein (1930) and Isaacs on symbolism and unconscious phantasy (1943), together with Milner (1952), as well as the work of Kubie (1953), tried in a critical but sympathetic way to suggest that what Klein was conceiving as unconscious phantasy activity in creating symbols could be better related to Coleridge's notion of imagination, differentiating it, therefore, from the psychotic, primary-process-related activity, which leads to what M. Klein had already called symbolic equation and Segal, whom Rycroft nonetheless does not quote, had called equations in her 1950 paper. Rycroft adds to the critical reappraisal of Jones' paper the observation that Jones had not been able to take into consideration the notion of the Ego as rooted in the Id that Freud had developed in his book *The Ego and the Id* (1923). There are many aspects of Rycroft's paper one could consider, but what I did find of some interest in what he has to say about symbolization is something that H. Segal had also tried to clarify, if the reader remembers what I pointed out regarding her attempts to differentiate between symbolic equation, symbols, symbol formation, and sublimations, and the important points she makes in her 1957 paper too about the way, in the case of psychotic people, they regress from having formed symbols to symbol equations or they can 'progress again' towards symbolization during treatment. Rycroft, who does not introduce clinical material, besides claiming that in all symbolizations one can, to a certain degree, find elements of the primary and the secondary process, at one point uses the expression 'desymbolization' to try to make sense of a process that tends to return to more primitive aspects of symbolization (Rycroft, 1956, p. 54). One can, as I do, disagree with the theoretical underpinning of Rycroft's views. However, his descriptive term, which more recently has been adopted, although in a different way, by N. Freedman (2002), who is one of the leading authorities in

America as far as symbolization is concerned, also seems to imply a sort of movement, which I do find relevant to the notes that I want to develop to conclude this paper.

As those rather heavy historical notes do, I hope, show, I have tried to indicate that the specificity and originality of the contribution that Klein and her followers have brought to the problem of symbolization is linked to the way they understand, ontogenetically speaking, the psychical apparatus and the drives and the unconscious emotions and primary phantasies linked to them since the beginning of life of us human beings. The great initial season of psychoanalysis when, beside Freud's research and discoveries, all his most significant pupils at one point started being fascinated by what the master meant by unconscious symbolization, was also characterized by the most daring phylogenetic speculations about the origins of symbolization, as understood by psychoanalysis. That was due to the courageous application of psychoanalysis to all sorts of fields of the human and natural sciences. As in so many other cases, due to the at times indiscriminate use of Darwin's and Spencer's evolutionary model, infantile way of thinking and symbolizing, unconscious symbolization of the dreams, adult way of thinking and symbolizing, adult severe psychopathological way of thinking and symbolizing and data coming from primitive ways of thinking studied by anthropologists were all compared and at times roughly equated together. That led to a vital, fermenting but also at times problematic and questionable psychoanalytical synthesis. Just think of the complex problem of the relationship between the primitive, the psychotic, the child. Analogies were often transformed into reductive identifications.

This flamboyant period of psychoanalysis, for various epistemological, cultural, sociopolitical, and historical reasons, which I cannot discuss here, was followed by an attempt to concentrate, as we have seen, on the ontogenesis of the process of symbolization and its clinical applications, in addition to what all this could mean for the understanding of normal development, particularly when M. Klein, due to the reasons I tried briefly to illustrate, started seeing the possibility of treating psychotic disturbances in children and later on, through her pupils, in adults too, if the therapist paid attention and tried to understand the earliest phases of the process of symbolization in the child and the adult. All this, descriptively and terminologically speaking, and partially at least dynamically speaking, had a long, bold history, which M. Klein inherited and developed. Today, even if we are unaware of this, we are still the heirs of this bold and long history and implications, as I have tried to show. Just think of the role played in our clinical work by the notion of the universality of the sexual symbols and of the primary unconscious phantasies. What seem to emerge as the pillars in the model of the psychic apparatus as conceived by M. Klein and her followers, even as far as the creative and complex rethinking of this model, represented by the work of Bion, is concerned, are: the schizoparanoid and depressive position and all that it involves, which I cannot repeat here. As regards the issues I am concerned with (and we have seen this, expressed in various degrees by Klein and all her followers), one has to be aware of the dynamic, fluid links between the two positions and the to-ing and fro-ing between them.

As I have also tried to stress, neither Klein, nor Rosenfeld nor Segal, nor even Bion, in spite of his attempts at one point to mathematize psychoanalysis through the use of what he called the 'Grid' (Bion, 1963), due to the qualitative nature of the phenomena they were describing, and their mobility, were able to describe with exact precision. They, inevitably, had to use an approximate and very often metaphorical language. *Pace* the at times understandable claims of the so-called empirical contemporary psychoanalysis,[33] had the Kleinians succeeded in finding an absolute and precise language, I have the impression that that kind of rigour would have become the *rigor mortis* of psychoanalysis.

There are, of course, problems even with the model of symbolization proposed by the Kleinians. I already drew the attention of the reader to the possible confusion (Steiner, 1975) that can arise because of the use of the same terminology, symbolic equation, to describe both normal and pathological development, due to the conviction of Klein and her followers that psychotic anxieties are present even in 'normal' people. Freud claimed the same, as far as neurotic anxieties were concerned. Although all the new developments concerning the study of projective and introjective identification in relation to the way the mother, but I would also add the father (Steiner, 1999), act as containers for the primitive anxieties of the baby, Bion's differentiation between psychotic and non-psychotic aspects of the personality and the insistence of Rosenfeld (1986) on the communicative aspects of projective identification can help to clarify this issue. This, in my opinion, is strictly related to the main problem that the Kleinian model seems to bring with it. By that, I mean: the lack of an explicit developmental model of the psychic apparatus, beyond the first year of the life of the baby. This complicates the issue. However, in the case of symbolization, I drew the attention of the reader (??) to some statements of H. Segal (1957) that seem to imply the existence of this model. Furthermore, one has to remember that access to the deepest layers of the primitive Id is only partial and one has, in one way or another, to accept the notion of Freud's *nachträglichkeit*, even if Klein's late notion of memory in the form of feelings (Klein, 1956) makes it quite clear that she and her followers believe that her and their model of the primitive psychic apparatus is based not only on bold fantascientific hypotheses as Kubie (1953) among others claimed.

If I can quote myself again (but of course I was, and am not, the only one!), think of the objections from classical Freudian psychoanalysts and others too when, in 1975, I pointed out some of the difficulties related to the lack of a development model as far as the problem of symbolization is concerned and even later on (Steiner, 1989, Rosenfeld, 1986), when I discussed the various types and intensity of the projective and introjective identifications in terms of a possible developmental model. I even tried, and I should have done more work on it, to hypothesize a sort of developmental model of the depressive position, pointing out that the elementary acquisition of language around the ninth month in the life of the baby did not exhaust the acquisition of language itself. And a mature use of the language by the child would imply a better and more articulated possibility of tolerating separation, and therefore of symbolizing via language (Steiner, 1975, 1982, 2002).

Perhaps all this could help to better formulate and understand what I am going to say. I want to start with a few questions. Does an intermediate state between symbolic equation and proper symbolization exist? Many of my clinical vignettes, to which I have now to refer, seem to imply it does, as I stated at the beginning of my paper. And how would it be possible to describe it? Without having to refer to Winnicott's (1971) idea of the transitional object, which seems to be at the core of Milner's view of symbolism (1952), and with which Klein disagreed, as I mentioned a few pages ago, in studying the work of the Kleinians and what I have just finished summarizing, it seems that this intermediate state can be postulated and perhaps described. It is difficult to link it exactly to a precise development phase of the child, for the reason I have just mentioned. But, certainly, it does imply a more mature and integrated self than that involved in symbolic equations, due to better, less malignant, massive use of projective and introjective identification and a less dramatically troubled and emotional relationship between the baby, or infantile part of adult patients, and his or her caregivers, mother, father and so on, during the first years of their life. That does not mean that this intermediate state is or cannot be pathological, and at times it can further desymbolize (to use the useful term created by Rycroft, 1956) itself, falling back into symbolic equations or, of course, can better resymbolize or symbolize itself, resulting in a more mature and functional symbol and sublimation.

Can this intermediate phase be better described from a phenomenological viewpoint, so that we can be more aware of what goes on clinically in some of our patients? My answer is a tentative one.

Looking at psychoanalytical literature, particularly what has been written on borderline conditions (Kernberg, 1985; Rosenfeld, 1986; J. Steiner, 1996), which to my mind this intermediate phase seems to often refer to, it does not seem to me that one can find many suggestions.

Years ago (Steiner, 1982), in a different context, I became very interested in what A. Green called the tertiary process[34] (Green, 1979), insofar as verbal communication is concerned. He thought that the tertiary process was one of the major characteristics of clinical communication and it implied a co-presence of primary and secondary processes; by that, I think he meant their different logic. Indeed, even from a Kleinian point of view, all that I have tried to remind the reader would be impossible to understand without implying the presence, for instance, of the primary process in the distorted symbolization created via projective or introjective identification, even in the case of verbal symbolic equation. In those cases, there is a massive prevailing presence of the primary process and its logic, due to all the confusion created by this logic, which seems to take over the patient.[35] The same, in a milder form, could be said of what I call the intermediate stage of symbolization. I still find Green's observations very important, particularly what he says about the constant blending of primary and secondary processes in the communication, I would say not only of the patient to the analyst, but also vice versa, because Bion's 'reverie', which the analyst has to constantly use, implies a free, although at the same time controlled, access to the primary process's logic. Yet, while observing the phenomena that I have tried to describe in my clinical vignettes, and bearing in mind what H. Rosenfeld (1986), O. Kernberg (1975) and J. Steiner (1996) wrote about the syndrome of borderline patients in general, it came to mind what I had condensed in my old 1975 book concerning the possible relationships between the notion of symbol in the work of the great American philosopher and semiotician, C. Pierce, and the notion of symbolism in M. Klein, particularly verbal symbolism. It had been the study of the work of the linguist R. Jakobson that drew my attention to the work of Pierce. Jakobson used Pierce to discuss and deeply criticise the notion of the total arbitrariness of the linguistic sign of de Saussure (Steiner, 1975, pp. 205, 209), something which I did find again extremely interesting, thinking of what Klein and her followers had noted regarding the presence of non-arbitrary transcultural and transgenerational elements linked to primitive object relationships, the unconscious phantasies originally expressed through body language, etc., and last, but not least, linked to the emotions, even in the most abstract and apparently arbitrary symbols. Here is not the place to discuss Pierce's complex thinking concerning symbolization (Pierce, 1955). Jakobson reminded us of it and synthesized Pierce's thinking using his famous notion of 'index', in which the relationship between the symbolized and the symbolizer is necessary and based on a natural 'contiguity', as in the case of fire and smoke. Then Jakobson referred to the notion of 'icon', in which there is a strong, very often perceptual similarity and relationship between the symbolized and the symbolizer, but, unlike indices, they are not so necessary and naturally linked together. Jakobson reminded us that Pierce was referring to visual, non-verbal ways of expressing oneself, even to paintings and statues. Then, finally, there is the verbal symbol that can never be conceived without indexical or iconic elements, although the conventional elements are predominant in the symbol. Incidentally, even the icon cannot be conceived without more or less strong indexical elements in it.

One should not forget that this is a classification that deals with the so-called normal way of understanding and communicating, and is a part of a complex semiotic model that Pierce had created, *which is, however, fluid and interconnected* (Steiner, 1975, pp. 185–193). Jakobson used this model to point out in an extraordinarily interesting and rich way the indexical and iconic components of language, stressing that poetry, for example, and artistic language in general, could not be conceived without the notion of icon (Steiner, 1975, p. 197). All this, curiously enough, appears to link verbal language also to the body and the way the body reflects itself in language. . . Furthermore, Jakobson was interested in describing a hierarchical system of communication, in which non-verbal, body-related gestures and visual language could be linked and absorbed, without losing their quality and specificity, into verbal communication. Of course, to be able to try to use all this in psychoanalysis, one should not forget the unconscious and all that it implies in Kleinian terms. Yet, with this proviso, it seems to me that what Pierce and Jakobson described as indexical and iconic aspects of communication, present even in verbal symbols, could perhaps help to better describe and understand that intermediate stage of communication between symbolic equations and symbols, which seems to me to be so evident in my clinical vignettes. I am quite aware of the danger in applying to pathology what was originally intended to describe normal communication, and also of the danger of falling into loose 'analogical' thinking. Yet, all that has been said by not only the Kleinians about the danger in isolating too much the notion of symbolism and symbolization in psychoanalysis from what is meant by all this in other disciplines should at least legitimate the attempt to put forward my hypotheses and see if there is something valuable in them.

The link between symbolic equations and indices as such does not seem to me difficult to find. Just think of the artificial and inexistent links felt and 'thought' as 'natural' that, due to the complex reasons M. Klein and her followers have put forward, schizophrenics and even paranoid or manic-depressive psychotic patients are able to establish between various things or people. My first three clinical vignettes speak for themselves, it seems to me.

But now think of my other vignettes. Here, in my opinion, there is a much more fluid and evident interplay between indexical, iconic, and symbolic stages of communication. In the fourth vignette, of course, there is the moment in which the symbolic equation or the artificial 'natural link' between breast and mastitis prevails so much that the patient cannot tolerate it but then the patient comes back and is more able to take in symbolic interpretations, although the 'iconic' components, the intense 'image' and the emotions connected by what for the patient the mother's breast meant played an enormous part in all further associations and for a very long period. The fifth seems to be a very good example of the strong, indexical, iconic components of the communication of this patient or of how I was felt and used by her. My words did not disappear totally but were kept in the background. The 'as if' characteristic of the verbal symbolic communication was reduced to a minimum: to use Werner's and Kaplan's (1967) famous terminology, the distance between the symbolized and the symbolizer shrank to the limit. What prevailed were body language and sensations, visual, tactile 'language', mixed with respiratory activities linked to the image of the mask used for the asthma attacks, but also to my speaking, all interacting together. However, I would not put this kind of communication in exactly the same category as the one in the previous vignettes.

In the sixth and seventh vignettes, both patients were aware of the 'as if' quality of what they did. Nevertheless, at the same time, the emotional and phantasized iconic elements attached to their behaviour and what they not only felt but imagined in their actions or ritual had such an almost indexical intensity that proper symbolization, thinking and not acting, was still difficult, due to the strong 'iconic' presence of what they were looking for in vignette six, or frightened of in vignette seven. But it was not something which one would call a proper delusion.

Even the eighth vignette is quite interesting. After all, the patient produced what one could call a 'classical' symbolic dream in which she incorporated the father's penis. But the unconscious pre-verbal visual phantasy linked to an action, the oral incorporation of the father or his penis, which was felt by me, via my countertransference, when I started opening my mouth in a certain way, something that both Jakobson and I. Fonagy, who wrote a marvellous book entitled *La Vive Voix* (1983) would have been interested in, seems to show that the reference to Pierce (and Jakobson's semiotic model) can be of some use.

What I also found striking, and still find striking, although more than thirty years have now passed since I came across it all, is that both Pierce and Jakobson (Steiner, 1975, p. 195) stressed how indices and icons are related to a static notion of time, whereas the symbol contains an *esse in futuro*, a 'to be in the future', a sense of time that can develop. This is again something very similar to what Klein, Segal, and even Jones, as well as Milner and Rycroft, have claimed concerning symbols in psychoanalysis. Indeed, the sense of repetitiveness, the lack of the sense of time as development, the fixity of the visual or body-language-related scenario of many aspects of the communication of my patients was something striking when the iconic indexical elements prevailed in their communication. Whether all this has something to do also with what Bion (1957, 1959, 1967) called 'iconographic thoughts' (see also Money-Kyrle, 1968, 1983), I do not know.[36]

What I want to finally stress is the following: even this model compelled me to use a qualitative, approximate language although, I repeat, the possibility of being better aware, descriptively speaking, of those intermediate aspects and stages of symbolization seems to me quite useful, clinically speaking.

Due to the clinical routine we use, too often we fall into the trap of using a jargon which does not seem to reflect the different ways and degrees of the 'as if' of the symbolization of our patients at different times, sometimes during the same session (see also Freedman, 2001, 2002). We refer to what they feel or imagine or report as 'concrete', or very often we presume that there is symbolization *tout court*. If what I have tentatively tried to point out succeeds in drawing the attention of the reader to the complexity and fluidity and various ways in which the process of symbolization takes place not only in our patients, but also in ourselves, that, for me, would already be a good result.[37]

Of course, I could go on discussing or even speculating on this fascinating issue. If the reader remembers what I observed in mentioning Freud's statements concerning the unconscious activity of the 'imagination', which creates symbols in dreams, and what I stated about Klein's symbolic function, later elaborated in great detail by Bion's model of the mental apparatus, one of the problems which seems to emerge from what I said is (and it was of course the main interest of Jakobson, from a semiotic linguistic point of view) whether it would be possible for us, as psychoanalysts, to come to a better, more refined description of what could be called an 'intersemiotic function', to use Jakobson's language, while bearing in mind the founding, cognitive role played by the unconscious emotions linked to the drives, which Jakobson ignored. By 'intersemiotic function' I mean a function able to register all aspects of human communication and able to make sense of them through verbal language and interpretation without losing contact with the immediacy of their non-verbal and pre-verbal components, related to all our perceptions, not only the acoustic or the visual ones. All this would probably mean another way of looking at Bion's alpha function. But that would be the task and subject of another paper.

Notes

1. Due to space and other constraints, I must quote these clinical vignettes out of the context of the personal history of the patients. This of course complicates what I want to say very much and can lead to distorsions and misinterpretations of which I am painfully aware.
2. 'Equus' in Latin means horse. The patient knew Latin and in his confusion created this odd play on words, whereas the day before it looked like a real pun. It is a well-known phenomenon that psychotic patients can do that and then suddenly regress to confusion.
3. During that session I managed to help the patient to lie down and to leave the scissors with me.
4. One should not forget that Jones' work depended on the work of Freud, Stekel, Ferenczi, and others, and discussions with them on the subject. Beside what was already said by Freud in his *Interpretations of Dreams* (1900) in the case of the little Hans (1909) etc., his hypotheses were confirmed by the work of his followers in various fields of applied psychoanalysis. If one nevertheless takes Freud's famous n.X lecture of the 'Introductory Lectures on Psychoanalysis' (1916–1917), in which he describes the theories of Sperber, which seemed to confirm his views concerning the prevailing importance of sexual symbolism in the dream, Freud insists on the fact that according to Sperber, language and inanimate tools were originally in prehistoric terms equated to sexual organs. In the German original edition of 1916, he uses the expression 'equivalent' (Freud, 1916–1917 [1948], p. 170), which in the English version already translated by J. Riviere in 1920 and later on by Strachey in the same way (1963) as 'equivalent' (Freud, 1916–1917, p. 167).
5. As far as the *Studies on Hysteria* (1895) are concerned, I have particularly in mind the case of Cecile M., in which Freud, incidentally, makes some

pioneering observations concerning the existence of a preverbal and non-verbal language that lies at the heart of the symbol (Steiner, 1975, pp. 8–9).

6. In a paper dated 1913 called 'An Evidential dream' S.E., vol.XII, p. 275, Freud claims that in the case of dementia praecox, the understanding of the dream's symbolization is easier than in the case of obsessive neurosis. In a note added to the 1925 revision of the *Interpretation of Dreams* (Freud, 1900, p. 351) Freud claims that often patients suffering from dementia praecox show a direct understanding of dream symbolism. But this note was published much later than Bleuler's observations in a paper in 1910, *Die Psychoanalyse Freuds* which I am referring to in the text. In that paper (p. 362), Bleuler claimed that his schizophrenic patients could understand symbolism without any effort. Later on, in his masterpiece *Dementia Praecox or the Group of Schizophrenias* (1911)(1950, pp. 402–424), Bleuler gave several examples of what could be called today symbolic equations. See also the classic research done by A. Storch in 1922 following partially in Bleuler's steps. It is interesting thinking of the importance that Abraham had for M. Klein, that in the same note where Freud quotes Bleuler, he quotes K. Abraham's book of 1909, *Traum und Mythus,* and the work of Kleinpaul, a non-medical polymath whose work Freud knew very well. One should not forget that Kleinpaul had already noted en passant in *Sprache ohne Worte* (1885) that children treat words like things, which contain many anticipations as far as what Freud, and later on M. Klein, observed about the primary process and the way children seem to be in contact with it, in their symbolic equations. Kleinpaul was well known to Freud's pupils too (Steiner, 1981, 1982). Freud, in *The Interpretation of Dreams* (1900, p. 303) and in *Jokes and their Relations with the Unconscious* (1905, p. 120), probably following Kleinpaul, had already observed that children tend to treat words as things. These linguistic tricks are 'the common source of these things in dreams and psycho-neuroses alike' (Freud, 1900, p. 303).
7. One has to say that Jung's *Wandlungen und Symbole der Libido* (1912) contains a very important and elaborate view of the function that symbolism has for the development of humankind. Jung, of course, desexualizes all the symbols and uses libido in a vague way. In 1946, Piaget, who was working on symbolism in the child, quoted Jung as much more interesting than Freud, whom he found too reductionistic. It is difficult to imagine two scholars and researchers more different than Piaget and Jung, but in this case it was not only their 'geographical' affinity – the town of Geneva beside Sabina Spielrein – that helped them to agree: it was their opposition to Freud.

8. My emphasis.
9. My emphasis.
10. Groddek (1922, p. 160) claimed that the Unconscious compels man to use symbols, and stressed that children had an intuitive knowledge of symbols (p. 163). This was not a new idea, but the stress on compulsion attracted the attention of M. Klein.
11. Interestingly enough, Freud never changed his views concerning phylogenesis. In *Moses and Monotheism* (1939), he beautifully summarized and confirmed fully his and his pupils' discoveries and hypotheses. Here, again, one can see that there exists an implicit analogy between primitive men and children and, I would add, adult psychotics: 'The symbolic representation of one object by another, the same thing applies to actions, is familiar to all our children and comes to them, as it were, *as a matter of course* (my emphasis). We cannot show to them how they learnt it and must admit that in many cases, learning is impossible. It is a question of an original knowledge, which adults afterwards forget.' Adult psychotic patients are an exception: remember Bleuler and others. Freud continued: 'It is true that an adult makes use of the same symbols in his dreams, but he does not understand them unless an analyst interprets them for him, and even then he is reluctant to believe the translation [. . .] Moreover, symbolism disregards differences of language. Investigation would probably show that it is ubiquitous and the same for all people. Here then, we seem to have an assured instance of an archaic heritage.' (Freud, 1939, pp. 98–99).
12. S. Langer (1942), a pupil of Cassirer, would later on not be so critical of Freud. I will come back to Langer's work because it played a part in the British psychoanalytical school of the Fifties and echoes of Langer can be found in Segal's work and Bion's too (Steiner, 2000).
13. Consider another statement always present in the tenth lecture of the *Introductory Lectures on Psychoanalysis* (1915). On page 163, Freud quotes von Schubert on the investigation of dreams to stress that 'the symbolic relation can go beyond the limits of language'.
14. Although Klein, like Freud, insisted also on the constitutional components of the personality even in the case of the baby.
15. It might be interesting to remember that during those years, using a different frame of reference, other authors were using the notion of symbolic equation too. For instance, in his 1936 paper entitled *Symbolic Equation*, Fenichel did not quote Klein, but referred to the very important paper by J. van Ophuijsen published in 1920, *On the Origin of the Feeling of Persecution*, in which van Ophuijsen describes oral-anal equations, referring also to the equations of the Wolf Man (Freud, 1914, p. 254).

Fenichel, in a paper of 1931, *Respiratory Introjection* (p. 221), stressed that the first equations were related to the respiratory function. M. Klein knew the work of van Ophuijsen, who worked in Berlin with Abraham, whom she quotes, as far as the process of 'equation' is concerned, in *Die Psychoanalyse des Kindes* (*The Psychoanalysis of Children*, 1932). In the German edition of her book, she uses 'identifiziert' (1932, p. 39), to describe the identification between 'penis' and 'faeces' made by the baby and adult patients too, and then also the expression 'gleichgesetz' (1932, p. 39), which in the English version of the book were respectively translated as 'identifies' and 'equivalent'. Van Ophuijsen therefore has to be remembered as one of Klein's sources too.

The term 'symbolic equation' perhaps originated with Fenichel, but I am not completely sure of that. It appears very often in the American psychoanalytical literature of the 1950s and 1960s. One need only consult the indexes of the *Psychoanalytic Quarterly* and the *J.A.P.* But no references were made to the way M. Klein understood it.

16. Particularly if one takes into consideration the role they play in the countertransference of the analyst.
17. In a very important paper published in 1961, Money-Kyrle questioned Freud's phylogenetical hypotheses concerned with primary unconscious phantasies, which had been at the core of S. Isaacs' paper published in 1943, *On the Nature and Function of Unconscious Phantasies* (King & Steiner, 1993). He claimed that what Freud called phylogenetic inheritance could be better understood as simply preconstituted aspects of the mind (Steiner, 2003, p. 43).
18. Lacan, although critical, appreciated many aspects of Klein's work (Grosskurth, 1986, pp. 376–377, 389–390). I have tried to show that what Klein was claiming concerning the depressive position and the role played not only by the mother but also the father was similar in some respects to what Lacan was proposing (Steiner, 1975) as far as mature symbolization was concerned.
19. See for instance Bion's very late work (1980, pp. 106, 109), in which he refers to Segal's 'violinist' and his symbolic equations.
20. In another paper, Segal will report the patient saying: 'Why? Do you expect me to masturbate in public?' Segal (1957 p. 49).
21. The diagnosis of autism could perhaps explain Dick's behaviour. D. Meltzer and Tustin developed later on their views about the way autistic children communicate, inspired by Klein, Bion, and E. Bick.
22. Bion (1958, 1967). See also the best description of this phenomenon in Bion (1962, p. 64). Bion will also describe the process of 'evacuation' of protothoughts and thoughts when the patient cannot think and elaborate

them, which seems to be another peculiar pathological form of projective identification, giving rise to pathological symbolic equations, particularly present in 'hallucinations'.

23. Deri, the Hungarian-American psychoanalyst who wrote a very important work on symbolism (1984), was one of the first in America to understand and clearly stress the importance of Bion's hypotheses concerning the link of primitive thinking and the preconscious.
24. I do not know whether Bion's views concerning something that is 'inaccessible', instead of being 'conscious or unconscious' (Bion, 1980, p. 105) could be linked to what I called 'grade 0 of symbolization'.
25. It is curious that in her description of Jones' contribution, Segal avoided mentioning Jones' use of the term 'symbolic equation' and no mention was made of Ferenczi. Later on (Segal, 1979), in her book on Melanie Klein in dealing with symbolism, she will mention Ferenczi (p. 67).
26. Which does not help to keep things clear in one's own mind, but probably she is referring to what I call normal symbol equations.
27. Bion, Learning from Experience (1962a) and Attention and Interpretation (1970).
28. She will amplify all this particularly as the possibility of using langauge by the baby in interaction with the mother in her paper *On Symbolism*.
29. In this paper, *Changing Models of the Mind*, Segal will use Bion's model of the contact barrier between the conscious and Unconscious, which allows a fluid repression, to claim that this notion of repression allows a constant process of symbolization to take place. By that, she means – still referring to Bion – 'constant transformation of beta elements into alpha elements'. The fluidity of the barrier, which in my opinion retranslates in Bion's terms an old conviction of Melanie Klein, 'allows the person to be in constant contact with his or her unconscious in a way necessary to be in contact with reality too' (Segal, 2001, p. 161).
30. I completely agree with H. Segal. Yet, I would still stress the importance of repression in 'normal' symbolization and sublimation, thinking particularly of the Arts – a great artist, although able to mourn, and freely in contact with the primitive phantasy life of the Unconscious, can disguise and creatively elaborate its symbols and primary phantasies through his or her creative capacities, in which repression still plays an important part. This is evident when artists openly make use of crude symbolism and primary phantasies as understood by psychoanalysts (not to mention the ridiculous reductionism of all sorts of psychoanalytical schools' criticism of the arts). That leads inevitably to banal reductionism and mechanic repetitiveness.

31. In my old book, as I have already mentioned, I discussed the possible links between some aspects of Klein's work and those of J. Lacan on the role played by what he referred to as the law of the father – and the symbolic order.
32. Milner agreed with Klein's view that symbolism was essential for sublimation and the growing of talents. However, in a letter to Milner commenting on her paper, Klein stressed that Milner was avoiding too much to consider aggressive destructiveness in idealizing this moment of illusion as necessary to the baby but also to the adult (Milner, 1952, p. 110). In her notes, Milner claims that she could not read S. Langer's *Philosophy in a New Key* (1942) when she wrote her paper on symbolism and that she regretted it. She was right, because Langer's book, incidentally known to H. Segal too, contained an interesting series of observations about symbolism that sometimes echo issues that were present in Klein's and Segal's work too. Think of what Langer says about the 'constant symbolic transformations as characteristic of our creative mind' (p. 42) and of the fact that symbols are 'the starting point of all intellection' (p. 42). What would M. Klein have thought of Langer's statement concerning the fact that 'symbols serve to let us develop a characteristic attitude towards objects 'in absentia' which is called thinking of or 'referring to' what is not here' (p. 31)? Langer seems to be describing symbolization in the depressive position!
33. Of course, I do not have anything against the attempt made, for instance by N. Freedman and his colleagues, to come to a more precise empirical description of symbolization (Freedman, 2001, 2002). It is interesting, nevertheless, that the champion of this empirical approach based on tests and measurements, P. Fonagy, who in my opinion, as well as borrowing the idea of mentalization from the French school (Marty & de M'Uzan, 1963; Luquet, 1981), has simply tried to retranslate into his own language, with distorting results, what the Kleinians mean by symbolic equation, symbol formation, and symbolization, inspired by cognitivistic academic psychology and attachment theory, practically eliminating the disturbing implications of the notion of the Id, as understood by Freud (1923) and developed by M. Klein and her followers, falls into the same irresolveable problems that any attempt to transform quality into quantity brings with it. In his *Reflective-functioning Manual* (Fonagy et al., 1997), he tries to grade the patients' responses to the Adult Attachment Inventory, but has to use Minus I or Negative RF, response grading etc., or expressions like that, which, although they appear so precise (the responses are graded on a scale between 2 and 10 points for the presence of mentalization), do not solve the problem.

34. I was studying some of the characteristics of jokes and I came to the conclusion that in order to understand them, we had to use what Green called a 'tertiary process'. Later on, I discovered that even the great and too often forgotten scholar, S. Arieti, had defined the logic of jokes in this way (Steiner, 1982, p. 161). It is not clear to me whether A. Green found the definition in the work of Arieti, whom he seems to know, or whether he came to his conclusions by himself.
35. Alongside the work of Bleuler (1911), Storch (1922), and Arieti (1955), etc., the observations of von Domarus (in Kasinin, 1964) on the logic of schizophrenic patients remain of major importance, phenomenologically speaking.
36. In a paper originally written in 1968, Money-Kyrle describes a sort of Kleinian developmental model of cognition and he differentiates very rigidly between a state of non-differentiation between the subject and object, a stage characterized by a rudimentary visual thinking, like that of the dream, and proper symbolization. Money-Kyrle claims he has been deeply influenced by Bion.
37. If the definition of 'thing' and 'word' representations (Freud, 1915, 1923) did not create problems, particularly concerning what Klein and her followers mean by 'symbolic equation' where the notion of 'representation' particularly in pathological cases, becomes problematic, one could try to formulate what I mean by this fluid intermediate state, as an intermediate state between thing and word representations. But one should bear in mind the complexity of the notion of repression in Freud and the fluid role played by the preconscious in the case of this intermediate state.

References

Abraham, K. (1909). *Traum und Mythus*. Leipzig and Vienna: Fischer Verlag.

Arieti, S. (1955). *Interpretations of Schizophrenia*. New York: Brummer.

Bion, W.R. (1953). Notes on the theory of schizophrenia. In: *Second Thoughts* London: Heinemann, 1967.

Bion, W.R. (1956). Development of schizophrenic thought. In: *Second Thoughts* London: Heinemann.

Bion, W.R. (1957). Differentiation of the psychotic from the non-psychotic personalities. In: *Second Thoughts* London: Heinemann.

Bion, W.R. (1958). On hallucinations. In: *Second Thoughts* London: Heinemann.

Bion, W.R. (1959). Attacks on linking. In: *Second Thoughts* London: Heinemann.

Bion, W.R. (1962a). *Learning from Experience*. London: Heinemann.
Bion, W.R. (1962b). A theory of thinking. In: *Second Thoughts* London: Heinemann.
Bion, W.R. (1963). *Elements of Psychoanalysis*. London: Heinemann.
Bion, W.R. (1965). *Transformations*. London: Heinemann.
Bion, W.R. (1967). *Second Thoughts* London: Heinemann.
Bion, W.R. (1970). *Attention and Interpretation*. London: Tavistock.
Bion, W.R. (1974). *Brazilian Lectures, Volume I*. Rio de Janeiro: Imago Ed.
Bion, W.R. (1980). *Bion in Sao Paulo and New York*. Pershire: Clunie Press.
Bion, W.R. (1992). *Cogitations*. London: Karnac Books.
Bleuler, E. (1910). 'Die psychanalyse Freuds. *Jahrbuch der Psychoanalyse, Vol.2:*
Bleuler, E. (1911). *Dementia Praecox or the Group of Schizophrenias*. New York:
Britton, R. (1989). The missing link. In: R. Britton, M. Feldman (Eds.), *The Oedipus Complex Today: Clinical Implications* London: Karnac Books.
Cassirer, E. (1927). *Philosophie der Symbolischen Formen, Volume III*. Berlin:
Cassirer, E. (1945). *Essay on Man*. New Haven and London: Yale University Press.
Deri, S. (1984). *Symbolisation and Creativity*. New York: International University Press.
Fenichel, O. (1931). Respiratory introjection. In: *Collected Papers, Volume I* London: Routledge and Kegan Paul, 1954.
Fenichel, O. (1936). Symbolic equation. In: *Collected Papers, Volume I*. London: Routledge and Kegan Paul, 1954.
Ferenczi, S. (1913). Stages in the development of the sense of reality. In: *First Contributions to Psychoanalysis* London: The Hogarth Press, 1952.
Fonagy, I. (1984). *La vive voix*. Paris: Payot.
Fonagy, P. and others (1997). *Reflective Functioning Manual*. London: University College London.
Freedman, N., & Lavender, J. (2002). On desymbolisation. *Psychoanalysis and Contemporary Thought, XXV, 2*
Freedman, N., & Russell, J. (2001). *Symbolisation of the Analytic Discourse*. Unpublished paper from the Research Programme of I.P.T.A.R., New York.
Freud, S. (1895). *The project for a scientific psychology. Standard Edition, 1.*
Freud, S. (1895). *Studies on hysteria. Standard Edition, 2.*
Freud, S. (1900). Die Traumdentung, G.W., Vol.II/III
Freud, S. (1900). *The interpretation of dreams. Standard Edition, 4–5.*
Freud, S. (1901). *On dreams. Standard Edition, 5.*
Freud, S. (1905). *Three essays on the theory of sexuality. Standard Edition, 7.*

Freud, S. (1909). *Analysis of a phobia in a five-year-old boy. Standard Edition, 10.*

Freud, S. (1911a). *Formulations on the two principles of mental functioning. Standard Edition, 12.*

Freud, S. (1911b). *Psychoanalytic notes on an autobiographical account of a case of paranoia* (Dementia Paranoides). *Standard Edition, 12.*

Freud, S. (1914) (1918). *From the history of an infantile neurosis. Standard Edition, 17.*

Freud, S. (1915). *The unconscious. Standard Edition, 14.*

Freud, S. (1916–1917). *Introductory lectures on psychoanalysis. Standard Edition, 15–16.*

Freud, S. (1916–1917 [1948]). Vorlesungen zur Einfuehrung der Psychoanalyse. *G.W.*, Vol. *XI*.

Freud, S. (1920). *Beyond the pleasure principle. Standard Edition, 18.*

Freud, S. (1923). *The ego and the id. Standard Edition, 19.*

Freud, S. (1924). *The loss of reality in neurosis and psychosis. Standard Edition, 19.*

Freud, S. (1939). *Moses and monotheism. Standard Edition, 23.*

Green, A. (1979). *Psychoanalysis and Ordinary Thought* Inaugural Lecture, University College London.

Groddek, G. (1922). *The Compulsion to Create Symbols*. London: Maresfield Gardens, 1977.

Grosskurth, P. (1986). *Melanie Klein*. New York: Knopff.

Isaacs, S. (1943). The nature and function of phantasy. In: P. King & R. Steiner (Eds.), *The Freud-Klein Controversial Discussions, 1941–45*, quoted, (pp. 265–319). London: Routledge and the Institute of Psychoanalysis, 1993.

Jones, E. (1916). The theory of symbolism. In: *Papers on Psychoanalysis* (pp. 87–152). London: Balliere and Tyndall, 1948.

Jung, C. (1912). *Wandlungen und Symbolen der Libido*. Leipzig and Wien:

Kasanin, J.S. (Ed.) (1964). *Language and Thought in Schizophrenia*. New York: Norton.

Kernberg, O. (1975). *Borderline Conditions and Pathological Narcissism*. New York: J. Aronson.

King, P., & Steiner, R. (1993). *The Freud-Klein Controversial Discussions, 1941–45*. London: Routledge and the Institute of Psychoanalysis.

Klein, M. (1923). Early analysis. In: *Love, Guilt and Reparation and Other Works (1921–45)* London: The Hogarth Press and the Institute of Psychoanalysis, 1975.

Klein, M. (1926). The psychological principles of early analysis. In: *Love, Guilt and Reparation and Other Works (1921–45)*. London: The Hogarth Press and the Institute of Psychoanalysis, 1975.

Klein, M. (1927). The importance of words in early analysis. In: *Envy and Gratitude and Other Essays* London: The Hogarth Press and the Institute of psychoanalysis, 1975.

Klein, M. (1930). The importance of symbol formation in the development of the ego. In: *Love, Guilt and Reparation and Other Works (1921–45)* London: The Hogarth Press and the Institute of Psychoanalysis, 1975.

Klein, M. (1932), Die Psychoanalyse des kindes, Wien Internationaler Psychoanalyt

Klein, M. (1935). A contribution to the psychogenesis of manic-depressive states' ego. In: *Love, Guilt and Reparation and Other Works (1921–45)* London: The Hogarth Press and the Institute of Psychoanalysis, 1975.

Klein, M. (1944). The emotional life and ego development of the infant with special reference to the depressive position. In: P. King & R. Steiner (Eds.) *The Freud-Klein Controversial Discussions, 1941–45* London: Routledge and the Institute of psychoanalysis, 1993.

Klein, M. (1946). Notes on some schizoid mechanisms. *International Journal of Psychoanalysis, 27:* pp. 46–72.

Klein, M. (1952a). The origins of transference. In: *Envy and Gratitude and Other Essays* London: The Hogarth Press and the Institute of Psychoanalysis, 1975.

Klein, M. (1952b). Some theoretical conclusions regarding the emotional life of the infant. In: *Envy and Gratitude and Other Essays* London: The Hogarth Press and the Institute of Psychoanalysis, 1975.

Klein, M. (1952c). On observing the behaviour of young infants. In *Envy and Gratitude and Other Essays* London: The Hogarth Press and the Institute of Psychoanalysis, 1975.

Klein, M. (1955). The psychoanalytic play technique: its history and significance. In: *Envy and Gratitude and Other Essays* London: The Hogarth Press and the Institute of Psychoanalysis, 1975.

Klein, M. (1963). Some reflections on 'The Oresteia'. In: *Envy and Gratitude and Other Essays* London: The Hogarth Press and the Institute of Psychoanalysis, 1975.

Kleinpaul, R. (1888). *Sprache ohne Worte.* Leipzig:

Kubie, L. (1953). The distortion of the symbolic process in neurosis and psychosis. *J.A.P.A., I*: 59–86.

Lacan, J. (1959). A la mémoire d'Ernest Jones: sur sa théorie du symbolisme. In: J. Lacan, *Ecrits* Paris: du Seuil.

Langer, S. (1942). *Philosophy in a New Key*. Cambridge, MA: Harvard University Press.

Luquet, P. (1981). Les changements dans la mentalisation. *Revue Française de Psychanalyse, 45*: 1023–1038.

Marty, P., & De M'Uzan (1963). La pensée opératoire. *Revue Française de Psychanalyse, 27* (supplément)

Milner, M. (1952). The role of illusion in symbol formation. In: *The Suppressed Madness of Normal Man* London: Tavistock and the Institute of Psychoanalysis, 1987.

Money-Kyrle, R. (1983). Cognitive development. In: J.S. Grotstein (Ed.) *Do I Dare to Disturb the Universe* London: Karnac, pp. 538–550.

Peirce, C. (1955). *Philosophical Writings*. Edited by J. Buchler. New York: Dover.

Piaget, J. (1946). *La formation du symbole chez l'enfant*. Neuchatel, Paris: Delachaux-Niestle.

Rapaport, D. (1951). *Organization and Pathology of Thought*. New York: Columbia University Press.

Rosenfeld, H. (1950). Notes on the psychopathology of confusional states in chronic schizophrenia. In: *Psychotic States*, London: The Hogarth Press, 1965.

Rosenfeld, H. (1952). Notes on the psychoanalysis of the superego conflict in an acute schizophrenic patient. In: *Psychotic States* London: The Hogarth Press, 1965.

Rosenfeld, H. (1986). *Impasse and Interpretation*. London: Routledge.

Rycroft, C. (1956). Symbolism and its relationship to the primary and secondary process. In: *Imagination and Reality* London: The Hogarth Press and the Institute of Psychoanalysis.

Sandler, J. (Ed.) (1987). *Projection, Identification, Projective Identification*. London: Karnac Books

Sechehaye, M.A. (1950). *Journal of a Schizophrenic*. Paris: P.U.F.

Segal, H. (1950). Some aspects of the analysis of a schizophrenic. In: *The Work of Hanna Segal* London: Free Associations, 1989.

Segal, H. (1957). Notes on symbol formation. In: *The Work of Hanna Segal* (pp. 49–64). London: Free Associations, 1989.

Segal, H. (1978). *Melanie Klein*. London: Karnac Books.

Segal, H. (1978). On symbolism. *International Journal of Psychoanalysis, 59*: pp: 315–319.

Segal, H. (2001a). *Symbolisation*. In: C. Bronstein (Ed.), *Kleinian Theory* Philadelphia: Whurr Publisher.

Steiner, J. (1996). *Psychic Retreats*. London: Routledge.

Steiner, R. (1975). *Il processo di simbolizzazione nell'opera di Melanie Klein*. Torino: Boringhieri.

Steiner, R. (1982). Es Ludens? In: F. Fornari, (Ed.), *La comunicazione spiritosa* Firenze: Sansoni.

Steiner, R. (1988). Paths to Xanadu. . . . *Intern. Rev. of Psychoan., 15*

Steiner, R. (1989). Rev. of J.Sandler ed., *Projection, Identification, Projective Identification*, Vol.70

Steiner, R. (1999). Some notes on 'The Heroic Self'. In: *International Journal of Psychoanalysis, 80.*

Steiner, R. (2000). *Tradition, Change and Creativity in Psychoanalysis*. London: Karnac Books.

Steiner, R. (2002). The depressive position and the beginning of the linguistic phonemic differentiations in the baby. A possible link between M. Klein and R.Jakobson. In: R. Lasky (Ed.), *Symbolization and Desymbolization* New York and London: The Other Press.

Steiner, R. (Ed.) (2003). *Unconscious Phantasy*. London: Karnac Books.

Storch, A. (1922). The primitive archaic forms of inner experiences and thoughts. In: *Schizophrenia* New York and Washington: Nervous and Mental Diseases Publishing Company, 1924.

Van Ophuijsen, J. (1920). Uber die Quelle der Empfindung des Verfolgtwerdens. *Int. Zeitschrift. Für Psychoanalyse, VI*:

Werner H., & Kaplan B. (1963). *Symbol Formation*. New York: J. Wiley and Sons.

Winnicott, D.W. (1971). *Playing and Reality*. London: Tavistock Publications.

CHAPTER FOURTEEN

The foreign language

Louise de Urtubey

The foreigner

My aim here will be to try to understand certain anxieties and defences when faced with a foreign language and what is foreign in general, both difficulties having, of course, common roots.

For at least two reasons, this article will be more than subjective: the first is that those who are unilingual (i.e. who only speak one language, their own), and their pathology, to which I referred some time ago (Urtubey, 1993), are completely different from my own 'language apparatus' (Freud, 1897) because, from the moment I gained access to the world of words, I acquired three languages (French, Euskara – Basque – and Spanish). Consequently, I may not understand these unilingual people well or perhaps feel that they are too different from me. The second is that, from the point of view of national identity, place of living, and learning, I have always been 'in between' (South America, where I was born, a bit by chance, prematurely, and France, where I have lived, if I add up the various periods, for almost fifty years). Furthermore, if I think about the transgenerational dimension, so well described by H. Faimberg (Faimberg, 2005), my family on my father's side, to which I am strongly attached, has been established for centuries with attachments on both sides, on the borders of two countries, France and Navarre, which has become since the sixteenth century, the Southern or Spanish Basque Country.

I thus accept, in advance, the particular partiality of my text, but is any piece of writing entirely devoid of it?

At the beginning of his research, Freud designated the unconscious as a foreign body which, long after its entry during a traumatic experience, persisted, thereby provoking disturbances on account of its incompatibility with the ego (at the time, this term more or less denoted the person). This 'body' did not become diluted in the psyche but remained 'enclosed' by repression, rejected by the ego, and inaccessible to the system conscious, but was still capable of acting by causing 'strange' effects, beyond the subject's conscious control.

The first clinical case described by Freud, that of the woman who wanted to feed her baby herself but was assailed by 'counter-ideas' announcing her future failure, and then actually impeding her from feeding the baby, presented all the symptoms of a refusal or of a simulation by someone refusing to carry out an action. Things continued like this until Freud intervened, and, under hypnosis, commanded her to successfully feed her baby. This occurred for her first two children. Freud notes that this family, with which he was acquainted, far from being grateful to him for the success of his intervention, distanced themselves from him and were rather reticent (Freud, 1895). This stemmed, it seems to me, from Freud's power over this 'foreign body' which, without realizing it, the lady had inside her and could not dominate in spite of her efforts. Freud probably seemed to her to be someone dangerous, perhaps endowed with magic powers.

In fact, the 'foreign body' is also Satan, particularly in cases of possession of a woman, generally speaking. This was seen on innumerable occasions during what the historians call the 'witchcraft epidemics' which were rampant in France and almost everywhere in Europe (without forgetting Salem in the nascent United States) during the fifteenth, sixteenth, and seventeenth centuries (Caro Baroja, 1961; Delumeau, 1978).

During those years, all of a sudden, women began recounting that they flew through the sky at night to get to the Sabbath feast in order to meet the devil, and to pay him homage by kissing his shameful parts before indulging in orgies, notably incestuous ones, with the other participants. Of course, the inquisitors took these delusions as plausible and, by means of their questions (and by means of *the* question) drove these women, generally country women and ignorant, to making such confessions. But, owing to hysteria, many of them identified with the symptoms of the others, and denounced themselves even before they had faced their inquisitors. Basically, victims and torturers shared the same fantasies, the former identifying with them, the latter projecting them. (Freud, 1894–1903)

The devil, just like the repressed foreign body, is supposed to dominate, to produce dangerous, evil, and uncontrollable effects. Freud himself, in his obituary on Charcot, underlines the similarity between hysteria with its incorporated foreign body and the earlier witchcraft, the unconscious replacing in the new science (psychoanalysis) the devil of yesteryear (Freud, 1893).

He was to return to this subject in another way in *The Uncanny*. There too, that which is foreign, unfamiliar, the *Umheimlich*, is evocative of the devil, in particular through the recollection of Hoffmann's tale where it appears in a more or less dissimulated way, first in the form of the subject's father, and then in that of the magician persecuting the hero to the point that the latter ends up by committing suicide (Freud, 1919).

Defences against 'the foreigner'

Whether unconscious or demon, the 'foreigner', that is, one who belongs quite simply to another country or was born there, is often more or less consciously feared, seen as dangerous. Already, he invades a country which is 'ours', either momentarily: 'Oh, these tourists, what bad manners they have!' or permanently: 'Oh, these immigrants, they are all dangerous!' (accused of being thieves, having the wrong skin colour, being rapists and profiteers). Or when we ourselves are abroad, we sometimes think that all the food is bad because nothing is as good as 'at home': the bread doesn't have the same taste as the bread at home, there is too much oil, the meat is overcooked, they eat raw, and even live fish, and so on. When one hears people speaking like this, one wonders, well, why do they travel then? It may be because what is dangerous is also attractive.

The foreigner is someone one does not understand: his language, his habits, his manners, his cooking. What one does not understand contains a danger: it's unpredictable, perhaps disordered, other, in any case.

What is more, he is necessarily totally different: he does not have the same habits (even if these are universal); he eats differently (in my experience of travelling, the 'local salad', composed of tomatoes and lettuce, is so called almost everywhere); the climate of the new country where the foreigner lives is different from that of his own country (in his own country it is hot, whereas in France it is never hot); in the past, syphilis was the Italian scourge in France and the French scourge in Italy, while in England one drinks excessively like a Dutchman and in Holland one drinks immoderately like an Englishman. All this is often expressed with at least a touch of scorn for 'the other'. This phenomenon, at the level of groups, was studied by Bion (Bion, 1962): the newcomer (s) is (are) dangerous and the 'invaded' group seeks to reject him (them), an experience which is confirmed each time one joins a group that has already been more or less formed, even for a short while: dinner, seminar, a doctor or dentist's waiting room, a cultural, artistic, religious or other type of association. The more outsiders there are in the constituted group, the stronger the reaction of rejection is. This is caused by anxiety about being invaded, which is at the origin of a phobia that is sometimes masked by a counterphobic attitude leading insiders to help these outsiders who are basically despised. What are people defending themselves against? Why this phobia? The phobia, of course, is an expression of anxiety related to the fear of being devoured, abandoned, and castrated.

Projection is one of the major defences against these fears. He is (they are) bad; I am (we are) good, well brought up, endowed with good manners, cultivated, civilized. Projection reveals itself when one attributes to foreigners our own shortcomings or difficulties: for example, the inhibition to learn a foreign language, which is rather characteristic of certain 'civilized' countries such as France and England.

Another typical defence is the negation of similitude: what is said to be different is often very similar. He has, in fact, the same habits, the same culture, as this is not the monopoly of one country, the one where one was born, but is more or less universal for those who have done equivalent studies. Moreover, French culture has exerted its influence – alas, long ago! – throughout a large part of the world, so that foreigners, too, are often impregnated with it. This similitude is denied.

Narcissism contributes in a large part to the rejection of the foreigner: I (we) am (are) superior. Whites are assumed to be more intelligent, English (or French, etc.) is believed to be superior. 'Northern' countries have a higher place than Southern ones (Italy, Spain, Greece, South America), where the people are lazy, terribly underdeveloped (perhaps Indians), have a siesta when it is very hot, for, as a colleague to whom I was trying to explain a bit of geography once said to me, even at the South Pole, the temperature is tropical. However, she did not believe me when I told her that this was not so.

In order to bolster one's defences and narcissism, one refers to the place of birth, by asking 'where were you born?' even if, for example, French is one's first language, acquired during the first months of life. As for me, I wonder what the importance is for someone of the place where he was born, except perhaps from an administrative point of view? We have no conscious memory of our birth, nor even, it seems to me, an unconscious recollection of what this country was like at that time, cold? hot? democratic? civilized?

Brassens' song about 'the idiots who were born somewhere' comes to mind. However, it is not a question of idiocy but of rationalizing prejudices against the projected bad object (foreign body, devil). Another country will necessarily be inferior, the teaching will not be so good. If the one who is speaking about this failed in his studies, for example, and feels hurt, it will be a relief to project this narcissistic suffering on to others, the foreigner. Freud pointed out the difficulty of accepting that the ego is not the master of his own house, that the unconscious foreigner dominates it (Freud, 1923).

Another defence is the denial of the foreigner's capacities: even if it is obvious that he knows a subject as well or better than his 'indigenous' interlocutor, the latter will not notice it consciously. He will be taught things that are obvious: an example from my own experience comes to memory here, concerning a lady who explained to me at length that 'French' streets had even numbers on one side and uneven ones on the other; she did not hear me when I replied that it was like that in all cities and in all countries where there were streets, and did not believe me either.

At other moments, the foreigner is perhaps not imagined as being inferior but as dangerous, because he might take your place (devour you), or be loved at your expense, while you are neglected (abandonment): already, he speaks at least two languages, is capable of venturing to change country, perhaps having to start his professional life over again; he will surpass you and will be superior to you (castration anxiety). If he dares to do that, what will he fear? Nothing, he's a serious and dangerous adversary, ready to despoil you.

Then projection comes into play: but really, why is he here, why didn't he stay there 'where he was born'? And what if he was expelled 'from his country', what if he was a fugitive from the law which had been pursuing him for good reasons? And supposing, here, amongst us (in our Association, our hospital, our Faculty), where 'we all get on so well together and never have conflicts', he started to stir up trouble, to put us all at loggerheads, and wanted to destroy us? And, why not, what if he were a terrorist?

Resistance to learning a foreign language

All these fears about the foreigner show an underlying wish for unity, for narcissistic fusion, non-differentiation. We should all be the same. If this is not the case, we are afraid and become anxious, defending ourselves by projection and the other mechanisms referred to above.

This fusion accompanied by clones, narcissistic images reflecting each other, implies a disorder of symbolization, which is impossible without a third party, without acceptance of the differences of alterity, of the sexes, and of the generations.

This disorder may concern the subject's whole person, in which case he will suffer from psychosis, or it may take root in a few particular aspects. Language, which is essentially symbolic, is one of the points on which this pathology hooks itself. If this pathology which is widely shared, probably owing to the play of identifications, is the only indicator of the impossibility or great difficulty in attaining symbolization, it will tend to be circumscribed and relatively minor, though it may worsen under predisposing circumstances.

We encounter it daily when we suggest to an analyst in training or even a colleague that they read a book or an article written in another language than French. Almost always, we hear the reply: Oh! But I can't read English!' (or German, Spanish, etc.). Sometimes this resistance to symbolize what is foreign is slight and disappears under the pressure of the teacher (one observes this phenomenon particularly in this context and one finds that the one who said he understood nothing in this other language, is finally able to read it without too much difficulty, with practice or when his wounded narcissism or castration anxiety in face of the danger have been overcome.)

But often, there is nothing to be done. They wait for the translation. Would the slowness with which these appear in French, to the point that there is still no translation 'in France' of the complete works of Freud in chronological order, be a symptom of this pathology? That several major English authors have been translated decades later (Bion, Winnicott, Racker, Rosenfeld), so much so that once they are accessible in French, readers find that their work is dated and that X, Y or Z have already said that, perhaps by citing them, though the source, written in a 'foreign' language, has been forgotten.

Words, accent, rhythm, intonation, resonance

I will now turn to one of the other aspects of the 'foreign language', which needs to be distinguished. First, the words are grammatically different from French words, in particular their 'sex' is not always similar or does not exist. The first case, among the idioms of 'civilized' people, is that of German: Freud pointed out that the sun was feminine in this language, but did not draw any particular conclusions from it (Freud, 1911). However, with regard to Schreber, he could have approached his pathology with reference to his mother and not only to his father, which might have changed his interpretation of the case.

In English, words have no 'sex'. Are we to suppose that the natives of the United Kingdom suffer from sexual non-differentiation? In any case, they do not suffer from a non-differentiation of the generations, because children are neuter (it), like an inanimate object. In German, there is a third asexual sex, the neuter, which is attributed, among many other objects, to children, as in English (*'the baby is here, it's crying'*, *'das Kind ist hier'*). Is this such an intense accentuation of the difference of the generations that it transforms the child into an object?

On the other hand, in English, domestic animals are in no danger of being considered as things and are given masculine and feminine pronouns depending on the case *('he's barking, she's calling'*, for dogs of masculine and feminine sex for example). Moreover, the English write 'I' with a capital letter – is this to be seen as a sign of accentuated narcissism? The Germans, on the other hand, write 'you' with a capital letter (Sie) – does this mean they are more respectful towards the other or, rather, do they thereby accentuate his difference or his distance?

These languages – like all the others – are pronounced with a particular accent. This is the most useful characteristic for identifying a person's origin, the region they come from, their social milieu, for certain sounds are particular to these conditions. I think that accent is the maternal mark of the language, because it is the mother who provided care for the child during the first months. In my view, the structure of the language, its spelling, its syntax, are more paternal, for they obey strict rules, laws of a sort.

The appreciation of accent is more subjective, and thus lends itself more to projections. There are specialists capable of distinguishing, by virtue of his accent, the origin of someone coming from one region or another or even from one district or another. In Paris, one distinguishes between the accent of the '16th' (one of the smart districts, particularly bourgeois) and, at the other end of the range, suburban sounds. But often, non-specialists get it wrong, or rather, project spontaneously. Not long ago, an English lady firmly believed, listening to my pronunciation in English, that I was Polish and sought to hide it (why?). Now, my accent in English is deplorable, but I have never spoken Polish. I don't know what this lady's reasons were, but it was definitely a projected fantasy on her part.

Intonation, the melody of a language, is characteristic and here, too, one can identify the origin of the person who is speaking, as well as his/her cultural level. For instance, the 'Parisian' accent with 'e's' added at the end of all the words, even those that end with a consonant, as well as a certain high pitch at the end of a sentence, fools no one as to the origin of the person who is speaking (they were perhaps not born in Paris but came there when they were little) or their cultural level, since this accent is not found at all in 'cultivated people' and even less in those who have been to university.

Intonation and sonority coincide. There is a tendency to believe, it seems to me, that in women high-pitched voices are more 'French' than lower-pitched voices; is this to say that sopranos are Gallic and contraltos 'barbarian'. I do not know what the physiological explanation for this particularity might be, but would tend to attribute it to a play of identifications stemming from early childhood or inherited from ancestors temporally distant but present via the transgenerational path, as H. Faimberg suggests (Faimberg, 2005). For example, this intonation used by a 'bourgeois woman' would, in fact, betray forgotten peasant origins.

Certain words are more 'civilized' than others. One can write them, whereas a different variety is accepted in spoken language only. This cultivated speech is narcissistically invested and represents a certain value when faced with the foreigner, who is supposed to be without it. It will be disconcerting to find that this is not the case, when, for instance, one tries to explain to a foreigner what he knows perfectly well, for example, the existence of the subjunctive. Here, too, it is a question of ignorance or of painful memories of childhood that are projected, because, in fact, the subjunctive is present in all our Western languages, and probably also in the others.

There is a link between this idealization of the language itself and of the capacity to use it correctly, and the difficulty of learning another language. Scorn hides other feelings: before the child could understand it, his parents, and adults in general, also spoke a foreign language. From this point of view, the foreign language is parental *par excellence*. The foreigner, this time, will dwell more in the superego than in the ego, from where he will prohibit the possession of that which belongs/belonged to the parents, in a sort of auditory primal scene. How does the *infans* hear? Can he distinguish human voices from other sounds? From barkings? From meowings? From thunder? From rain?

We have learnt quite recently that the baby recognizes *in utero* the father's voice. Does that mean that it can distinguish between the human and the non-human or the thunder of the father's choleric voice?

The particular difficulty when faced with the 'foreign' language

The mistakes made when expressing oneself in a foreign language are accompanied by a sort of stubbornness, either anal or narcissistic. There is a wish to make the foreign language yield to one's one language and one is quick to point out that in French (in Spanish, English, etc.), it is not like that.

Basically, I think that underlying this there is an important disturbance of symbolization, namely, that the subject is attached to the idea that a word means one thing and nothing more: 'une table' is 'une table', 'una mesa' in Spanish means nothing, 'a table' in English means nothing either. There is a capacity to 'pre-symbolize' between two terms: the object and the word that corresponds to it. But there is no place for a third element (the foreign word). The failure to achieve a symbolization between three elements constitutes a disturbance that is close to psychosis or completely psychotic, if it is not the result of identifications, that is. Does this allow us to suppose that in cases where learning a foreign language is impossible, fragile narcissism and/or excessive primary and secondary identifications are involved? In any case, there is an ego-functioning which hates external reality and only accepts what it sees fit to eat, to introject (Freud, 1915), or which is so fused with that of its parents that it enjoys no freedom. Once outside its narcissism or its identifications, it cannot 'return', after traversing the disorganizing foreign territory, the different idiom, towards its own psyche, its own language.

In earlier articles, I have raised the question of the possible existence of a word-system specific to each language, so that the person who speaks several languages would possess as many systems of word-presentations. My reasoning was based on the fact, observed in myself and in several other multilingual people, that a slip of the tongue in one language does not lead to the same in another; and that the forgetting of a word in one does not have its counterpart in another. On the contrary, the multilingual person faced with a memory blank overcomes it by having recourse to another language. One might suppose that it is because the associations with the forgotten words, more or less traumatic, split off or repressed, are different in each language. I tend to think this is the real reason, rather than supposing that there are one or several word-systems. I had taken as an example my forgetting, in Spanish, of the name of a fur, instead of which there came to my mind the word '*escarabajo*' (beetle, scarab, a disagreeable but harmless insect). I overcame the difficulty by searching in French where I found nothing, and then in English where I found 'squirrel', which I easily translated by *écureil*, the real name of the fur in question being Siberian squirrel. On thinking about it now, while associating, I find that '*escarabajo*', an unpleasant insect, takes me back to an infantile phobia of flying insects, a path that leads me to many other more personal associations, linked in the last instance to the primal scene. On the other hand, 'squirrel' was not associated with anything particularly traumatizing, but rather with the pretty English books of tales for children read by my English governess, who only arrived at our home when I was eight, whereas the word *écureil* was no doubt familiar to me before and associated with pretty little animals (birds, pigeons, lambs), observed with joy in the country, but also with ambivalence because they represented possible future little brothers or little sisters.

I will relate another example of this attachment, but it would really be better to say of this force pushing the foreign to be and remain foreign, thereby receiving the projections of what is disagreeable in oneself. About thirty years ago, shortly after I had started to work as a psychoanalyst in Paris, I had a young female patient, a French teacher in a *lycée*, who suffered from various hysterical symptoms but had, as it materialized later, a difficulty in symbolizing. The daughter of émigrés from Eastern Europe, she had lost her mother early on in life and lived with her elderly father who had great difficulty speaking French and with whom her relationship was difficult. She protected herself by speaking 'very quickly' so as to 'reduce him to silence', a method she employed very successfully. As was easily foreseeable, she used the same method with me, especially as she expected me not to speak like the Lacanians (her sister was in analysis with one), and also because she had been told I was a foreigner. I once repeated the word 'table' which had appeared several times in a dream. She replied that she did not know what this word meant, perhaps in Spanish ... but she did not speak this language. I spelt the word but she asserted that she did not know it at all. Not in French, in any case.

In order to be able to interpret, I chose a method aimed at reducing the anxiety from which she suffered in front of the foreigner, which was increased owing to her bad relationship with her father and the early death of her mother. Speaking very quickly – and even though she was a French teacher – she eventually made some slips of the tongue. I detected one in her use of the imperfect of the subjunctive, which I pointed out to her, and which, to my surprise, she admitted she had made. As a result, she withdrew her projection on to me as a foreigner which then appeared instead in her dreams, concerning the origin of her parents, their misfortunes during the war, and in the country where they had lived before. Was this an interpretation or the fruit of my countertransferential irritation at being transformed into an ignoramus? Perhaps, but it had a heuristic success.

This was certainly not the only occasion on which I have felt the force of the projection of the unfamiliar on to me, leaving aside methodologically my probable participation in these occasions owing to my untypical situation (foreigner but citizen, and multilingual, but with a long French familial and personal past).

I would like to emphasize again the instinctual thrust, so to speak, of the projection of these occasions. On the one hand, it is felt by the ego of the interlocutor to be a force of the kind which is sometimes seen emitted by psychotics; on the other hand, in the case of patients 'stuck' to their identifications, there is a fixation to the projection (to the point of not knowing the word table). Such a projection can only be archaic in origin. I will make the hypothesis that it comes from earliest childhood, and is experienced in the face of the mysterious, enigmatic (in Laplanche's sense, Laplanche, 1987) language of the parents. At the time, the anxiety about the primal scene was not symbolizable, so that this sector remained split off but capable of showing its effects if the occasion presented itself: when someone speaks a foreign language and, perhaps, worse still, if, in French, she 'should' speak incorrectly but expresses herself like everyone else, the projection comes back to the sender and disorganizes his/her psyche.

References

Bion, W.R. (1962). Group Dynamics. *International Journal of Psychoanalysis, 33*: 235–247.

Caro Baroja, J. (1961). Las brujas y su mundo. *Revista de Occidente.*

Delumeau, J. (1978). *La peur en Occident*. Paris: Fayard.

Faimberg, H. (2005). *The Telescoping of Generations*. London: Routledge.

Freud, S. (1887–1904). *Sigmund Freud Briefe am Wilhem Fliess*. S. Fischer Verlag, 1986.

Freud, S. *On Aphasia*. London and New York, 1953.

Freud, S. (1892–1893). A case of successful treatment by hypnotism. *Standard Edition, 1*, 117.

Freud, S. (1893). Charcot. *Standard Edition, 3*, 9.

Freud, S. (1895). *Studies on hysteria. Standard Edition, 2.*

Freud, S. (1896). The aetiology of hysteria. *Standard Edition, 3*, 189.

Freud, S. (1911). Psychoanalytic notes on an autobiographical account of a case of paranoia. *Standard Edition, 12*, 3.

Freud, S. (1915). Instincts and their vicissitudes. *Standard Edition, 14*, 111.

Freud, S. (1919). The uncanny. *Standard Edition, 17*, 219.

Freud, S. (1923). *The ego and the id. Standard Edition, 13*, 3.

Green, A. (1984). Le langage dans la psychanalyse. In: *Langages*. Paris: Belles Lettres.

Laplanche, J. (1987). *Problématiques V*. Paris: PUF.

Laplanche, J. (1987). *Nouveaux fondements pour la psychanalyse*. Paris: PUF.

Urtubey, L. de (1988). Dites tout ce qui vous passe par la tête, tout comme cela vous vient et dans la langue où cela vous vient. *Revue française de psychanalyse, 2.*

Urtubey, L. de (1993). Des unilingues. *Revue française de psychanalyse, 3.*

INDEX

Page references in italics indicate illustrations.

For Product Safety Concerns and Information please contact our EU representative GPSR@taylorandfrancis.com Taylor & Francis Verlag GmbH, Kaufingerstraße 24, 80331 München, Germany

Batch number: 10726011

Printed by Printforce, the Netherlands